The Great African Society

The Great African Society

A plan for a nation gone astray

Hlumelo Biko

Jonathan Ball Publishers
Johannesburg & Cape Town

First edition published in trade paperback in 2013 by
JONATHAN BALL PUBLISHERS (Pty) Ltd
A division of Media24 (Pty) Limited
PO Box 33977
Jeppestown
2043

12/03/2013

Reprinted in 2013

Paperbook ISBN 978-1-86842-521-1
eBook ISBN 978-1-86842-522-8

Cover design by Michiel Botha, Cape Town
Design and typesetting by Triple M Design, Johannesburg
Printed and bound by CTP Printers, Cape Town
Typeset in 10.5/15pt ITC Stone Serif Std

Twitter: www.twitter.com/JonathanBallPub
Facebook: www.facebook.com/pages/Jonathan-Ball-Publishers/ 298034457992
Blog: http://jonathanball.bookslive.co.za/

Contents

To my children Luthando and Lewatle
God willing, you will one day live in the great African society.

Preface

There is a growing public debate about the type of society South Africa is becoming and who or what is to blame for the failure to live up to its lofty ideals. The ANC Youth League has represented my generation in this debate, calling for economic freedom in this lifetime through nationalisation. Young intellectuals like Vuyo Jack, Itumeleng Mahabane and Eusebius McKaiser have been urging a more nuanced form of socio-economic redress grounded in an understanding of South Africa's constitutional framework and our macro-economic constraints. Many young people I have spoken to seem torn between an emotionally charged response to the nationalisation argument, the sub-text of which is that it is black people's turn to enjoy the spoils of the country, and a more reasoned view that any form of redress has to happen in a manner that does not set South Africa's overall economic development back a few decades.

My generation's contributions to this debate have been hampered by the fact that many of us have not taken the time to repay the investment made in our education (by our families and taxpayer money). I feel particularly guilty of this failure to repay this investment, because the investments made in me by my parents involved the ultimate form of sacrifice. Our failure to adequately contribute to the current debate can easily be misconstrued as a form of acquiescence to some of the terrible things being carried out in the name of South Africa's youth. If we care about our future we have to assume custodianship of the direction our country is being steered in. This involves having uncomfortable debates with our elders.

The Great African Society represents my attempt to show that today's economic redistribution debate is a continuation of the inter-racial battle for scarce economic resources that has been fought over the last two centuries. This book seeks to flesh out the socio-economic consequences of this battle for today's society, particularly the tendency for the private and public sectors to view each other as adversaries as opposed to allies in the creation of shared growth. Ultimately the book attempts to plot a different path forward predicated on achieving economic freedom for all South Africans. This work champions the targeted use of private sector capacity to deliver goods and services to poor communities as part of a reorganised form of Black Economic Empowerment as a central platform for a new social compact. I believe that our inability to correctly frame our challenges in the context of our history leads to a short-sighted form of analysis that often lends itself to false validations of long-held racial superiority or inferiority complexes.

My generation is the bridge between the generation responsible for our liberation and the generation of 'born frees'. We will be left with the burden of explaining to our children and grandchildren why we could not take the platform given to us by Presidents Nelson Mandela and Thabo Mbeki to generate shared economic prosperity. It will not be enough for us to say that the previous generation overstayed their welcome and that our calls for a generational mix within the country's leadership fell on deaf ears. We have to roll up our sleeves and contribute to the current struggle for economic prosperity in meaningful ways. Our professional lives will not provide refuge against the future backlash by less privileged members of our generation as they rebel against a society that gives them welfare grants instead of economic freedom. My hope is that my book can offer courage to some and information to others to use their talents to make their own contributions. Freedom lingers sparingly in societies that do not nurture her.

1

The Elusive Rainbow Nation

The rainbow nation built under the leadership of the great President Nelson Mandela is facing grave threats. Though South Africa has much to be proud of and many massive achievements to celebrate, it has failed to honestly face its socio-economic legacy, leading to a social fabric that is very thinly knit.

Yet, as most critics are told by supporters of the governing party, the ANC has successfully doubled the middle class, drastically reduced illiteracy, built over 2 million new low-income houses, created a social grant system that supports 16 million people and electrified most of the country while successfully providing fresh running water to tens of millions of South Africans. As amazing and indeed monumental as these achievements are, they don't begin to describe the hard work that has gone into rebuilding a state bureaucracy that previously catered for less than 15 per cent of the country to one that can be responsive to the needs of close to 50 million people. Rome was certainly not built in a day – so why should South Africans not be more patient with the status quo? The answer to that question is probably better initiated by another: Why is it that after 18 years of being liberated more than half of South Africans are living in poverty?

There are no easy answers. First, there is a crucial distinction to make between a society that is unequal, and a society displaying signs of inequity. An unequal society is one in which, comparatively speaking, everyone is at varying levels of economic progression, with significant gaps between rich and poor. Inequity, however, includes the prospect that not all members of society are treated equally in their efforts to move from their current economic state towards prosperity. This nuanced difference points to the perpetuation of an injustice that holds certain citizens back while supporting the progress of others. To evolve from a society characterised by the framework of inequity towards a functional, equitable meritocracy, South Africa needs to be able to analyse its history honestly and apply the principles of restorative justice in the construction of policy for its future.

Equity for the minority: the apartheid legacy

Apartheid was a tool used by white governments to divide scarce resources amongst South Africa's white people at the expense of the indigenous majority. This process was facilitated by a legislated 'othering' of blacks that sought to strip them of any rights they had to the country's resources. The resources themselves were used to finance the incredible infrastructure citizens still enjoy, subsidising the country's development for the benefit of a minority.

In 1994 South Africans acknowledged the fundamental flaw of this development model, and agreed that it had to be changed radically. The country went about setting the foundations of change to its socio-political structure – from an economically isolated inward-looking authoritarian state, to a globally integrated outward-looking centralised bureaucracy. Institutions were set up to help deal with the past and ensure a fairer future for all. Of all these none is more important than the national constitution.

What was neglected was a proper diagnosis of the structural problems resulting from the development model of the last 60 years, to identify what specifically about that development framework was broken and more importantly, how to fix it. In 1994 the focus of analysis was on apartheid as a perverted system of government that was put in place by Afrikaner fundamentalists blinded to reality by racism. In this narrative British imperialism's role as an uneasy facilitator was regarded as an unfortunate confluence of agendas.

In reality, however, apartheid had been a rational mobilisation tool for white Afrikaner supremacists in order to win political power and to deliver patronage to a growing number of poor and unskilled Afrikaners struggling to attain employment. These Afrikaners saw black population growth in urban South Africa as a major hindrance to their economic advancement – *swart gevaar* (black danger) became the rallying cry that resonated with their constituency. They also saw a possible future marginalisation of the *volk* if indigenous African interests could one day be aligned with British imperial interests.

Over the course of the preceding century or so, the patient British colonial government had allowed the Afrikaner Voortrekkers to act as trailblazers in the harsh interior, while exercising their 'right' to annex any valuable land that might be deemed strategic because of its mineral content or geographical proximity to trading routes. This gave the British Empire a method of expanding the imperial economy without having to use significant British resources. Black people were merely pawns in a game of resource accumulation between imperialist and settler demands. Like any other game, imperialism/apartheid took on a dynamic of its own, with the players of the game moving the hapless pieces in a contest for unequally distributed opportunities and resources.

During the twentieth century, South Africa was incorporated as a country, divided amongst its new shareholders and opened for business with the rest of the world through global economic integration. Its rich resources, including former shareholders who now served as cheap labour, made it a very globally competitive economy. Its customers turned a blind eye to how it operated so long as it remained a reliable supplier and a safe investment destination. It was only in the 1970s that the 'global shareholders' of these international customers started making uncomfortable noises about their trading partner. The tens of thousands who died under apartheid over the years served to turn global sentiment against the government while weakening the resolve of the Afrikaner electorate.

To be sure, the work of the liberation movement gradually made apartheid as a policy impossible to implement. The growing support for a sanctions campaign and more tellingly the increasing reluctance of the international banking community to roll over the South African sovereign debt were testimony to the relentless work of the African National Congress (ANC) and internal activists in highlighting the plight of black South Africans. Global discomfort with the apartheid government's modus operandi ultimately contributed significantly to the undoing of the apartheid regime.

To assign such a passive role to black people in this story will anger many of South Africa's struggle veterans, who would have an amplified view of their role as political agents for change. There is no doubt that were it not for their role, South Africa would not yet be a free society. But I firmly believe that viewing history through the lens of rational resource accumulation, with its skewed allocation to white people as a motive and apartheid as a modus operandi, offers a more useful perspective.

The perspective of resource accumulation enables an analysis of South Africa's historical socio-economic development process and the structural impacts that have proven difficult to tackle in the post-apartheid era. To date the focus has been on a diagnosis of the racial symptoms of apartheid, resulting in a weak prescription of a Truth and Reconciliation Commission with a narrow mandate focused on racist-motivated crimes against humanity, and prescribing a cocktail of Black Economic Empowerment and affirmative procurement as a remedy for South Africa's economic ills. If the desired outcome behind BEE as a policy was broad-based economic empowerment of previously disadvantaged South Africans, then so far it has failed. To reverse the de-industrialisation currently taking place in South Africa while attempting to address the many sources of inequity within the society requires a powerful social re-engineering mechanism.

Social re-engineering for the future

The key difficulty South Africans face with addressing inequality arises from a lack of shared understanding of what liberation from apartheid was supposed to achieve. The middle and upper classes (black and white) view liberty as a combination of freedom of expression, freedom of movement, universal suffrage and the constitutional protection of their property rights. Under this definition, liberty has been achieved; they are part of a small cohort of liberated South Africans. For the centrists in the ANC, liberation meant the end of white minority political rule in South Africa. They subscribed to Kwame Nkrumah's maxim that liberation movements should 'seek first the political kingdom and the rest will follow'. They too view South Africans as a liberated people. The left wing of the ANC – namely the Alliance partners of Cosatu and the SACP – share Chris Hani's view that 'liberation should free the poor from hunger and landlessness'.[1] By this definition 1994 represented a first step in a long process of liberating South Africa.

Apartheid was a massive social engineering project that lasted (in its official form) nearly 60 years. What we need now is a similarly ambitious social re-engineering project, if pitfalls of the current path are to be corrected and new ones avoided. The reality is that the country has massive assets – a combination of public infrastructure, mineral wealth, agricultural heritage, natural beauty and human capital – which were sold off to the private sector after being unlawfully accumulated at close to no cost by the state (most South African land was taken from blacks using the *'terra nullius'* principle, meaning that the territory had never been subject to the sovereignty of any state). What is now South Africa Inc, with its trillions of rands in wealth, needs to proceed with a massive redistribution programme, or else risk a rapid and unprecedented devaluation of its assets.

The process of devaluation has already begun, driven by a new value system that has captured South Africans as a result of a growing realisation that the post-apartheid system is not fair. This value system has supplanted 1994's idealism, manifesting itself in new police officers who view their badge and gun as apparatus with which to extort favours from the very people they are supposed to serve, in the new 'business mechanic' who bribes officials to win a tender, and in the teacher who makes his students perform sexual favours in exchange for good grades. Equally disturbing is the increase in institutionalised corruption of state-owned enterprises as ANC party 'deployees' adjust to a free-for-all environment.

The only way to stop this runaway force is to convince everyone that the system can be made fair and that the rule of law (which must be focused on the egalitarian socio-economic undertakings encapsulated in the Bill of Rights) can offer them legal opportunities for self-improvement – in other words, that they too will be given an opportunity to join the ranks of truly liberated South Africans. Such an environment would allow them the means through which to acquire skills to pursue careers in their chosen trades and be fairly compensated for an honest day's work while living dignified lives.

The test of whether a society is successful has to be when ordinary citizens are capable of success through hard work alone and not through extraordinary gifts. So far post-liberation South Africa has consistently failed this test. It has tended complacently to measure its success on the basis of the achievements of exceptional black people. This illusion of fairness flies in the face of evidence that South Africa is one of the world's least fair and most unequal societies. People who know that apartheid has robbed them of an opportunity to excel in life cannot be expected to wait another 50 years for the governing party to build a better life for all. They have lost patience. The increasingly common xenophobia attacks, the almost monthly service delivery strikes, the growing numbers of so-called wildcat strikes in the mining industry, the millions of instances of crime committed against all citizens, and the rampant corruption which prevents many government departments from successfully executing their mandates are leading indicators of societal decay.

The failure of Black Economic Empowerment to be a significant catalyst for broad-based poverty eradication calls for a moment of pause and reflection about South Africa's societal outlook on re-distributive economics. What is it that led most citizens to think that selling shares in white-owned companies at small discounts to well-connected black businessmen (and I use this term in its loos-est sense) would translate to sustainable wealth creation amongst a broad class of black people? Whether one believes it was the in-fluence on policy makers of the discredited theory of trickle-down economics, a corrupt need driven by the new black elite with the support of big business to create a patronage network, or the result of a severe disconnect with poor South Africans, the damage is done.

According to South Africa's most popular BEE ratings agency, Empowerdex, black South Africans own 1.6 per cent (R81 billion) of the JSE's value, which stands at R5.2 trillion. This amount is the unencumbered portion of the shares. When you add the portion still encumbered the percentage rises to a total of 5.75 per cent. All the different BEE codes are aimed at a percentage of between 10 and 25 per cent, depending on the industry. The fundamental flaw in the empowerment legislation is that the so-called transfer of wealth comes with a transfer of liabilities to people with underlying assets (the shares that they are sold as part of the BEE deal) that they don't control and with dividend streams that are earmarked for debt repayment usually structured over five to ten years. There are few multiplier effects that come from such a policy. The 'em-powered companies' often don't change their corporate behaviour. These new shareholders are usually preoccupied with the reality of having to find cash for working capital and therefore as BEE 'investors' are often unable to add any real value to their investee companies. There is little indication that BEE has any job-creating effects. What South Africa needs to do is to press the reset button on redistribution and find alternative channels to achieve more sustainable results that have greater multiplier effects.

The country needs to give all firms that have already agreed (through industry empowerment charters) to participate in the current BEE policy an alternative avenue for redressing the wrongs of the past. This alternative set of channels needs to be under-pinned by a desire to create a society that is genuinely owned by its citizens. Such a society needs to provide a trampoline for the ma-jority of its citizens to jump on so that they can get to level ground before putting in place a social safety net. To successfully achieve this some home truths need to be accepted by the key players.

Central to a national turnaround strategy:

❏ South Africa's corporate sector needs to realise that what Archbishop Desmond Tutu refers to as the 'powder keg of South African poverty' threatens to blow up in their faces and drastically devalue their aggregate assets. They need to fast-track the money spent on redistribution, incorporating this type of corporate spending into the long-term incentive struc-ture, so that executives' performance on empowerment can be incorporated as part of the creation of shareholder value. Without this, the mining industry will be the first of many to experience the erosion of long-term shareholder value as a result of a failure to correctly share the economic upside with the broader communities within which firms operate.

❏ Unions need to recognise that they have performed dismally by the index of job creation. They have to take responsibility for their role in creating the jobless growth model that the country currently has. If they do not, alternative collective bargaining mechanisms with more radical agendas will pursue a more reckless strategy through which to achieve higher lev-els of economic welfare for their members.

❏ The government needs to acknowledge that its bureaucratic machine cannot handle the redistributive demands of its electorate. The problems in South Africa cannot be resolved within the current service delivery limitations of provincial and local government in particular. Therefore it needs to create massive public-private partnerships (PPPs) run by the private sector in areas which require urgent attention.

Instead of pushing forward aimlessly with the implementation of agreed BEE targets, South African corporations need to be challenged to contribute the balance of their BEE pledges in cash directly to government-sponsored PPPs designed to impact the education and health care sectors as well as facilitating an integrated widespread mixed-income housing programme.

If the Empowerdex measure of how much BEE has been achieved amongst listed firms is any indication of progress made to date, there is at least another 10 per cent worth of BEE transactions to be undertaken by listed firms. This translates to roughly R500 billion worth of capital that is available for redistributive initiatives. If the government were to allow firms to invest this capital directly, rewarding early movers by lowering their aggregate tax bill, we would have the makings of an economic sea change that could turn South Africa into a First World country in two generations.

South Africa has to get four things right in order to unleash unprecedented prosperity:

❏ First, we must reverse the massive assault that apartheid inflicted on our education system.

❏ Second, we must focus on the immediate critical need to overhaul the national maternal and child care system to make sure that no child stays home sick or, worse still, dies because of a preventable or curable disease.

❏ Third, we must create a sustainable country-wide mixed-income urban housing model that will reverse the stated apartheid policy of making cities uncomfortable for black people to live in. As a society that embraces urbanisation, South Africa should reject the idea of any child being raised in a shack in 2013 and beyond.

❏   Fourth, we should realise that our greatest export to neighbouring African countries is our world-class infrastructure. Their greatest export to South Africa is a superior workforce trained both domestically and in the West. Therefore, as part of our economic development policy, we should strive to facilitate the movement of as many African business headquarters to South Africa as possible. The country's world-class infrastructure, combined with a globally competitive service sector, should make it an attractive base from which African entrepreneurs can launch their global ambitions. The aggregate of these efforts will be a major boost to job-creation efforts.

Many of the enabling policy frameworks necessary to carry out these recommendations are available to law makers. We have had no shortage of commissions of inquiries, advisory committees and think tanks coming up with a variety of solutions geared towards solving our most vexing problems. What has not been on display is a consistently long-term-focused, people-orientated leadership that can sift out those suggestions that are in the interest of the broader population.

Another key deficiency is the incapacity of the South African leadership to cast aside convenient political alliances and to put in place policies that have been proven to have worked in other parts of the globe. Time and again the government has pandered to the interests of narrow constituencies in its decision making on major aspects of the economic regulatory framework.

Luckily, over 15 years (until 2009 the macro-economic environment was regarded globally as sound to conservative) of ANC-directed macro-economic framework has built South Africa a reputation as a forward-thinking, fiscally prudent country, creating leeway for more bold policy steps today. What is needed is a combination of goodwill, determination, honesty and hard work. These are values that all great societies possess. To create the Great African Society, South Africans have to confront structural inequality as the challenge of this generation. A focus on policy solutions addressing the four key pillars listed above will give citizens, businesspeople and government officials a chance to create a globally competitive and fundamentally sustainable economic growth programme that will create an eruption of new home owners, qualified graduates, entrepreneurs and perhaps a few more Nobel prize-winning writers and scientists.

2

The Making of South Africa

Every country's history has its scholars and biographers, taking various paths of information discovery, emphasising different historical actors and prioritising specific dates. They may be writing about the same sets of events, but much depends on interpretation and selective vision, reflecting the various mythologies that affect that society's thinking. At any given time one or more dominant mythologies tend to reflect the way the ruling group sees things. This is what has happened in the study of every society – be it the Roman Empire, ancient Egypt or the French Revolution. These dominant mythologies become reference points against which contemporary scholars highlight and refine their areas of interest. To be sure, once in a while a piece of literature is produced that substantiates a contrarian view. In so doing humanities scholars have created rich bodies of history with various perspectives that can be studied and debated by generations to come.

The history of the formation of South Africa is still too fresh for a definitive narrative to have effectively formed; in fact historians are still trying to adequately replace the pernicious manipulations of apartheid history books. This allows anyone studying the period the opportunity to make contributions to what will one day be a fuller history. This book seeks to enrich, through contextualisation, some of the current debate on how South Africa's socio-economic problems were formed and how apartheid and post-liberation governments managed to entrench them.

The current consensus amongst historians is that the Mfecane, which started in 1818, marked the beginning of a fundamental reshaping of tribal settlements in southern Africa. This reshaping might one day have created a unified South African kingdom were it not for the defeat of the Zulu King Cetshwayo at the hands of the British in 1879, which left indigenous black people fractured and vulnerable to the divide-and-rule strategy. Historians generally agree that after the formation of the Union of South Africa on 31 May 1910, the Natives Land Act of 1913 was a major milestone in the establishment of black people's subordinate land rights, cementing a process of land dispossession that was initiated by the Dutch East India Company when in 1703 it overturned the ban on grazing in close proximity to the colony in the Cape, freeing up the burghers to move deeper into the interior.[1] It is widely accepted by historians that Afrikaner nationalism, led by white supremacists determined to marshal the ascent of their *volk* to the top of the South African class structure, led to the policy of apartheid or separate development from 1948 until the country was liberated in 1994.

What is not yet well understood about South Africa is why, despite seemingly insurmountable socio-economic challenges, both its citizens and its friends continue to bestow expectations that it will be a special nation. What is it that has allowed South Africans to overcome so much in such a relatively short period of time? What changed this country from a nation under low-intensity civil war to one consisting of multiple ethnicities and 11 official languages living side by side in relative peace? Some scholars and commentators have referred to the entire settlement in 1994 and the events preceding the settlement as a miracle. Others have explored the liberation process from the point of view of the key actors in the apartheid government and pointed to international pressure, sanctions and fear of full-scale civil war as reasons for the settlement. Some scholars have looked at the liberation process from the point of view of exiles or inziles, the Black Consciousness Movement or liberation groups in their entirety. Reasons for the negotiated settlement are as varied as the end of communism, economic unsustainability of apartheid, skilled leadership from liberation leaders or a combination of these factors.

These studies have left two key questions unresolved. First, what is behind South Africa's so-called miracle – in other words, what led up to the specific type of resolution the country's leaders chose to end apartheid with? Second, why are our political achievements so far ahead of our economic ones? Is there a substantiated basis upon which South Africa can claim exceptionalism from the post-liberation shortcomings of other African countries?

Before attempting to answer these two questions in the subsequent chapters of this book it is important that I define what I believe to be South Africa's chief political achievement. I believe this achievement to simply be the non-coercive creation of an organic bottom-up united South African nation through a socialised nation-building process that lasted more than 60 years. This view is borne out by the fact that the negotiated settlement of 1994 was focused on the facilitation of the inclusion of a small minority of South Africans who missed out on this nation-building process because of their inability or unwillingness to join the liberation movement. The economic realities of post-apartheid South Africa have turned on its head which population group is now marginalised in South Africa, but this should not obscure the fact that in 1994 the victors were the majority of the population who joined hands in celebrating something they had – collectively – created for over half a century.

One of the biggest gifts South Africa received from Europe was the opportunity through the struggle against imperialism, colonialism and apartheid, to leapfrog major steps in the process of nation building. It goes without saying that the extended colonisation by white settlers facilitated the building of unmatched (on the African continent) economic infrastructure and durable, functional

14

institutions. Part of the endowment of the struggle against apartheid is less tangible and is easy to overlook. Black South Africans (a category that includes coloured, Indian, Cape Malay and Chinese South Africans) were forced to put aside tribal, ethnic, linguistic and religious differences in the formation of a unified opposition to white domination. The process of creating that unified opposition started in the early 1930s and was eventually completed by the late 1980s. It overcame huge obstacles put up by the apartheid government along the way.

The process of mass mobilisation against apartheid sheltered South Africa from what would have been years of intra-ethnic subjugation, exploitation, conflict and polarisation that would have taken place had the natural development of Africans not been interrupted by European invasion. The virtual absence of ethnic conflicts and atrocities among black South Africans means that the creation of tribally inflicted scars has been avoided – scars that would no doubt have been harder to heal than those inflicted on blacks by relative strangers. The relative absence of such scars has provided this country with the platform on which to build a nation state that could legitimately strive for an egalitarian, non-racist, non-sexist and meritocratic society. South Africans could do so because, by and large, all those who had fought for the freedom finally obtained in 1994 were rich in the sense of moral high ground that their struggle occupied and were filled with hope and a common bond endowed by struggle. In addition, those who had fought in the struggle for freedom were also united by their lack of material wealth and a long history of self-sacrifice.

Most black South Africans took great pride in spurning the materialistic patronage networks that were developed in the so-called Bantustans as proof of the illegitimacy of Bantustan leadership and its elitist value system. It was with a sense of pride that black people carried their lack of material wealth. To many it was a badge of honour. Black people understood that this was not how they wanted to raise their families but they wanted economic progress to be accompanied by real freedom and not the illusion of it.

15

Many African countries share the experience of colonial oppression and liberation. But the brutality, length of time and directness of apartheid rule, combined with the broad-based, uniquely decentralised format and national pervasiveness of South Africa's liberation struggle, have conspired to create a special opportunity to build a well-resourced nation from the ground up.

By undergoing this organic national democratic revolution for change from an autocratic society to one aspiring to egalitarianism, South Africa avoided the fate of some post-liberation African societies where change was orchestrated by a top-down constructivist ethos. Francis Fukuyama's analysis of the origins of political order highlights some interesting correspondences: 'Social order was not, according to Friedrich A Hayek, the result of top down rational planning; rather, it occurred spontaneously through the interactions of hundreds or thousands of dispersed individuals who experimented with rules, kept the ones that worked, and rejected those that didn't. The process by which social order was generated was incremental, evolutionary, and decentralised; only by making use of the local knowledge of myriads of individuals could a working "Great Society" ever appear.'[2]

Equal opportunity oppression

Indigenous Africans tried to fight white domination in their disaggregated tribes, communities and villages. The first to attempt to resist colonisation were the KhoiKhoi and the San, who were relatively easily managed by the Dutch East India Company shortly after its 'settlement' of the Cape in 1652. The *trekboer* encroachment on what later became known as the Eastern Cape led to a series of conflicts with the Xhosa starting from 1779 that were to last nearly 100 years but ended in defeat. These uprisings were met with brutality and subjugation that was consistent throughout the country. Whether one looks at the Battle of Blood River in 1838 where the Zulu put up a brave stand against the *trekboers*, or the

16

Bambatha Rebellion in 1906, these independent forms of rebellion were courageous but ultimately ineffective in preventing white domination.

Even the formation in 1912 of the South African Native Congress (the name was changed to African National Congress in 1925) had as its core objective the battle for inclusion into white-dominated South Africa rather than outright liberation. As historian David Welsh mentions, 'The membership of the early ANC was rooted in the educated Christian class, products of mission schools who were the sole providers of education for Africans at that time.'[3] It was not until the 1930s that a leadership emerged that understood the nature of the oppressive system contemplated by Afrikaners, and the implications of such a system for all black people, regardless of tribe or ethnicity. They began to articulate a form of African nationalism that would transcend intra-African differences in the formulation of a movement that would undertake a national struggle for liberation.

These leaders included Dr AB Xuma and Chief Albert Luthuli, who demanded a suspension of tribalistic or ethnic-related obstacles to African unity and exalted a form of peaceful and dignified rebellion against white domination. They spoke to a newly urbanising black population, forced by the Native Land Act of 1913 to come to the towns and seek employment. These towns, developed because of the formation of industrial-scale mining in places such as Kimberley and the Witwatersrand, were melting pots for ethnic and racial diversity. It was in Johannesburg that young rural men like Oliver Tambo and Nelson Mandela met street-smart township youths like Walter Sisulu, recognising that their worlds had changed for ever and that if they wanted to survive, they had to use both brain and brawn to earn a living in South Africa's urban metropolis.

These young men, led by Anton Lembede, were to take the message and fine tune it by sharpening the distinction between what South Africa was in the early 1940s and the country they wanted to live in post-liberation. They internalised Chief Luthuli's message and pledged to spread the new message of hope among an

African population that was becoming hopeless. It was through their evangelical work that the first dissemination of this philosophy of nationhood began to take root. Along the way, priests, community leaders and celebrities began to be the carriers of this new message of African nationalism.

The young men also decided to use the ANC as a vehicle to establish the more militant and Africanist ANC Youth League in 1944, which through Anton Lembede's fiery rhetoric managed to break the class barrier previously distancing the masses from the ANC because of its relatively elitist roots. The young lions' display of defiance through public protests gained the ANC legitimacy as the pre-eminent front through which the war against apartheid would be waged. Throughout the 1940s and 1950s, ANC leaders were giving the message of cross-tribal and ethnic unity just as the apartheid government was beginning to put together policies that were based on ethnic segregation.

In response to the 1952 Defiance Campaign, in which leaders such as Nelson Mandela burnt their passes and defied various other apartheid laws, the government showcased their zero-tolerance policy with mass detentions. This had the effect of further endearing the young nationalists to the broader population, creating even greater receptivity for their message of unity and solidarity. This repressive response against the young African nationalists enabled people like Nelson Mandela and Bram Fischer to put aside ideological differences about communism or socialism and link arms to fight together for a common cause. In so doing it opened up the creation of an alliance between the ANC and the South African Communist Party that would greatly radicalise the ANC and legitimise the SACP as a party.

The introduction of the Communist Party as the ANC's partner in the liberation movement brought with it the extra advantage of the communists' propaganda skills. 'Newspapers' were started around the country disseminating the message of liberation to both literate and illiterate South Africans. The message focused on how to interpret the oppression the majority of the population was subjected to and more importantly how to contextualise the motives behind such oppression. This mass propaganda highlighted the principle that each South African was not alone in his or her suffering and humiliation. The suffering and humiliation were made not just more tolerable, but also more meaningful. It was in suffering together that black South Africans first learnt to define themselves as a group that transcended their families, neighbourhoods, villages and townships.

After the gradual formation of the Congress Alliance – the ANC, the Coloured People's Organisation, the South African Indian Conference, the white Congress of Democrats and the SA Congress of Trade Unions – in the early 1950s, black South Africans were able to memorialise their ambition to create a democratic, egalitarian, non-racist, non-sexist and economically just society in the form of the Freedom Charter. Drawn up at the Congress of the People in Kliptown and accepted in 1955, this was to be the people's constitution, espousing democratic values far in advance of the laws under which the voting members of the South African public lived.

The closening of the relationship between the ANC and the SACP and its various proxies (such as the Congress of Democrats) when it was banned under the Suppression of Communism Act of 1950 enabled white South Africans like Joe Slovo, Albie Sachs and Ruth First to join not just the struggle for liberation, but also the leadership of the liberation movement. This forced many black leaders to deal with racism in a way that many apartheid leaders would only get to do 40 years later.

The participation of black leadership in the Communist Party – which had been multiracial since its inception – changed racial perceptions amongst the black community. It facilitated a more nuanced view of race relations and resulted in black people not responding to apartheid oppression with the same blanket hatred for white people that many of them had for black people. It facilitated the removal of racism from liberation politics and forced people in the struggle to think harder about the type of society they wanted to build. That black people could not replace one racist regime with another became clear as they saw white and black liberation leaders treated the same by apartheid leaders when they threatened the system in any way.

Throughout the country small groups of freedom fighters congregated, sharing with each other different modes of rebellion, different world views and different tactics on how to win liberation. That their struggle was not being won on the streets (as evidenced by the massive numbers of South Africans arrested in the Defiance Campaign) was immaterial to the underlying process of national consolidation of effort that was taking place. All black people, whether they had a car or were able to build double-storey houses, were equally oppressed and forced to live together by the Group Areas Act of 1950. This inability to unilaterally move away from one's community because of an improvement in individual circumstances forced a community improvement mentality among the well-to-do black people, leading to the enhancement of an overall value system of ubuntu that was to defy normal socio-economic class divisions. The more oppressive the laws passed under apartheid, the more people saw that the system was intolerable for them however well they were doing relative to a different group of oppressed South Africans. This new-found revolutionary spirit was reflected in the Sharpeville massacre, when a group of roughly 6 000 black people, supporters of Robert Sobukwe's Pan Africanist Congress, risked their lives to protest compliance with apartheid pass laws in 1960.

The spirit of revolution that had begun to penetrate the workforce brought home to Africans the meaninglessness of their titles and workplace seniority: their relative wealth meant nothing, because on their way home they all became 'kaffirs'. Apartheid was an equal opportunity system of oppression, which meant that, unlike other African societies that were dominated by the British imperialist system of indirect rule, class distinctions didn't create divisions in social relations between black people in South Africa. To be sure, there was a big differentiator, which was one's level of education, but this status did not give those more educated a right to live somewhere else or allow them to not be disrespected by less educated white people, or travel without a passbook.

The Rivonia Trial, which began in 1963, put on display the immense intellectual capacity of leaders like Nelson Mandela, allowing the masses to begin a long journey towards ridding themselves of preconceptions about the intellectual superiority of white authority figures. The mark of the liberation movement's success was that the leadership vacuum caused by the fact that the armed struggle had forced most of the ANC/SACP leadership into prison or exile did not lead to stagnation of the development of African nationalism. The message of struggle for a greater, more equal South Africa had already taken root. Young South Africans could now idealise heroes such as Nelson Mandela, Govan Mbeki, Robert Sobukwe and Walter Sisulu, to name just a few. These leaders in prison represented a set of aspirations for freedom which could no longer be suppressed and their personal struggle to survive in bondage showed the level of sacrifice needed from all black South Africans for liberation to be achieved. It also created a level of prestige that came with being arrested, serving time in prison or even facing police brutality. Repression played the same role as military national service did for free societies in generating camaraderie and a spirit of nationalism.

In South Africa's prisons leaders used their jail sentences as opportunities for teaching, mentoring and guiding young black South Africans. These incarcerated young leaders were inspired to go back to their communities and teach, mentor and guide other young leaders who would go on to impact millions of lives. It was in jail that ideological differences between different layers of the liberation movement were ironed out and set aside.

A new generation

A new, more intellectually combative brand of young student leaders came in the late 1960s to fill the domestic leadership vacuum in

South Africa. They were led by charismatic personalities like Steve Biko, Barney Pityana, Mamphela Ramphele, Mosibudi Mangena and Malusi Mpumlwana. They had a philosophy called Black Consciousness (BC), which served to infuse self-confidence and self-worth in black South Africans. These leaders recognised the growing feeling of despondency that had crept into the spirit of black South Africans as a result of the repression of the Defiance Campaign. This despondency was in response not just to the de-pleted local liberation leadership but also to an increase in the pettiness and indignity forced on them by the apartheid regime. Indignities were aimed at breaking people's spirit, leading them to slowly abandon the aspirations of being part of the creation of a new, more equal society.

The BC Movement focused not only on nation building but on the preparation of individuals for what the leadership felt would be an extended period of repression by the white regime. Indeed, the personal costs of participating in the struggle for freedom were becoming too high for individuals and their families. BC advo-cated psychological liberation of oppressed black South Africans in order for them to become agents for change in their communi-ties. This was a cornerstone for nation building for other forms of leadership to build on, bringing back the spirit of public confron-tation with symbols of authority such as the rejection of Afrikaans as a medium of instruction at black public schools, culminating in what is now known as the Soweto riots in 1976.

Another great addition from the BC Movement to the cause of nation building was a more inclusive and positive definition of being black, which gave future leaders like Pravin Gordhan, Jakes Gerwel, Trevor Manuel and Mac Maharaj in the Indian and col-oured communities a tool to erase the remaining ethnic barriers to the unification of the black South African liberation movement. Adding further strength to the resolve of black South Africans was the knowledge that somewhere in the bush on South Africa's border men like Chris Hani, Joe Modise, Jacob Zuma and Tokyo Sexwale were taking up arms, under the banner of Umkhonto we

Sizwe (MK), for their liberation. These acts of bravery emboldened young men and women to be equally brave in their interactions with figures of authority who they no longer felt were invincible.

Following the banning of the BC movement by the apartheid regime in 1977, the spirit and ideologies of the various liberation movements became fused together and brought closer to the community. The establishment of the United Democratic Front in 1983 saw the various liberation vehicles – more than 600 of them – united under one umbrella led by Archie Gumede, Oscar Mpetha and Albertina Sisulu, with Popo Molefe as general secretary and Patrick 'Terror' Lekota as publicity secretary. Throughout the 1980s this movement saw a decentralisation of the liberation struggle that made the movement more effective in leadership development, community outreach programmes and ultimately national unity for the sake of one common cause. It was during the 1980s that black South Africans merged into a nation joined by tens of thousands of white people who supported the liberation movement. Faith-based leaders such as Archbishop Tutu, Njongonkulu Ndungane, Bishop David Russell and Allan Boesak used their moral base to drive the message of unity, self-sufficiency and principled struggle to both the liberal and conservative members of the black community.

Black workers signalled their ability to organise themselves in a disciplined fashion, starting with strikes in 1973 that made a strong statement to corporate South Africa and ultimately increased the awareness of business of the need to deal with unions. These strikes led to the concessions of the Wiehahn Commission in 1979 legitimising the role of black organised labour unions (which merged into Cosatu in 1985). This laid the platform for unionists such as Cyril Ramaphosa, Jay Naidoo, Marcel Golding and Johnny Copelyn to lead a new terrain of resistance. The men and women who worked in the belly of apartheid's economic beast saw the effects of this new representation in the form of new safety regulations, some improvement in wages and general workplace treatment. However the greatest effect was in areas such as leadership development, financial literacy and the upward mobility that these new skills gave to a new group of fast-learning mine workers, textile labourers and manufacturing workers as preparation for the future. Leaders like Mbhazima Shilowa, Kgalema Motlanthe, Gwede Mantashe and Zwelinzima Vavi serve as testimony of this success. The connection that these leaders made with the everyday ordeal of deep-level miners shaped their perspective of what would be considered fair labour practice in the South Africa they were fighting for.

In exile, leaders such as Oliver Tambo and Thabo Mbeki, joined by African statesmen from the newly liberated neighbouring African countries, redefined the practice of African diplomacy. These two leaders created alignments with both sides of the Iron Curtain, operating equally comfortably in London, Havana and Moscow. They skilfully positioned the apartheid government as a brutal, repressive and undemocratic regime, undermining its international legitimacy and in so doing paving the way for sanctions. They were also able to use the murder of leaders such as Steve Biko and the incarceration of leaders such as Nelson Mandela, Govan Mbeki and Walter Sisulu to give their cause an overwhelming moral authority. In the 1970s and 1980s, under the shuttle diplomacy of Oliver Tambo and Thabo Mbeki, African nations became more emotionally involved in the South African liberation movement, building mutual goodwill that withstood years of the apartheid regime's increasingly desperate attempts to claw back the initiative.

South Africa's liberation was a process, not an event. South Africans had to become a united nation within an oppressive regime to liberate themselves. Ironically, it was white South Africans who were liberated by the negotiated settlement to join the nation that was already built through struggle, and thus experienced for the first time the graceful, inclusive, visionary and moral leadership of men like Nelson Mandela and Thabo Mbeki. President Mandela put his finishing touches on a unification process that had been going on for 60 years, which now included white South Africans who previously either could not or chose not to participate in the struggle.

Ubuntu

The concept of ubuntu represents the ability to place the welfare of your fellow human being at the centre of your decision-making universe. According to Archbishop Tutu, 'Ubuntu speaks particularly about the fact that you can't exist as a human in isolation. It speaks about our interconnectedness. You can't be human all by yourself and when you have this quality – Ubuntu – you are known for your generosity.'[4] It manifests itself in the use of empathy as a moral compass to help one navigate around everyday trade-offs. The concept is simultaneously well known and under-appreciated in the way that it elevated interpersonal expectations within apartheid South Africa's African society. It is the antithesis of the foundational American value of capitalism as representing an exercise in rugged individualism. For capitalism to be sustainably practised in a society that values ubuntu, it has to operate in a people-centric manner.

The ultimate compliment paid by an elder to a member of the community was *unobuntulamtu* (that person is people-centric). This term conveyed an elder person's admiration for an act or a personality that was consistent with their idea of a person placing other people at the centre of their decision-making universe. That person paused to ask themselves: 'How is this action going to affect the lives of my fellow beings?' Similarly, the ultimate insult that could be hurled at a member of apartheid South Africa's African society was *akanabuntulamtu* (that person is individualistic in his or her actions). African societies are famous for raising their children by committee, so this concept, reinforced as it was from household to household, became a powerful mechanism in creating self-governing behaviour in young children. The preferences of the society were made clear early and often in terms of what was regarded as model behaviour.

Well before 1994, the concept of ubuntu was seriously challenged by the adoption of a capitalistic lifestyle amongst Africans as they were forced by the urbanisation and accelerated industrialisation of South Africa to adjust to the new rules of the game. The national liberation movement helped generate the fortitude within Africans to defend this people-centricity against the assault of individualistic capitalism, but unfortunately they were unprepared for its effects on post-apartheid society. This lack of preparedness opened the way for a massive readjustment of priorities and values that has left many rudderless in their navigation of a post-1994 capitalist South Africa.

Like most modern societies, South Africa elected for a separation of church and state, which together with the social upheaval that came with managing a transition to a liberal democratic capitalist society (from an authoritarian faith-based society), created massive challenges. The floodgates were opened to drug dealing, gang activity, materialism, anti-religiousness and increased inequality within African communities as overwhelming assaults on the dominant value system. Strong, unified family structures closely linked to their rural or extended urban family roots managed to repel many of the negative effects of such forces, but single-parent, poor and isolated urban families were the first to feel their brunt.

I believe that South Africa's dominant value system coming out of the liberation struggle was that of community-based ubuntu. The majority of South Africans carried with them aspirations to lead their lives in a way that resulted in the improvement of what they considered to be their community. The enduring institutions in the poorest parts of South Africa were community centres or those enterprises (whether for or not for profit) in which the community considered itself a stakeholder. These 'community-owned institutions' thrived and those considered alien by that community failed to survive for very long. Firms like Coca-Cola and South African Breweries who were successful marketers in the majority of communities understood this impulse, choosing not to fight it but instead to unleash their corporate strategies in a manner that benefited from its functionality. Successful NGOs around South Africa became skilled in community engagement methods that resulted in a feeling of ownership and connectivity with their causes, while the ANC built a branch network that thoroughly entrenched the party's brand throughout the country.

From the moment sanctions were lifted and major corporations begun unleashing a significant marketing push into South Africa, a new consumer-centric set of attitudes began to take shape. This emerging consumerism coincided with the advent of democracy in 1994, ushering in a new era where people began to robustly embrace consumer products that they had been forced to live without for most of their lives.

The western corporations spearheading the push into post-apartheid South Africa came from societies that were founded on the bedrock of a value system that believed in rugged individualism. This is the phrase that Herbert Hoover, during his time as the President of the United States, used to describe the idea that each individual should be able to help themselves out, and that the government is not needed in the economic space – a deep-seated value that affects all aspects of American society.

What started as an emerging attitude morphed into a set of values that were in direct conflict with ubuntu. At the same time, the forces of urbanisation, upward social mobility and intermarriage created an alternative cosmopolitan set of values that lived side by side with ubuntu.

It is impossible to passively resist such active assaults on one's value system for long periods of time. Part of what South Africa currently struggles with is the search for an active repellent of the attack on this most sacred of values. The solution to this problem is to be found in actively embracing the struggle against poverty and inequality as the national struggle for economic liberation of this generation. This new struggle should be fought as passionately and diligently as the last liberation struggle was fought. It is only through the active engagement of all South Africa's citizens in this war on poverty that we can rediscover the spirit of ubuntu. In short, South Africans have to embrace people-centricity as a guiding principle for a national battle for shared prosperity.

Unfortunately the spirit of ubuntu has not facilitated an economic settlement between white-dominated corporate South Africa and the black-dominated government. Instead the country has found itself generating jobless GDP growth to the increasing frustration of labour unions, the governing party and – most importantly – ordinary men and women. This frustration first manifested itself in the form of a stubbornly high crime rate that took on a particularly violent manifestation. Next it showed itself in acts of xenophobia that were uncharacteristic of a nation liberated with the help of her neighbours. Recently the advent of so-called service delivery protests and the conflict between striking miners and the police in the North West Province's platinum-mining area has forced onto the national agenda the issue of genuine societal economic equity. All throughout this period the tension between business and labour has intensified with each wage negotiation and confidence between the two sides erodes with each work stoppage. Making matters worse is the increasingly cavalier manner in which corruption manifests itself in the public sector.

In their study of why more equal societies almost always do better, Wilkinson and Pickett remark: 'It has been known for some years that poor health and violence are more common in more unequal societies. However, in the course of our research we became aware that almost all problems which are more common at the bottom of the social ladder are more common in more unequal societies.'[5] They go on to identify the following problems shared in common between unequal societies (some of which, like the United States, are very wealthy) and some of the poorest in the world: low level of social trust, high incidence of mental illness, high incidence of teenage births, homicides and imprisonment.

South Africa is not doomed to follow the path towards social imbalance in order to push forward with policies that ensure high incomes for its very wealthiest. The country has choices and its policy makers are alive to their risks. Much as many wish to dislocate these dangerous trends from our history, solutions to these societal ills have to be grounded in a thorough understanding of how history continues to inform their impulses.

3

A Pre-owned Society

To truly understand the nature of the economy inherited by the ANC in 1994, one has to go back in history to contextualise how Dutch and British imperialism shaped South Africa's socio-economic development, the pressures that led to war between the Afrikaners and the British and how this conflict shaped the country's distribution of wealth. At the centre of it all was the contest for a share of the colonial spoils.

The Dutch East India Company founded a shipping station at the Cape of Good Hope in 1652 with the aim of producing fresh provisions for their fleet as it travelled to and from the East Indies. The early history of this colony was of extreme poverty with the colonialists finding it hard to live comfortably on the land. Slaves from the East were provided by the Company, but the settlers also subjugated the local population, using them as servants and domestic workers. Historian Thomas Pakenham makes the introduction:

The settlers were mainly Dutch Calvinists, with a leavening of German Protestants and French Huguenot refugees. To Africa these Pilgrim Fathers brought a tradition of dissent and a legacy of resentment against Europe. They called themselves 'Afrikaners' (the people of Africa) and spoke a common language, a variant of Dutch that came to be called 'Afrikaans'. The poorest and most independent of them were the *trekboers* (alias Boers), the wandering farmers whose search for new grazing lands brought them progressively deeper into African territory.[1]

These Afrikaners immediately identified themselves as legitimate owners of whatever land they colonised and whichever slaves they took over. Hermann Giliomee, author of a seminal study on the Afrikaner people, noted that they were 'among the first colonial peoples to cut most of their family and community ties with Europe and to develop a distinct sense of self-consciousness; they made the new land genuinely their own'.[2] This stunningly simplistic claim to land ownership made for a complicated history between the burghers and the British when they took control of the Cape Colony from the Dutch East India Company.

Over the first 100 years of European settlement in South Africa, three systems of land title were applied in different parts of the country. The first was traditional or customary law, which recognised ownership of land by different tribes. Key to this form of land title was the tribe's history of occupation and its displayed control of a territory through clear demarcations and/or landmarks that served as boundaries.[3] This was summarily replaced by Dutch and British legal customs when it suited the interests of the colonisers.

Both the Dutch and the British refused to recognise traditional or customary law as a form of land title. At the centre of the land issue lies the question: did the societies created by the indigenous tribes have ownership of the land that they occupied prior to the arrival of European settlers and therefore what is the legitimate legal justification for European settlers' land title? PJ Steytler's article on the traditional ownership of land explains:

During all this time the black people continued to use traditional tribal law to regulate their land rights in the areas they occupied. Their traditional law was officially recognised by the white authorities as the legal system applicable to black people in black areas.

Traditional law was written up and recorded in great detail by law-yers and anthropologists such as Seymore, Kerr, Junod, Schapera and Van Warmelo. Traditional law, or 'native law' as it was referred to at the time, was not only administered in tribal courts and in the Native Commissioners' courts but was also applied by the Supreme Court and even the Magistrates' courts in certain circumstances. According to traditional law the tribes had ownership on the land they occupied because of their history and long occupation. These rights, according to their law, were equal to registered land owner-ship in the Deeds Office.[4]

This selective application of when and where customary law was applicable facilitated the transfer of the majority of the country from African ownership to white (both British and Afrikaner) ownership in a systematic state-sponsored wealth transfer that was both illegal and unethical.

The Afrikaner justification for this entitlement over the land and the labour that was needed to work it was based on two mutually reinforcing principles: that indigenous blacks had no religion and that they were barbarians. Their Calvinistic form of Christianity taught them that they were God's own special people, sent to Africa to bring civilisation to the land. Under the Dutch, as Giliomee explains, there existed two categories which classified inhabitants of the colony and impacted heavily on their rights: Company servants, burghers and slaves were the first category; the second equally important category was either heathens or Christians.[5] Slavery would later be abolished and the British would arrive to reconstitute the class structure in the colony to reflect their own norms, but indigenous Africans were consistent in their occupation of the bottom of the food chain. This position was morally justified by the Dutch and later British failure to recognise African belief systems as legitimate forms of worship, thus classifying them as non-believers, a charge which was added to their lack of demonstrated civilisation.

David Welsh's *The Rise and Fall of Apartheid* traces the phenomenon to its roots: 'By the end of the nineteenth century all of the African polities in what was to become the Union of South Africa had been brought under white control, either by conquest or, in some cases, by treaty. The frontiers of white settlement had rolled forward inexorably; even the most redoubtable of the indigenous chiefdoms could not indefinitely withstand the pressure of guns and horses of frontiersmen, or colonial and imperial troops. Three interrelated issues dominated the black/white encounter: security, land and labour. Among Dutch and English farmers an insatiable land hunger was accompanied by an equally insatiable demand for labour.'[6]

The British annexation of the Cape in 1806 had everything to do with its strategic value relative to the route to India. The interior was of little interest, so in 1852 and 1854 the independence of Transvaal and then the Orange Free State was allowed. In 1870, however, the discovery of diamonds in the Kimberley region put a new complexion on the matter, and the northern Cape was swiftly incorporated into the British-controlled Cape Colony. The gold rush in the Witwatersrand began in 1886, and thus began the real scramble for control of South Africa and its resources, with intensifying imperial ambitions on the part of Britain matched by the first stirrings of Afrikaner nationalism, as Welsh notes.[7]

It is important to recognise that the plight of indigenous South Africans was not materially better under British indirect rule prior to the formation of the South African Union. Indeed British imperialism had the same racist undertone in the way that it viewed indigenous people, and was very blunt about their economic role as primarily a source of cheap labour. Cecil John Rhodes, prime minister of the Cape Colony from 1890, saw the question of African labour chiefly as an employer and founder of the diamond company De Beers. Giliomee records that: 'On 7 August 1894 the Bloemfontein *Express* reported a speech by Rhodes on the reserves, stating "that certain parts of the country must be home of the natives. Not everyone must have a piece of land, but it must be a place where people could go back to after working." The economic function of the reserves always predominated.'[8]

Afrikaner nationalism was to create an opposition to British imperialism stronger than Britain had seen from most of her colonies. At its centre was the Afrikaners' single-minded belief that they were fighting a just war and that God was on their side in this battle to create a nation of their own. Indeed the British added legitimacy to the Afrikaners' feeling that their claim to South Africa occupied a moral high ground by reneging on their agreement to the self-governing of Transvaal as a territory, issuing an ultimatum to Paul Kruger to step aside as an independent leader or go to war with Britain. Pakenham puts it in a nutshell: 'The war declared by the Boers on 11 October 1899 gave the British, in Kipling's famous phrase, "no end of a lesson". The British public expected the war to be over by Christmas. It proved to be the longest (two and three-quarter years), the costliest (over £200 million), the bloodiest (at least twenty-two thousand British and twelve thousand African lives) and the most humiliating war for Britain ...'[9]

The war ended with the Peace of Vereeniging in 1902. Surrender to the British was humiliating in many ways for the Afrikaners, but it did not quell their desire for national sovereignty. It did however put an end to their ambitions to unilaterally operate outside of British imperial interests. The Boer republics had been decimated: in addition to perhaps as many as 6 000 or 7 000 men killed in the field, 28 000 women and children died in the concentration camps. The whole of South Africa was now under British rule.

The Second Anglo-Boer War had profound implications for the future of South Africa. First, the British came to greatly admire and reluctantly respect the will of Afrikaners to make South Africa their home. Second, the war created a proud history of resistance which, with the folk stories about the Great Trek and the victory over the British in the First Anglo-Boer War on Majuba Hill, sealed a strong nationalist sentiment for the Afrikaner people. Third, the Afrikaners established themselves in the imperial pecking order in South Africa as a firm second below British interests. Finally, the human and financial costs of this war left the British convinced that the best way to control their South African interests was through a more sustainably indirect form of divide and rule. Reconciliation between Boers and British was paramount; at the insistence of the Boers, who were adamant that political rights for Africans were unthinkable, a clause to the Treaty of Vereeniging specified that: 'The question of granting the franchise to natives will not be decided until after the introduction of self-government.'

The British used generosity as a moderating tool over the Afrikaners by granting independence to the Transvaal and then the Orange River Colony in 1906/7, followed by full independence for the Union of South Africa in 1910. This generosity came out of a high degree of confidence on the part of Britain in an imperial system of indirect rule that had been perfected over centuries across the globe. The system made allowances for a leading indigenous ethnic group to be trusted with political custodianship as long as they handed over a lion's share of the local wealth. In South Africa the leading ethnic group was to be the Afrikaners, who were increasingly flexing their new-found political muscle.

As former president Thabo Mbeki put it in a speech entitled 'The historical injustice', written in 1978, 'British capital subdued this petrified and arrogant individualism during the Anglo-Boer War. In 1910 Boer and Briton entered into a social contract in which the Briton undertook to help ease the Boer out of the Dark Ages while promising to respect his traditions. For his part, the Boer pledged not to resist the advance and domination of British capital. Between them, Boer and Briton agreed that they would share political power and, finally that the indigenous African population would not be party to this contract but would be kept under the domination and at the disposal of the signatories, to be used by them in whatever manner they saw fit.'[10]

Of course Afrikaners were not ready to completely subordinate their aspirations for both economic and political independence to those of Britain. While moderate Afrikaner leadership thrived under the new arrangement with Britain, other potential leaders – chief among them JBM Hertzog, one of the Afrikaner leaders of the Orange River Colony – were not shy about using more populist strategies to gain political ascendancy within the newly independent state. Welsh explains:

> Language was critical since it was a vehicle of Afrikaner nationalist aspirations and the emblem of their identity as a *volk*, but other issues were closely associated and were to constitute much of the stuff of Afrikaner politics for many decades. Hertzog's slogan, 'South Africa First', encapsulated many of the nationalists' grievances and aspirations. It meant that South Africa's interests should take precedence over those of the Empire, and, as a corollary, that South Africa should be governed by those 'imbued with the South African spirit' and not by those he contemptuously called 'foreign fortune-seekers', referring to English speakers who although living in South Africa, regarded Britain as home, showed greater loyalty to the Empire than to South Africa, and typically viewed Afrikaner rights with contempt.[11]

The Afrikaner political constituency demanded tangible results out of their new status as top of the South African pecking order. They were frustrated by increased competition from an urbanising black population. The rural farmers were alarmed by the decrease in supply of African farm labourers, which increased the average wages they had to offer to attract their services. The politics of economic redistribution dictated that the newly empowered Afrikaner electorate wanted to see tangible economic results, which meant that either the British would have to make allowances for a bigger share of the economic pie going to Afrikaners, or more likely that the African non-voting public would have to suffer cutbacks in the amount of benefits they were to share under the new political dispensation. In the words of Moeletsi Mbeki in his *Architects of Poverty*: 'The Afrikaner elite to which the British handed state power in 1910 on the formation of the Union of South Africa were a class of property owners, latifundists who owned vast tracts of largely undeveloped land. In order to develop the land they needed cheap and plentiful labour, markets, transport to the markets, finance and knowledge and they used state power to address these needs.'[12]

The Natives Land Act of 1913 was the first of many laws designed to benefit the new Afrikaner elite at the expense of the African majority. This was a devastating policy for the wellbeing of a huge portion of the rural black agricultural class that had been making a living on their land for many generations. Welsh spells out its significance:

> Apart from the sacred and symbolic significance of land on which ancestors were buried, it was also the vital economic underpinning of traditional society. Alienation on so large a scale, combined with taxes that required men to go out to work as migrants, sounded a death-knell of self sufficiency and the beginning of the incorporation of Africans into white-controlled society as a subordinate colour-caste. It was a major instrument of black disempowerment. It was not only self-sufficiency that ended; the ability of African peasant farmers to market surpluses to the growing towns also declined and was finally extinguished.[13]

This Act restricted the African population to 7 per cent (later 'improved' to 13 per cent) of South Africa's land overnight by a stroke of a pen. In the words of PJ Steytler:

> When 19 June 1913 dawned there still were huge tracts of unsurveyed land all over South Africa. Surveyor-General maps before then show large portions of our country as 'unsurveyed and uninspected government land'. According to domestic and international law of that time, unregistered land of this type was generally regarded as terra nullius, ie land belonging to no one. In South Africa this was a legal fiction because all of it was occupied by tribes who owned the land, in terms of traditional ownership title. The fiction was never the less maintained by our courts. Then the general legal consensus was that government could do whatever it wanted with 'unregistered government land'. It could have it surveyed and cut up into farms. The newly-created property entities could be transferred to private persons or companies through 'Crown Grants' or 'Grondbriewe' registered in the Deeds Office. From 1914 onwards government had

huge portions of the raised land surveyed and transferred to white farmers and companies through this process. Government even allocated ownership to itself by having certain farms registered in its name in the Deeds Office.[14]

Though many Africans had made peace with the presence of a domineering white population, they had no idea what was to come out of the new peace settlement between the warring white colonialists. Many Africans had supported the British throughout the Anglo-Boer War in the misguided belief that they would be granted protection and self-determination by Imperial Britain. Despite losing close to 20 000 lives in the war, black people were left to fend for themselves by their erstwhile British 'allies'.

The concentric circle paradigm

To understand the esoteric workings of the imperial capitalists' indirect control system, and appreciate the way this system metamorphosed into the apartheid system as formally adopted in 1948, it is useful to look at this system through a dynamic set of class distinctions that regulated relations between the power centre in Britain and the periphery in South Africa. It is useful to analyse this imperial system through the prism of five concentric circles that categorise the class distinctions and display the relationship between the core and the periphery.

The outer layer contains **consumers**, who spend their lives on a virtual treadmill working nearly 12 hours a day, often commuting long distances in order to put food on their families' tables. These consumers serve as the cheap labour that underpins imperial capitalism. Their lives have to be lived in the hope that such subsistence will allow their children opportunities to get better educated and lead more fulfilling lives. Though this group contained the majority of the African (Black, Indian and coloured) people from the early 1920s through to 1960, this layer also contained a large portion of the Afrikaner community who served as artisans, mine workers, plumbers, subsistence farmers and builders. Giliomee explains: 'In a racially homogeneous society the Afrikaner poor would have become the urban proletariat and worked their way up from that position. But there already was a proletariat of between 200,000 and 300,000 male Africans who moved from the reserves to the towns and cities as migrant workers. Employers paid them as single men, arguing that the reserves provided for their family's subsistence. Africans did the unskilled work at a rate far below that for which whites were prepared to work.'[15]

The second layer of the imperial concentric circle paradigm is the **intelligentsia**, men and women who are teachers, priests, journalists and political bureaucrats who shape public opinion through their intellectual contributions. This layer is also made up of the professional class – doctors, lawyers, accountants and engineers who study at a high level in order to achieve their status in society. In a typical British colony this class would be made up of knowledgeable men who had studied in Britain or at colonial British missionary schools.

The form and substance of this education served to undermine nationalism and keep it in check by inculcating an allegiance to the superiority of the British model of society. To a large extent even missionary teachings enforced this notion of English superiority, especially in the Western and Eastern Cape. This layer of the British imperialist paradigm served to soften the cruelty of the system by providing hope to the 'privileged' members of the consumer layer that their children would have a better life than they had been offered. It was also essential in using religion as a mass demobilisation tool.

The third layer of these concentric circles is the **capitalist layer**, made up of industrialists, business owners, and corporate managing directors. In South Africa this layer was initially dominated by the commercial farming community and the mining sector. They formed what some Marxist scholars have termed the military industrial complex (a term first used by US President Dwight

Eisenhower). Moeletsi Mbeki explains: 'South Africa is well endowed with natural resources, especially minerals and metals. This has created a unique South African form of capitalism. The South African economy is dominated by the extraction of minerals from the ground, processing them into metals through the use of electric power and chemicals and selling them to the rest of the world. Most assets of the economy are devoted to these activities, which also account for most of the country's exports ... Among the weaknesses of the Military-Energy Complex ("the MEC") is its dependence on wasting non-renewable assets, dependence on imported technology and capital and overexposure to volatile world markets. Most importantly however a key characteristic of the MEC is its dependence on abundant, cheap and unskilled labour.'[16]

What allowed this system to function to the benefit of Britain was the system's reliance on British capital and the technological capacity of British multinational companies. The roles are clearly divided between cheap indigenous labour and a cohort of mining professional management drawn from British and Afrikaner settlers. All these actors were relying on British (and the broader Commonwealth) capital markets to provide the projects with funding, and British technology to endow the projects with the necessary mining and mineral processing equipment.

Closer to the core lies the fourth layer within the imperialist concentric circle paradigm, that of the **affluent upper class**. These were largely the shareholders and financiers behind the huge mining companies. At the level of the colonies they were often faceless wealthy families – and to this group went the bulk of the spoils. They intermarried and created dynastic partnerships which sometimes allowed, after years of service, members of the capitalist class to ascend to the layer of the affluent. They made and broke the reputations of many of the professional class, using their long reach into the intelligence networks and their ability to become big donors to faith-based organisations and schools as influence-generating control mechanisms. Ultimately their biggest trump card was their proximity to members of the imperial establishment who sat at the core of the system in a layer that housed **British imperial power**.

The Super-Afrikaners

By creating the Broederbond in 1918 the Afrikaner elite were able to form their own increasingly independent power structure that focused on the use of state power in creating alternative institutions. Its members simulated the ecosystem that the imperialist concentric circles represented, by creating a closed forum focused on the advancement of the socio-economic interest of their people. This allowed them to control the deployment of knowledge and capital through trusted individuals who acted as intermediaries for the state and more importantly provided access for other Broederbond members. Indeed, at the heart of the Afrikaner empowerment project was the willing use of state funds to educate Afrikaner youth (at the expense of the black population), finance Afrikaner entrepreneurs, affirmatively procure from Afrikaner businesses and develop the capacity of Afrikaner businesses.

None of this would have generated the desired results were it not for their shared (with British interests) access to South Africa's abundant and cheap labour. As Giliomee explains, 'The government drew a distinction between two types of labour. Those who performed "civilised labour" had to be remunerated in such a way that they could maintain "the standard generally recognized as tolerable from the European standpoint". Those employed as "uncivilised labour", invariably workers who were not white, required wages to afford only the bare necessities of "barbarous and underdeveloped peoples".'[17] From the outset, Afrikaner politicians such as JBM Hertzog knew that their chief constituency was poor Afrikaners who wanted to work their way out of poverty with the help of the state. The need was great, as Welsh explains:

The Great Depression that began in 1929 hit South Africa with a vengeance, conditions being made even worse by some of the worst droughts in living memory in the early 1930s ... Rural distress among whites had assumed alarming proportions. The 'poor white' problem, already discernible in the late nineteenth century, immensely exacerbated by the Anglo-Boer War and festering throughout the early decades of the Union, now became a crisis. (That African rural distress was of even greater proportions was predictably adjudged by white politicians to be a lesser concern.) A major investigation by the Carnegie Commission showed that of the white population, approximately 1.8 million in 1931, over 300 000 were 'very poor'. Since the great majority of poor whites were Afrikaners this meant that nearly one-third of all Afrikaners were afflicted by deepening poverty.[18]

The moderate Afrikaner coalition government of 1934 between Hertzog's National Party and Jan Smuts's South African Party made two fatal political mistakes. Firstly they failed to read the winds of change when it came to an increasingly self-assured brand of Afrikaner nationalism, and in so doing failed to secure the support of the elite Afrikaner Broederbond. Jan Smuts was a Cambridge-educated, moderate visionary and war veteran who had over time became an ally of Britain in her times of greatest need. He was largely disconnected from the Afrikaner nationalism that facilitated the formation of the Broederbond. Most importantly, he and Hertzog had lost touch with a major constituency in the Afrikaner community, the farmers. Consequently the coalition failed to understand the political consequences emanating from support of the British efforts in the Second World War, alienating further the Afrikaners who were reeling from the crippling effects of the Great Depression. Added to this oversight was the inability of the coalition to focus on the economic agenda of poor whites (particularly poor farmers). The Broederbond threw its weight behind the formation of the Herstigte Nasionale Party (HNP).

'Once [the HNP was] in power ... English speaking bureaucrats, soldiers and state employees were sidelined by reliable Afrikaners, with key posts going to Broederbond members (with their ideological commitment to separatism). The electoral system itself was manipulated to reduce the impact of immigrant English speakers and eliminate Coloureds.'[19] At its height the organisation had more than 19 000 members from all walks of society. From 1948 till 1994, every prime minister or state president was a member of the Broederbond. Moeletsi Mbeki charts the organisation's advance:

> The Afrikaner elite were primarily interested in state power and in using that power to advance its economic interests, particularly its agricultural interests, and to develop an Afrikaner professional class to provide the skills required by the public and parastatal sectors. The upliftment of poor whites was part of the effort to create a supervisory, managerial and technical class ... In order to achieve its objective, the Afrikaner elite promoted the emergence of state-owned enterprises such as the Electricity Supply Commission (Escom, now Eskom), the South African Railways and Harbours corporation (SAR&H, now Transnet), Land Bank, the South African Broadcasting Corporation (SABC), the Iron and Steel Corporation (Iscor, now ArcellorMittal), the Industrial Development Corporation (IDC), the telecommunications provider Telkom, the Development Bank of Southern Africa (DBSA), the Armaments Corporation of South Africa (Armscor) and the South African Coal, Oil and Gas Corporation (Sasol).[20]

None of this would have been possible without the massive subsidies generated by taxation of the black majority population. Indeed since the earliest colonial years tax policy had become progressively more efficient at forcing rural people into the labour system and generating revenue for the state, which was used to finance the development of an economic infrastructure that indigenous people were structurally locked out of. Cargill's study of Black Economic Empowerment measures progress:

> Mapping the period from 1948 to 1975 ... Afrikaner control of the private sector ... [increased] from 6% to 21% (a 15% increase) in

27 years. The mining sector's proportion of private sector owner-ship increased from 1% in 1948 to 10% in 1964 to 18% in 1975 (a 17% rise), largely due to the acquisition from Anglo American Corporation of General Mining and Finance Corporation by Afrikaner capital. The percentage growth in participation is fairly consistent for other key sectors. Liquor and catering escalated from 20% to 35%; finance from 6% to 25%; and manufacturing and con-struction from 6% to 15%.[21]

Throughout this period Afrikaners simultaneously built great educational institutions and solid government-supported com-panies, encouraged affirmative (in favour of other Afrikaners) pro-curement, and facilitated the emergence of a strong commercial farming network through cheap state finance and government protection. They were thoroughly successful at using state buying power to increase their share of economic activity.

The period after 1950 was one of unprecedented prosperity for white South Africans. The white population became almost entirely urban and employed in white-collar rather than blue-collar occupations. The proportion of Afrikaans-speaking white workers in agricultural occupations fell from 30 per cent in 1946 to 16 per cent in 1960 and 8 per cent in 1970. The proportion in blue-collar and other manual labour remained stable through the 1950s but fell rapidly in the 1960's and 1970's. Conversely, the proportion in white-collar em-ployment rose from 29 per cent in 1946 to 65 per cent in 1977. This was a period of widespread upward mobility into the middle and managerial classes.[22]

Black South Africans missed out as Afrikaners took advantage of the largest economic boom in the history of South Africa, which saw the entire economy fundamentally transformed from domina-tion by mining and agriculture, to a sophisticated industrialised middle-income country.

Though the Afrikaner state was intervening heavily in the

favour of Afrikaner business, many officials in government and the Broederbond knew that they would have to prepare Afrikaner children for a time where they would be much less sheltered from competition. This, combined with the Afrikaner's conservative Calvinistic culture, which emphasised sacrificing short-term pleasure for long-term rewards, led the elite to focus heavily on education. 'Between 1912 and 1926 spending on education as a proportion of the budget and the number of white pupils had doubled... In 1943 one estimate said that the state would have to multiply its current spending on black education thirty-six times to bring it to the level of white education; 60 per cent of black children were not in school at all.'[23]

Giliomee sums it up: 'In the first twenty-three years of apartheid, between 1948 and 1981, the South African economy grew at a rate of 4.5 per cent. This was about the average for a group of twenty comparable middle-sized developing countries.'[24]

So, with a combination of smart long-term policies, brutal repression of the majority of the population, cross-subsidisation through under-spending on Africans and (proportionately) over-taxing Africans, and luck, the Afrikaners were able to claw their way out of poverty and beat the British at their own game in the use of state power to circumvent imperial domination.

The timing of Afrikaner penetration closer to the core of British imperial concentric circles ensured that the prosperity generated by the commodities boom-driven industrialisation of South Africa benefited the larger Afrikaner community. Fortunes were built during this period and the national coffers were bolstered, allowing further investment in the education of new generations of both Afrikaner and English-speaking whites at the expense of other South Africans, preparing the next generation of white South Africans for the brutally competitive (post-1994) economy.

Preparing for reform

In the twilight of the apartheid era many Afrikaners were torn between a sense of pride in the nation that they had helped build and
shame at the cost of Afrikaner development to the broader black
population. It must have been clear to even the most unrecon-
structed of racists, looking around at the wide gaps in standards of
living, that this was not a sustainable political system. The signs
were everywhere for willing observers to see. According to Hirsch,
'The average per capita income (in 1994) of whites was 9.5 times
higher than [that of] Africans... When measured in 1989, 52.7% of
Africans were living below the poverty line, compared with 1.6%
of whites... In 1993 the poorest 10% of the South African population received 1.1% of the population's income, while the richest
10% received 45%.'[25]

The ANC-led liberation movement spent more than 70 years,
both internally through mass resistance and externally through
sanctions and armed struggle, initially pushing back against the
post-Vereeniging pro-Afrikaner reforms, and later in outright defiance of apartheid. These efforts finally paid dividends because
economic conditions facilitated the climate for a negotiated settlement. A key event in this process had nothing to do with South
Africa. In 1971 the world dropped the gold standard as a method
of underwriting the value of the world's currencies, and the price
of gold began to decline. Since gold is a major South African export, its 'commoditisation' was a game changer for the fortunes of
both British and Afrikaner mineral interests.

The introduction of sanctions, thanks to the ANC's clever use
of the symbolism of President Mandela's incarceration to project
a human face of the plight of the black South African, was the
straw that broke the camel's back. In September 1985, the country experienced a debt crisis brought about by a mismatch in the
maturity structure of the country's private sector debt. Rustomjee
explains: 'Compounding the situation, Chase Manhattan Bank refused to roll over its loans, alarmed by increasing violence and

the stubborn refusal of the apartheid government to agree to any political change. What followed was an escalating set of financial sanctions that cut off South Africa from global capital markets.'[26]

The combination of the fall in gold prices, a massive disinvestment and sanctions regime and an increase in the cost of managing the apartheid infrastructure (largely because of the increased budget allocation to the 'Bantustans') crippled the economy. Pippa Green's biography of Trevor Manuel gives a snapshot of the turmoil at the time:

> Capital fled and new capital cowered. Government's consumption spending grew from 15 percent of GDP in 1983 to 21% a decade later. In the first five years of the 1980's, foreign debt rose from 20 percent to 50 percent of GDP... By then, the deficit was heading to higher than 8 percent, or about R30 billion, in a shrinking economy. By 1994 – when the democratic government was slated to take over – the interest charge alone would be R20.7 billion (or more than 18% of expenditure), and the interest bearing debt R186 billion (or an astonishing 42 percent of GDP).[27]

It became inconvenient to the newly wealthy Afrikaner business elite for their businesses to be exposed to this type of negative business environment, so both the business and the Broederbond communities began lobbying the National Party for change in the form of a negotiated settlement. As Ruben Richards states, 'My view ... is that the ultimate struggle in South Africa was never really about race. Rather it was about who controlled the money. Race was used as an instrument in the hands of the oppressor to achieve economic power and control. When one race conquers another, the winning racial group generally designs systems to benefit its own racial index and support base.'[28] If one interprets South Africa's post-First World War history through the prism of both an inter- and intra-ethnic scramble for resources – that is, English-speaking whites versus Afrikaner whites versus the rest of South Africa's ethnic groups – race becomes a secondary rather than primary explanatory tool for the historical events leading up to the establishment of the apartheid regime.

In South Africa the mythology went as follows: Afrikaners are the chosen race, they should get control over all South Africa's resources, they should use that control as a way to empower Afrikaners at the expense of others. As whites became better educated and more prosperous, the logic became inverted. Blacks were portrayed as inferior to whites and expected to be satisfied with whatever scraps the system afford them. As the church, the state and the education system all participated with increasing missionary zeal in this justification mechanism, the fate of black South Africans was increasingly doomed. They got progressively less because the system recognised them as less and less human, resulting in terribly low levels of education and even worse economic prospects year after year.

4

The Great Fraud

The current *Oxford English Dictionary* definition of apartheid – 'a policy or system of segregation or discrimination on the grounds of race' – covers, on the face of it, the discriminatory, systematic and racist nature of apartheid, but the description doesn't begin to describe the strategic intent behind the policy, or the socio-economic impact of its execution. Over the years the blurred battle lines along which the liberation struggle took place obscured the original line in the sand drawn by poor Afrikaners demanding that their political representatives design a system of rule that would redistribute wealth in their favour. By 1994 South Africans were tired of inter-racial fighting, anxious to join the international community of nations, naïve about the extent of the socio-economic damage inflicted on their country and eager to join hands with each other towards a better, more inclusive future.

The nation anticipated the release of Nelson Mandela with a sense of euphoria within the black community and amongst members of the white community who had fought side by side for liberation. Among those who were active or passive supporters of the apartheid system was fear about the uncertainties associated with change, combined with a resigned preparation for payback in the form of punitive black rule. To their surprise – not having experienced President Mandela's leadership capacities prior to his incarceration, or been able (because his statements were banned) to read or listen to articulation of his moral approach to reconciliation whilst he was incarcerated – he came out, in keeping with the long-standing policy of the ANC, embracing non-racialism and reconciliation as the national priority number one. For Mandela, uniting South Africa was essential to cementing its future ability to redress the socio-economic hardships of the past.

Mandela worked feverishly to make sure that no South African would feel inferior or superior to another. Crucially this approach was based on the premise that such a balanced and gracious treatment would build political capital that the ANC could later use to bolster its redistribution agenda, by enabling it to call on the support of white business for both the RDP and Black Economic Empowerment (BEE).

One of the compromises made by the ANC negotiating team at the Convention for a Democratic South Africa (Codesa) was to have a Government of National Unity that was tasked with an interim power-sharing arrangement that could allow for a gradual transfer of power from the National Party to the ANC. Jo Ansie van Wyk maps the process:

> Accommodation of old elites was done in various ways. First, the protection of apartheid and Bantustan government officials was provided for in the 1993 Interim Constitution. In addition, Joe Slovo's 'sunset clause', which, inter alia, offered employment protection to the predominantly white Afrikaans bureaucracy... Some of the old elites were maintained in their government positions. Second, the pact included leaving the structures, powers and functions of the old state institutions intact. This compromise by the ANC was premeditated to prevent conflicts with the old elite. Once in the Union Buildings, ANC elites initiated and prepared to implement its agenda to overturn the legacy of apartheid, which was often met with opposition from the NP members of Cabinet and the predominantly NP-supporting government bureaucracy. The NP attempted to protect

THE GREAT AFRICAN SOCIETY

its bureaucratic interests and the ANC attempted to appoint officials from its elite.[1]

Across the country the goodwill that Mandela generated from this high road approach created a sense of hope and anticipation that through his leadership he could literally will the nation towards unity, peace and prosperity. This approach led many to believe that the ANC and specifically Mandela's leadership of the party was the best thing that could have happened in South African politics.

President Mandela's vision of a non-racial South Africa was rooted in a commitment to correct the socio-economic wrongs of the past but was not accompanied by significant economic hardship for white South Africans. To be sure, the new government's economic team, guided by Deputy President to-be Mbeki, pushed successfully for the retention and broadening of the progressive tax system that would have higher income generators pay a disproportionate share of the tax. This would be accompanied by an improvement in the professionalism of the South African Revenue Service (SARS), which increased the national tax receipts enormously year after year.

To Mbeki would fall the unenviable task of reconstructing almost every government institution. To transform the personnel, legal frameworks and ideological thrust of all these institutions while simultaneously facing a budget crisis worsened by debts taken on by the previous governments and the harsh economic realities that came from entering globalisation with a fundamentally uncompetitive economy, required superhuman strength. This was the curse of post-liberation leadership. The electorate did not think they were electing politicians, they believed they were electing heroes. So by definition the expectations were of extraordinary action within an unreasonable time frame, without consideration for the resource constraints. In the case of Mbeki, those expectations were not unfounded, since he was widely regarded as one of the brightest Africans of any generation. As a development economist who had been steadily mentored by the cerebral Oliver Tambo, he was trained for leadership under such circumstances.

The leadership of President Nelson Mandela and Deputy President Thabo Mbeki came at a very challenging time, based on changes in the geo-political and global economic landscape. The slow decline of the communist regime in Russia was accompanied by a dynamic interconnectivity between countries that had been largely facilitated by reductions in trade barriers (facilitated by the General Agreement on Tariffs and Trade), the steady decline between 1980 and 1993 of global transportation costs and the offshoring of manufacturing from European, Japanese and American firms towards developing countries which had increasingly educated populations able to produce high-quality goods and services from a lower cost base.[2]

Unfortunately for Mandela and Mbeki, their economic team completely misdiagnosed the nature of the apartheid wounds. They focused on the symptoms (unemployment, poverty, the lack of housing, malnutrition) rather than analysing the nature of the disease (systematic socio-economic incapacitation). Perhaps, snowed under by multiple accounts of the developing mythology of the political miracle of reforming racists turned agents for reconciliation, the team took their eye off the economic incentives for apartheid. Perhaps the spirit of political euphoria clouded the critical reflection necessary to weed out the political concessions on offer in order to evaluate the economic concessions not given.

Whatever the reason, the ANC's economic thinkers lost sight of the need to actively restructure the economy upfront as a precondition for long-term stability. An economy structured on the basis of cheap labour supporting a commodities-based industry was no longer able to be internationally competitive in the era of globalisation. In this new era the international capital markets rewarded the countries that invested heavily in their national intellectual capital, servicing high-tech industries that relied on high total factor productivity. In short, South Africa needed to have the fiscal flexibility and the foresight to invest heavily in the rapid skills development of her citizens to make the country more globally competitive.

What could not be dismissed as either accidental or a bureaucratic oversight was the massive compromise agreed to in Codesa's smoke-filled rooms to appease fears of apartheid-era public sector employees, which would affect South Africa's future economic development choices profoundly:

> Toward the end of its rule, the apartheid government in South Africa converted its contributory pension system for employees in the public sector from one that effectively functioned as a pay-as-you-go (PAYG) scheme to a fully funded scheme... The most far-reaching effect of the adoption of a fully funded pension scheme is that it led directly to a dramatic increase in national debt, as the public servants of the previous regime consciously indebted the state in order to safeguard their own pensions and retrenchment packages in retirement. In 1989 the total debt of the South African government stood at R68 billion rand, of which R66 billion was domestic debt and only R2 billion was foreign. By 1996 it had grown phenomenally to R308 billion, of which R297 billion was domestic and R11 billion was foreign debt. The servicing costs for these debts rose from about R12 billion in 1989 to more than R30 billion per annum in 1996. During the same period, the assets of the Government Employees Pension Fund (GEPF) grew from R31 billion to R136 billion.[3]

This amounted to one of the greatest frauds in world history. Such massive liabilities, accumulating over a short period of time, were in many cases the result of inflated retrenchment packages to the civil servants of a regime globally condemned for having purposefully overseen a systematic underdevelopment of the majority of its people. Because the nature of the debt was 'internal', most South Africans were blind to its cause and effects:

> In effect, the government is indebted to itself through the fully funded pension system [the Government Employees Pension

Fund], as the transition from a PAYG system to a fully funded one implied that former contributions to the public pension schemes had to be securitized via government bonds that were deposited in the newly created pension fund. Furthermore, contributions of current employees were directed into the pension fund while current pensions had to be financed out of the budget. This costly transition had detrimental implications for social investment, especially in the areas of education, health and welfare.[4]

Settlement in smoke-filled rooms

The leadership of the ANC while in exile had with a few exceptions operated in a manner that was inclusive, democratic and dignified. This exemplary leadership role endowed the organisation with the undeniable status of custodianship of the ambitions of the majority of the country.

The ANC's leaders returned from exile and prison as heroes of the liberation struggle eager to achieve liberation and ascend to the status of the ruling class. The irony is that the formation of the national identity of the country had not been experienced by its future leaders who were either in exile or in prison. The result was a disjuncture between the values and beliefs of a people who saw themselves as individual victors of a liberation struggle that they carried the life scars of, and a leadership that came from outside the society to claim a victory. Thus the spoils of this victory were earmarked for insiders of a political party that was led by outsiders. This disconnect between the lived reality of ordinary South Africans and the majority of their senior leaders facilitated the cold-blooded compromises that only detached leadership can make as the price of attaining political power.

South Africa's official history conceals not only the economic intentions behind apartheid, but also the political expediency of the ANC-led negotiation team in agreeing to create an effective economic straitjacket for future policy making. This dual deception created a settlement that was difficult to judge at face value. If you accept the logic that on the one hand you had a group of individuals representing a repressive racist regime who were ready (despite their control of a strong military) to acknowledge their faults and cede control to a leadership of sworn enemies, then calling it a miracle is entirely justified. At the same time, viewing the 1994 settlement as a carefully calculated pact by members of two groups of political elites interested in the orderly transfer of power accommodates a more cynical evaluation of the settlement.

At one time, history books tended to assert that apartheid came about because Afrikaners developed a racist loathing for black people which led them to choose to create a policy of separate development. Then, pioneering work led by Marxist scholars such as O'Meara, Johnstone, Wolpe, Davies and Morris in the 1970s began to shed light on the role of cheap labour in encouraging the creation of and sustaining the apartheid regime. Liberal historians such as CW de Kiewiet explored how the socio-economic privileges associated with white supremacy were drivers of segregationist policies that developed into full-blown apartheid. In addition, political economy scholars began in the 1970s to talk about a deliberate policy of underdevelopment. Economist Francis Wilson added specific insight into how labour policies towards indigenous South Africans were designed to give maximum benefit to the country's mining companies. Unfortunately the discipline of the underdevelopment school of Political Economy lost steam and the publication of works of this nature ceased around the fall of communism (though some great work in this area has been published from the late 1990s onwards). In fact, the dominant economic thinking in the 1980s was directed to studying how apartheid was slowing down the development of South Africa.

Economists focused on the opportunity costs of the apartheid regime to the country. Some went as far as to say that the apartheid years represented the 'lost years' of South Africa's development. The reported economic failure of apartheid was an important source of 'proof' to Marxist scholars that capitalism was doomed to fail; that evidence of its long-run success in the economic development of its intended beneficiaries (namely the Afrikaner population) was ignored. This misguided interpretation of South Africa's history has led to the often false conclusion that apartheid didn't work, that the policy cannibalised itself because it was doomed to fail from the beginning, and that by some miracle the apartheid regime realised the futility in its attempt to develop whites separately from Africans.

By obfuscating the real agenda behind apartheid, South African citizens (along with the rest of the world) failed to understand the true reason for the apartheid government's readiness to negotiate. As we have seen in our brief and necessarily schematic examination of the development of the Afrikaner people, it is clear that as they got richer and more integrated into the British-dominated economy, the rationale behind the apartheid project ceased to exist. But this was because of the success and not the failure of the policy.

> The gradual admission within the Afrikaner Broederbond that the revolutionary conditions in South Africa could only be peacefully resolved through the political participation of the black population at all levels was revolutionary in itself. It is the reason why in 1984-85 members had already begun to discuss in groups within individual cells how a new constitution could be developed. They envisaged one that foresaw a fundamental change of system in the sense of a political transformation, but which also took the interests of the Afrikaners into account as much as possible within this process.[5]

The lack of focus on the economic rationale behind the apartheid government's negotiation strategy led the ANC to approach the negotiations, both formal and informal, without sufficient preparation as regards the level of economic concessions they thought could legitimately be won. Critically the ANC did not, as would be expected given the type of crime committed against black South Africans, seek reparations even as a negotiating ploy. Nor did it negotiate significant debt holidays or debt restructuring from local and international debt holders. It is fascinating that the ANC had nationalisation as its only economic redistributive tool prior to 1990. Even this policy tool was not fleshed out in any real detail so as to provide serious policy options. Questions about whether the nationalisation would be with or without compensation, which industries the programme would focus on, and who would manage the nationalised firms, were not adequately dealt with. On the other hand, there had been active preparation by Afrikaner nationalists for life after apartheid for some time. 'In 1985 there were 35 different teams in the Afrikaner Broederbond, usually consisting of four to ten "brothers", producing policy papers on any theme remotely touching upon Afrikaner Broederbond interests.'[6]

The ANC was clearly not prepared for the barrage of lobbying, corporate bullying and sometimes outright bribery to protect the hard-won economic gains from apartheid. As Cyril Ramaphosa's biographer shrewdly noted: 'Relly [Chairman of Anglo American] also understood that nationalisation was an immense practical task, requiring carefully planned administrative and legislative programmes. He returned [from a meeting with ANC leaders in Lusaka] confident that the ANC's leading economic thinkers, such as Thabo Mbeki, had no practical strategy for turning the idea of state ownership into a credible programme of nationalisation.'[7]

The combination of the ANC's lack of preparedness and overeagerness for power with the lack of good faith and honesty from the apartheid negotiating team on economic issues, resulted in one of the biggest frauds ever. 'Crudely put, the ANC would enjoy relatively unfettered majority rule, subject to certain constitutional constraints; and whites would be allowed to continue their domination of the private sector, subject to very important qualifications aimed at redressing inequality, including affirmative action, black economic empowerment, land redistribution and restitution, and a progressive levelling of inequalities in the provision of services by means of an expanding floor of enforceable minimum rights.'[8]

Apartheid became a crime with no perpetrators and only victims. Overnight, simply by subjecting themselves to the Truth and

Reconciliation Commission and admitting their racism towards blacks and complicity to the apartheid ideology, everyone could become a victim of apartheid. South Africa began to create a fetish of race relations studies. National healing was the buzzword of the decade, with even the richest members of the society claiming a need to cure themselves of the ills of apartheid racist thinking, paving the way to entry into 'citizenship' as a guiltless member of the new South Africa.

Even though the TRC recommended modest payments to certain affected families, the Commission, against the advice of many of South Africa's most respected academics at the time, did not touch on issues related to economic crimes by the apartheid regime. The result was that South Africa was a country poised in many ways for a giant sweeping under the carpet of a big piece of its socio-economic history, by emphasising racism as opposed to economic expediency as the driver of apartheid. It became inconvenient to both the old and new governments to discuss in detail the true nature of apartheid crimes.

The crime of apartheid is defined by the 2002 Rome Statute of the International Criminal Court as inhumane acts of a character similar to other crimes against humanity 'committed in the context of an institutionalized regime of systematic oppression and domination by one racial group over any other racial group or groups and committed with the intention of maintaining that regime'.[9] Note the emphasis on the character of the crime and its institutional nature. The legal definition as well as the dictionary definition are silent on the economic crimes as well as, more importantly, on the economic motivation behind these crimes. By allowing the TRC to be structured in a manner consistent with this view, the ANC missed an opportunity to debunk the mythology of separate development and the fallacy behind the argument that its motive was racial – and even more importantly, missed the opportunity to extract reparations.

With a more accurate analysis of the economic motives of apartheid and a more comprehensive approach to the socio-economic

THE GREAT AFRICAN SOCIETY

truth and reconciliation needed to heal the nation, it would have become clearer to policy makers that the under-development of African indigenous education was the weak underbelly of the economy in need of immediate remedy. A fairer settlement would have resulted in a quantification of what it would take to correct this historical challenge, and how business (and well-to-do South Africans) should partner government in financing remedial action.

We need to understand and appreciate the massive strategic opportunity the ANC missed, and to do so requires a calibration of the nature of these crimes. Nattrass and Seekings set the scene: 'First, no other capitalist state (in either the North or the South) has sought to structure income inequalities as systematically and brutally as did South Africa under apartheid. Explicit racial discrimination affected earnings and income directly and blatantly. Black people and white people with the same qualifications were paid different wages for performing the same job especially in the public sector.'[10] Over a period of more than 40 years these represent staggering injustices. 'In the late 1960s the maximum pension paid to an African person was a mere one-seventh of the maximum payable to a white pensioner.'[11] These low African pensions directly subsidised the pensions of the higher-paid majority Afrikaner civil servants.

The legacy of pass laws dictated the skills sets and competency limitations of generations of African workers, resulting in their inability to market themselves in the new South African economy. This historical fact is a large contributor to South Africa's structural unemployment problem, which is currently blamed generically on a 'skills gap' (as if people have chosen to have the wrong skills). 'These [the pass laws] were defended in the parliamentary debates [of the apartheid government] on the grounds that they allocated labour efficiently in a period of full or nearly full employment. But they confined a large portion of African labour to two low-productivity, low-wage sectors of the economy; farming and mines. The result was high intersectorial wage differentials for African but not for white workers.'[12]

Not only did African workers subsidise white workers by being forced to accept low-wage, high-risk employment and lower pensions. They subsidised the economy by maintaining the productivity of the traditional sector (mining and farming) while white workers were trained (again using capital raised from taxes generated from Africans) for higher value new economy jobs. Thus the industrialisation of South Africa was buttressed by subsidies extracted from African people. For the majority of urban African labour to be forced through a cruel tax structure to enter into migrant labour (because they could not lawfully bring their families) on the mines for minimum-wage mind-numbing work was devastating to the development of the African family structure.

Worse still for black people was the knowledge that the only way their children's future could be secured was by the toppling of the brutal system. 'By 1960, the number of white students passing matric was sixteen times the total number of coloured, Indian, and African students who passed… By 1970, the secondary school enrolment rate reached 90 percent among white children; among African children, it had risen to only 16 percent despite growing fourfold in the previous decade.'[13] The policy of Bantu Education took pride in the systematic underdevelopment of black people, robbing them of basic problem-solving skills and replacing those with a steady diet of rote learning. During the course of apartheid, two generations of Africans went through this system.

The country robbed tens of millions of South Africans of the most basic of human rights, the ability to seek a better life for one's offspring. Tens of millions of Africans were denied rights to get a bank loan and buy a house in a neighbourhood they could afford to live in through the Black (Urban Areas) Act passed in 1923, together with the Group Areas Act passed in 1950. So the surest way to building wealth, home ownership, was denied to most African people. Apartheid ensured that poverty would be a condition that was passed from one generation of Africans to the next.

So, why did South Africa not have a settlement that was fairer?

Why did liberation leaders fail the poorest people by not only failing to negotiate appropriate reparations but also subsequently choosing an economic development path that forced them to compete with a global labour force that was light years ahead of them in their ability to out-perform them on every available metric?

Interestingly, Israel made a case in the 1950s that it should be compensated by the German government and its allies for the plunder of property by Nazis in the Second World War and the economic cost of absorbing nearly half a million Jewish people into the Israeli state. 'The Luxembourg Treaty helped Israel achieve a level of economic stability between 1953 and 1964. The Treaty was divided into four separate agreements, one specifically pertaining to Israel. The Israel agreement, otherwise known as the Shilumim, committed West Germany to pay Israel 3 billion Deutsche Marks (about $800 million) over a twelve year period.'[14] It is amazing to think that Germany was asked to pay such a large sum in reparations and the apartheid government was allowed to walk away without paying a cent. Instead, its then leader was awarded a Nobel Peace Prize for having the good grace to bow out while he was on top. With so many educated leaders in the ANC steeped as they were in European history one can only guess that they knew about these figures but chose to ignore them for purposes of political expediency.

It is interesting to note that in a speech given in 1978 Thabo Mbeki was already aware of the prospective dangers of a settlement that did not resolve the economic challenges posed by the apartheid system of wealth distribution. 'The charge of traitor might stick if we were to advance a program of equality between black and white while there remained between these two communities the relations of exploiter and exploited. But we have already said that our victory presupposes the abolition of parasitism and the re-integration of the idle rich as productive members of society as well as our writing off the debt of the white worker and farmer so that they can start again afresh, as equals with other producers, in law and in every other respect, without the heavy weight of blood money in their pockets and on their consciences.'[15]

If we go back to the analysis of the imperial concentric circles (explored in detail in Chapter 3) and how these concentric circles were pierced by the organisational capacity and single-mindedness of the Afrikaner Broederbond through the active use of state power, we can better understand the source of the pressure for a non-reparations-based settlement. The intellectual layer of the imperialist concentric circle's paradigm was by 1980 full of apartheid-era operatives (members of the security forces, political bureaucrats, journalists, university lecturers and professionals). Through active recruitment and affirmative action Afrikaners were playing a disproportionate role in all facets of the economy, permeating decision-making structures and therefore ensuring that they were actively involved in all major nodes of influence. Their prosperity hinged on their inclusion in the next regime, so they were the first to 'test the waters' with regards to meetings with senior ANC leaders.

The capitalist layer of these concentric circles consisted by the late 1980s of both British and Afrikaner business people, who operated businesses that had been built on the back of the apartheid system either directly (through state tenders or other government contracts) or indirectly (through participation in the military industrial complex or government-run import substitution programmes). Many of these businesses had been superbly managed by skilful businessmen who had learnt to operate in the internationally hostile sanctions environment. Ironically, many initially prospered from sanctions by buying exiting European and American companies at fire sale prices. 'In the isolated conditions of the 1980s, compounded by the growing disinvestments by foreign firms, a small number of South African conglomerates seized almost total control of the economy. By the end of the decade, five groups controlled companies worth close to 90% of the stock market value of all public companies based in South Africa.'[16]

These two layers within the imperial concentric circles combined with the charity organisations supported by members of the affluent layer of society (now joined by the likes of the Ruperts, the

Malherbes, the Hertzogs and the Graaffs), began forming informal and formal networks with key ANC leadership. Mark Gevisser describes one of the earliest meetings:

> A month before Dr Frederik van Zyl Slabbert's visit to Lusaka in June 1987, a group of South African businessmen and editors had met the ANC leadership at Kenneth Kaunda's game farm in Zambia. The liberation movement packed a high-powered delegation, but the South African visitors only had eyes for Mbeki. 'I'd be happy to have that guy as my president,' said Anglo American chair Gavin Relly of Mbeki as they were flown back in the company's private Gulfstream. Writing about the encounter, *Sunday Times* editor Tertius Myburgh cited one of his fellow-travellers: 'I'd rather have Thabo Mbeki at my home than Ted Kennedy'... 'After I had contact with him,' journalist Max du Preez has written, 'I would return to South Africa and tell everybody who would listen: Thabo Mbeki is going to play a major part in our future, and a better man you can't get.'
>
> The ruling Afrikaner elite might have expected such sentiments from 'soutpiele' such as Relly or 'verraaiers' such as Du Preez, but by early 1988 even one of their own seemed to have been turned: Willie Esterhuyse, the unimpeachably establishment Stellenbosch academic who had been approached by the National Intelligence Services (NIS) to serve as a an intermediary between the ANC and the government, reported back to his handlers: 'I'm prepared to trust my life to this fellow.'[17]

Aside from the fact that Mbeki was undoubtedly one of the most intellectually impressive of the ANC leadership and that his diplomatic, urbane approach must have been a welcome relief for business leaders who had inherently low expectations, there must have been substance behind the comfort expressed by these hard-nosed businessmen. There must have been some powerful assurances made, either explicitly or implicitly, by President Mbeki to these men in order for them to be that comfortable with his leadership, and the potential for his future presidency.

The corporations that benefited the most from apartheid, firms such as Anglo American, Gensec, Old Mutual, Sanlam and Shell, began funding conferences (attended by ANC leadership) on economic scenarios, overseas trips and study for key ANC technocrats, all in the hope of further influencing the settlement in their favour. The aggregate of these efforts was the elite pact entered into in 1994. Though many South Africans were unaware at the time, black South Africans had already given away their moral authority for a proper financial package of reparations or the hope that the new government could muster up huge public sector investment to help invest in education so that they could compete in the new South Africa. Hope was instead placed on a market-based economic solution, with limited state involvement.

In the marathon negotiations leading up to the first election in 1994, the ANC managed to secure several key political concessions from the National Party. These related to the adoption of a unitary state (with some pseudo-federal features) instead of the strict federalist government framework sought by the National Party. Importantly, the ANC also fought against futile efforts to have the Government of National Unity made permanent (instead of what ended up being a temporary GNU which lasted just under four years). The ANC's razor-sharp focus on political freedom and the control of state apparatus as quickly as possible led the party to make concessions on the economic redistributive power of the state that have resulted in 15 lost economic years for two thirds of black South Africans living in families ravaged by unemployment.

As previously described, not only did the ANC fail to secure any real reparations for poor people, the party was also hoodwinked into accepting liabilities (such as the huge pension fund liabilities associated with paying inflated pensions to apartheid-era public servants) that resulted from apartheid's subsidised development. In addition, South Africans also had a government that looked at governing through the prism of a free-market-centric outlook, which meant getting the budget as close to balanced as possible, at the developmental cost of the majority of the population. With the best bureaucratic management team in the world, such an equation would prove unmanageable. But against the reality of a first-time government made up of a majority of dedicated men and women who had no track record in the jobs that they filled, the task proved even harder.

The RDP and GEAR

The gap between the pro-poor rhetoric and the pro-rich reality of South Africa's macro-economic policy framework has become more apparent each year that the ANC has been in power. There was a false dichotomy created by both sides of the Codesa negotiating table in order to prepare the grounds for an elite pact. Simply put, the ANC had two options: lead a populist government that acquiesces to populist sentiment to deliver the spoils of liberation to the people through nationalisation, or follow the prudent path of responsible macro-economic management with some aspects of a welfare state (what was called the mixed economy).

As Nigel Gibson puts it: 'Indeed, post-apartheid society has created the type of integration that Biko would have abhorred: an artificial integration where a Black middle class views advancement in terms of a shrewd mixing of "ubuntu" rhetoric with possessive individualism. At the same time, South Africa's masses of poor people, many politicised by the long anti-apartheid struggle but marginalised from post-apartheid polity, have been quick to understand that the betrayal of "the struggle" is not simply a moral issue but a social phenomenon.'[18]

Presented with the false dichotomy between either nationalisation or prudent fiscal conservatism, the black population trusted a combination of the moral leadership of President Nelson Mandela and the technical skill of Deputy President Thabo Mbeki to manage the nuances of taking this 'more responsible' route. What was not explained at the time was that Mbeki had spent considerable effort on quietening any alternative economic viewpoints from the left of the ANC. The labour unions under Cosatu reluctantly supported this compromise on one condition: that a programme of Reconstruction and Development, the RDP, was created through the management of a fund that was to be controlled by an independent Ministry – headed by Jay Naidoo – that would carry out the agenda of redistributing wealth through targeted programmes. In Naidoo's words: 'Its goal was to transform the state and bring about economic growth through an infrastructure strategy that aimed at addressing the massive backlogs in the provision of basic infrastructure to areas where the black majority lived. It was also the platform to drive the modernisation of the economy that would be the basis for efficiency and business development through a comprehensive reform of industrial strategy to create jobs, meet domestic demand and build a competitive export sector.'[19]

This new interdisciplinary approach operated as a fund that drew money from the treasury and facilitated donor capital into targeted interventions in the economy. The left in the ANC thought that it served as a useful initial platform from which to build. As Naidoo explained: 'The RDP worked to link growth, human resource development, reconstruction and reconciliation into a "unified programme" held together by a broad infrastructure programme that would focus on creating and enhancing existing services in the electricity, water, telecommunications, transport, health, and education and training sectors. In particular, we realised that we had to tackle youth unemployment.'[20] For the left in the ANC this was an essential accompaniment to the various market-based reforms envisioned by neo-liberal market fundamentalists. They would no doubt have refused to be part of the settlement of 1994 were it not for these concessions.

However, Naidoo's ministry was short-lived: 'On 28 March 1996, barely a month after returning from India, the office of the RDP was officially shut down. As Minister, I was not informed before the decision was made, nor were satisfactory reasons given to me for closing the Ministry – barely 23 months after the RDP programme was set up with the enthusiastic blessing of President Mandela and all the Alliance partners.'[21]

Importantly, had the RDP been left to operate it would have been the logical recipient of a financial settlement aimed at repairing the effects of both colonialism and apartheid. By integrating its functionality into other government departments, the economic effects of apartheid could not be segmented and accounted for, as they would be obfuscated by the national budget.

The ANC's decision to scrap the RDP programme and replace it with the Growth, Employment and Redistribution programme (GEAR) represented a watershed for South Africa's economic development. This programme was a move towards an orthodox macroeconomic policy as was being prescribed by the International Monetary Fund to developing countries all over the world. If RDP represented watered-down concessions to the left, then GEAR represented the free-market-centric view of how economic policy over the next ten years was to look. In short, there would not be any structural redistribution except for that allowed under the auspices of BEE.

The Department of Finance's summary document gives the key components of GEAR as:

❑ a faster fiscal deficit reduction programme to contain debt service obligations, counter inflation and free resources for investment;

❑ a renewed focus on budget reform to strengthen the redistributive thrust of expenditure;

❑ a reduction in tariffs to contain input prices and facilitate industrial restructuring, compensating partly for the exchange rate depreciation;

❑ a commitment to moderate wage demands, supported by an appropriately structured flexibility within the collective bargaining system;

❑   an exchange rate policy to keep the real effective rate stable at a competitive level;

❑   a consistent monetary policy to prevent a resurgence of inflation;

❑   a further step in the gradual relaxation of exchange controls;

❑   speeding up the restructuring of state assets [including privatisation];

❑   tax incentives to stimulate new investment in competitive and labour absorbing projects;

❑   an expansionary infrastructure programme to address deficiencies and backlogs;

❑   a strengthened levy system to fund [industrial] training on a scale commensurate with needs.[22]

The last point led to the emergence of the multi-billion SETA system, which unfortunately failed to produce more than 15 000 artisans a year compared to the 30 000 that were produced under apartheid.

Economists Shahid Yusuf and Kaoru Nabeshima researched the policy choices made by governments in Singapore, Finland and Ireland, and the impact these policy choices had on their global competitiveness and overall GDP growth. What their research showed is that for lower- and middle-income countries, capital investment can explain 45 per cent of growth (since 1989), with labour and total factor productivity accounting for 29.6 per cent and 16.3 per cent respectively.[23] What this implies is that South Africa, already operating from a low skills base because of its apartheid legacy, failed to adequately stimulate its economic growth through heavy capital investment, squandering the opportunity to pull the policy lever most responsible for GDP growth.

With anaemic public sector investment throughout the 1990s, the hope was that foreign direct investment would bring the desired capital investment to drive economic growth. Policy makers chose instead to pay off apartheid-era debt while the government was trying its best to stretch a fiscal budget towards the needs of a previously under-serviced majority population. This trade-off meant that the first ten years of post-apartheid South Africa were preoccupied with reactive policy making, incapable of matching the heavy capital investments its peers such as Brazil, Singapore and Ireland were making.

Under Presidents Mandela and Mbeki a strangely exaggerated national sense of self-sufficiency developed which sought independence from the West's developmental finance institutions at the ultimate cost of dependence on the West for investment in the form of portfolio investments and foreign direct investment. The logic went something like this: We will not take on World Bank or International Monetary Fund debt for the purpose of rapid anti-poverty programmes because these programmes come with strings attached called structural adjustment programmes. These structural adjustment programmes will force us to liberalise beyond what we are comfortable with and at a pace that is too quick for us. Therefore, we have to go it alone. Going it alone, according to this logic, entailed making sure we were a desirable destination for foreign direct investment. Being a desirable destination for foreign direct investment meant having pro-business domestic policies, liberalised local markets, low inflation, low public sector debt, high interest rates and an independent reserve bank.

In practice, to international investors 'pro-business' meant not saddling business with any of the heavy burdens that come from redistributive policies. That means lower taxes and some government subsidies, and not having an overly robust competitions authority. Liberalised local markets meant facilitating international competition by dismantling apartheid-era import substitution programmes. Also, joining the global trade organisations as a middle-income country without the protections that come from developing country status meant that South African businesses were immediately thrust into the 'dog eat dog' world of globalisation by signing on to the General Agreement on Tariffs and Trade. Black businesses therefore had none of the traditional support mechanisms that apartheid created for Afrikaner businesses.

Another mind-boggling feature of South Africa's liberalisation policy was allowing businesses that had profited under apartheid, such as Anglo American and Old Mutual, to create dual listings in the United Kingdom, effectively exporting a huge portion of the national wealth base (not coincidentally back to the circle of British imperial power) with little financial gain for the country, given that that the money they raised through these listings went largely to international acquisitions.

Given the earlier decision not to reschedule the country's sovereign debt, most of which was owed to local institutions, the Finance Ministry began to aggressively pay down this debt. The idea was that the short-term belt tightening required to do so would pay dividends in the future. Seemingly irrelevant to the leadership of the new government was the fact that this was ultimately related party intergovernmental debt, given that the government was guaranteeing and subsidising pension liabilities of current and past civil servants. David Hemson provides an interesting example: 'In the period 1991-92 the state's contribution increased from R4.4 to 11.6 billion to provide pension insurance to civil servants. The pension fund assets grew exponentially from R31 billion in 1989 to R136 billion in 1996 after a dramatic super contribution by the state. This debt was incurred by issuing bonds to Public Investment Commissioners (PIC) to invest in the state's pension fund.'[24]

Actions taken by the Reserve Bank to prop up the value of the rand added further insult to injury. South Africa's Reserve Bank is constitutionally protected to act independently without fear of government influence, as agreed to in negotiation with the ANC.

Outside of the right to hire and fire governors (the 'market' carried a veto over the ANC in this regard because they could at any stage devalue the rand if they did not believe in the quality of the appointee), the government was powerless to impose either the priorities of the Reserve Bank or the instruments through which it effected those policies.

The preoccupation of the Reserve Bank Governor, Chris Stals, 'with low inflation and a strong currency seemed to override the commitment of the SARB to co-operate with the GEAR strategy. His fixation was never more evident than in the middle of 1998 when panic emanating from the Asian and Russian crisis hit South Africa. Stals intervened massively to try to retain the value of currency at close to five rand to the US dollar. He did this largely through swaps in the forward market. As soon as traders became aware of this, they bet heavily against the rand. Stals lost, the rand fell by 20% to R6.70 to the dollar, and the real bank rate was forced up to 14%.'[25]

Throughout their entire terms, Presidents Mandela and Mbeki's governments continued to support a pro-strong rand overall macro-economic environment. To keep the rand strong, the Reserve Bank had to put an emphasis on inflation targeting, which also meant high interest rates, increasing the cost of borrowing for local business people just as many black businessmen and women were entering the economy or families were buying cars and houses for the first time. The interests of these first-time market participants were quite literally subordinated to those of international investors who wanted the higher yield coming from high interest rates, and the interests of local business people whose assets were trapped in rands by exchange control and who wanted a stronger rand to protect the value of their businesses and savings relative to international currencies.

So after all this sacrifice, did the much-vaunted foreign direct investment arrive? The answer one would probably receive from many of the free-market-centric economic teams is no ... but, followed by any number of excuses: Asian crises, Russian crises, or the unpredictability of markets. The reality is that the market is no fool. It quickly worked out that the slave-like adherence to policies that were only good for investors in the short term had to be at the expense of poor people, and that therefore the best way to invest in South Africa was in the short-term capital markets in the form of portfolio capital flows that can be yanked out at the slightest sign of trouble. So that when the day of reckoning came and the socio-economic realities had to be faced the investors would be able, at the press of a button, to pull their capital out of the country and head for greener pastures.

Meanwhile the government of Mandela and Mbeki had effectively agreed to an economic liberalisation programme that was tougher than any structural adjustment programme that the Bretton Woods institutions would have put together. In this case, however, South Africa did not receive any money from the World Bank or IMF. South Africa, unlike countries such as China, took all this downside by putting in place conservative macro-economic policies and missed the upside of both a boost of capital and the benefit of micro-economic advice to design comprehensive coherent sets of targeted policy initiatives aimed at resolving specific development challenges.

Not everyone was a loser in this new deal. Big South African corporations made out like bandits. On the one hand, throughout the apartheid years they were the beneficiaries of years of protected growth, but they wisely also prepared themselves throughout the negotiation period for the onslaught of international competition. Hence, on the other hand, they emerged from a process of streamlining and selling non-core businesses at generous premiums to both local and international buyers with strong balance sheets ready to do vertical acquisitions or grow organically. The other windfall was that the new black consumers afforded them customers hungry for all of their goods and services.

As if this was not enough, perhaps unexpectedly, BEE (characterised in the mid- to late 1990s by sales of minority interests to black-led investor groups) provided liquidity opportunities for these companies that had the added benefit of access to the new political elite. Many of the big South African corporates quickly got comfortable with the status quo and felt economically protected by the 1994 settlement and the rights entrenched in the constitution to protect their apartheid gains.

As Ruben Richards states: 'BEE has, in fact, worked brilliantly and as originally designed. BEE has created a new class of super-wealthy black aristocrats, as intended. It is now widely acknowledged that BEE has not benefited the masses, who, it seems were under the impression that BEE would be the solution to the rampant economic inequalities inherited from past generations of colonial and apartheid white-minority economic protectionism.'[26]

BEE attempted to create a market-based government-regulated redistribution of wealth, which would appeal to the black aspirational community while remaining palatable to business. It was launched with great fanfare by the ANC when it created the first BEE investment vehicle, called Thebe Investment Corporation (in which the ANC was a big shareholder through its treasury department's proxy, the Batho Batho Trust). The roots of BEE date back to the fundraising meetings between the ANC and the black business community in the late 1980s. 'By 1988, the term "Black Economic Empowerment" or BEE, as it would become universally known – had become something of a buzzword among black businessmen; Nafcoc [which was then the unofficial black business council] now demanded that "tangible expression and meaning" be attached to it.'[27]

BEE legislation had at its core the principle that the white establishment 'empowered' the new black investors who were the acquirers of shares in their companies. This set up a policy that encouraged a beauty parade where black businessmen had to 'prove themselves worthy to be empowered'. This process is as disempowering as any the apartheid government could have thought of. Instead of white businesses looking to be the active providers of reparations, the BEE legislation sought to make so-called black investors (many of whom started with no capital) the suitors, putting them in an awkward negotiating position. So the logic for this policy was to allow all South Africans the ability, if they so wished (with the added incentive of the state's affirmative procurement policies), to negotiate their own 'redistribution'.

By failing to provide the umbrella of an economic TRC over this voluntary redistribution programme, the new ANC-controlled state transferred its weak negotiating hand to the black investors who (in the beginning at least) only had relationships to offer the private sector in exchange for shares. Success or failure in BEE deals was left to chance instead of being embedded in the policy framework, leading to uneven results and delayed redistribution. According to Nigel Gibson: 'In other words, all the struggles, all the sacrifices that are made, the pain endured, all the beatings, disappearances and tragedies can be a waste of time if the struggle simply results in another form of domination, the transfer of political power from colonial authorities to a nationalist party, and the exclusion from politics of the truly historical protagonists, the very damned of the earth in whose name the struggle was fought.'[28]

I regard the great fraud to be the combination of the lack of an economic Truth and Reconciliation process which could have arrived at a fair economic settlement for apartheid's worst-affected indigenous people, the acceptance by the ANC of huge apartheid-era liabilities that drastically constrained the policies of the government under its leadership, the failure of the De Klerk administration to be honest about its bankrupting of the state prior to the hand-over of power, and the inappropriately conservative free-market-centric choices made by Presidents Mandela and Mbeki.

The ANC, in its rush for power, chose power over the people instead of power of the people. The leadership, in their policy-making decisions, chose self-sufficiency of the leadership over self-sufficiency of the people, and ultimately history will judge them harshly. Meanwhile, the rest of society is left to pick up the pieces and deal with some of the consequences resulting from the settlement. Elites in South Africa need to make a decision about whether they want to cling on to the gains they have today at the expense of long-term socio-economic stability, or to embrace the giant progress to be made by reaching for collective gains that can be jointly generated tomorrow.

5

After 1994 – Unintended Consequences of the Settlement

For 10 million South Africans who are in the middle class or richer there are few better countries in the world to live in. South Africa is a beautiful destination for tourists, but even better to live in when one has the means. Around the country incredible hospitality groups have put together a collection of some of the very best hotels in the world. Amazing chefs run world-class restaurants in most of the city centres. The country has also become a golfer's paradise, offering unparalleled scenic golfing experiences. Rural South Africa has a picturesque charm that is truly breathtaking. Certain parts of the country, such as the Stellenbosch winelands, the Drakensberg Mountains, Hogsback in the Eastern Cape, God's Window in Mpumalanga, Zimbali outside Durban and of course Table Mountain in the Cape, are enchanting and awe-inspiring regardless of the number of times one has visited them.

South Africa has had the luxury of a good platform to build on. The apartheid government set up the platform by creating a highway and rail network around the country that enabled long-distance commuting. In addition local banks, pension funds and insurance companies which had their money trapped in South Africa throughout the sanctions era, had little choice but to significantly invest in suburban and metropolitan infrastructure. These financial institutions built high-rise buildings, shopping centres and residential developments. The state-owned enterprises such as Transnet, Eskom, Airports Company of South Africa (Acsa) and Telkom helped build the railways, power stations, ports, airports and phone lines to make South Africa more functional.

The post-apartheid government has continued investing in infrastructure at as fast a rate as the annual budgets permit. Despite reducing fiscal deficits from 9.1% in 1993 to 2.5% in 2000, it has managed to generate enough revenue to continue investing in the economy, by professionalising the South African Revenue Service.[1] There was a tremendous effort by President Mbeki's economic team to build the economic infrastructure of the marginalised. 'For example, the number of housing subsidies approved since 1994 reached 2 million in 2004, while the portion of households with access to electricity rose from 32% in 1994 to over 70% by the early 2000s.'[2]

The ANC's market-friendly policies have given confidence to local private sector property groups to invest and construct additional world-class developments. These, combined with the urban charm of recently revitalised inner-city areas such as Newtown in Johannesburg and the Cape Town CBD, have greatly enriched the nature of the South African tourism experience. The post-apartheid investments are most telling in Soweto, which has been transformed from a labyrinth of interconnected housing zones into a suburb incorporating the best and the worst of liberation-era culture. South Africa's investment in tourism infrastructure such as waterfront developments, game parks, outdoor sports and museums have the added value of providing recreation and entertainment facilities for all.

Throughout the history of South Africa, dating back to the colonial days, the country has been a sports-crazy nation. Consequently even during apartheid both black and white South Africans made time for sports in well-to-do areas. Sports facilities have been up-graded and multiplied, leading to an embarrassment of riches when it comes to sports grounds. Every city has multiple rugby and soccer stadiums as well as cricket and tennis facilities. Most suburban private and Model C schools have sports facilities and sports programmes that make South Africa globally competitive in rugby, athletics, soccer, tennis and cricket, to name a few. Over the last 15 years since its re-admission to the international sporting world, the country has had many occasions to show off its sport-ing infrastructure.

South Africa has successfully hosted both Cricket and Rugby World Cups, but the crowning achievement has been the hosting of the 2010 FIFA World Cup. As host nation it had to build four world-class stadiums and undertake four major stadium upgrades to meet FIFA specifications. The country also built a new airport in Durban, an entirely new rapid-rail system in Johannesburg and upgraded all of South Africa's international airports. These were all built above specification, below official FIFA budgets and well within the official timelines. The quality of the event and the level of service given to international visitors spoke to the organisa-tional capacity of the nation. This was a massive public-private partnership requiring planning, discipline and some give and take from all participants.

Given the quality of infrastructure and the quality of life offered by the hospitality industry it would be possible to make an ar-gument that the roughly 10 million lower middle- to upper-class South Africans live in a first world environment. Almost 5 mil-lion of that middle class now comprise black people. This figure is flattering because of the liberal definition used by Statistics SA to define middle class (according to a 2006 household survey), namely families that live in formal housing, have a water tap in their dwelling, a flush toilet in their dwelling, electricity or gas as a main cooking source and either a landline or a family member with a cellphone.

By this definition of middle class, South Africa increased its middle class from 23 per cent of its households in the 1998-2000 survey to 26 per cent in the 2004-2006 survey.[3] Broken down by skin colour (using the government's way of categorising citizens), the biggest jump in middle-class households was in the urban black category, which moved from 15 to 22 per cent.[4] A large part of the praise in terms of increasing the numbers of the middle class needs to go to the management of the economy by President Mbeki's economic team and their emphasis on affirmative action. Having said this, the disparities in wealth in South Africa are glaring. There are 83 per cent of white households living in the middle-class category, 75 per cent of which have monthly expenditure topping R2 500, while only 1.4 per cent of rural black families qualify as middle class and a statistically negligible number of them have monthly household expenditure of above R2 500.[5]

South Africa should have taken its lead from another country suffering from high levels of inequality and battling to responsibly respond to its socio-economic challenges while paying off relatively large sovereign debts. Throughout the 1980s and for some of the 1990s Brazil held the dubious honour of being the world's most unequal society. Brazil faced historical socio-economic challenges of a large (mainly northern) poor population most of whom were descendants of slaves. A legacy of uneven geographic economic development had locked large chunks of the country out of its economic development path. Resulting rapid urbanisation put pressure on urban infrastructure, creating large urban slums in the main cities.

Unlike South Africa, Brazil opted to use the help of the World Bank in mapping, quantifying and partly financing a set of social programmes that helped make an enormous dent in poverty levels and stimulate growth. 'The World Bank found that a transfer of 1.6 percent of total income in 1995 would be sufficient to accomplish the task. That would translate to less than 5 percent of the income received by the wealthiest 10 percent of the population.'[6] By instituting a set of very well-crafted conditional grants called Bolsa Familia and a disability grant called LOAS, Brazilian policy makers were able to generate staggering results over the next 12 years. 'The Gini coefficient has declined from 0.594 in 2001 to .552 in 2007; the Theil index (a measure of intra-group inequality) has declined proportionally more, from 0.72 to 0.61 respectively. The ratio of the richest 10 percent to the poorest 40 percent has fallen from 22.9 to 17.1...'[7]

Unfortunately some of the same free-market-centric policies referred to in Chapter 4 prevented similarly aggressive action by the South African policy makers, resulting in an increase in the skewed distribution of income streams both between and within race groups. In fact South Africa has become one of the most unequal societies in the world by almost any statistical measure.

The combination of factors leading to the settlement in 1994 (which I have labelled as the Great Fraud) has had six major unintended consequences: persistent (structural) unemployment; acute fiscal and budgetary constraints; special-interest-based democracy; an over-compensatory sense of national self-sufficiency; unresolved psychological effects of apartheid; and resentment about societal injustice. It is necessary to unpack these unintended consequences and reflect on how they affect the socio-economic development of South Africa.

The jobless economy

South Africa has a chronically underskilled labour force. According to Nattrass and Seekings, 'In South Africa at the end of apartheid, poor households did not for the most part lack labour power (they lacked the kind for which there was strong demand in the economy – skilled labour). Poor households were poor largely because their members did not have jobs; when they did have jobs they were low-paying ones. Poverty and inequality in the distribution of incomes were due to inequality in the distribution of jobs and skill.'[8] If one looks at the statistics between 1994 and 2000 it becomes clear that the economy mostly generated jobs in the informal sector.

According to various OHS/LFS surveys, about 9.5 million people were employed in 1995, with about 8.3 million in the formal sector. According to Hirsch, 'By 2003 about 11.5 million people were employed in South Africa, with about 8.2 million in the formal sector. The increase in employment came largely from domestic workers (0.3 million), subsistence farmers (0.4 million), and the rest of the informal sector (1.4 million).'[9] This simply meant that as South Africa's middle class was expanding the economy was shedding jobs as fast as it was creating them; the unwanted black unskilled labour force were left to serve as domestic workers and temporary construction workers for the elite class.

The free-market-centric economic policies of the Mandela/Mbeki presidencies accentuated South Africa's structural economic unemployment problem. 'According to the broad measure of unemployment, which includes not only people who are actively looking for work but also discouraged-job-seekers, the unemployment rate was almost 30 percent in 1993.'[10] If we accept that this meant, by and large, that 30 per cent of the country's labour force had inadequate skills, then that means that South Africa sought to retrain from scratch a third of its labour force.

After considerable pressure from people like Cosatu's Zwelinzima Vavi, President Mbeki and his administration had to acknowledge that, left to its own devices, the market was not prepared to absorb the current labour force because it lacked desirable skills. This led to the passing of the Skills Development Act, No 97 of 1998. Among the listed purposes of this Act were to develop the skills of the South African workforce, increase investment in education and training in the labour market, encourage worker participation in learning programmes and assist the labour force in finding work.

The Skills Development Act was funded from the proceeds of a skills levy of between 0.5 and 1 per cent of the total wage bill of South African employers. Those who could submit a detailed training plan to the Department of Labour qualified for a 20 per cent rebate from the levy. The surplus was supposed to be disbursed through Sector Education and Training Authorities or SETAs. These industry-specific bureaucracies took a further two to three years after the promulgation of the Act before they got functional.

This piece of legislation should have been part of the settlement process in 1994, tackling apartheid's legacy of Bantu Education and chronic suppression of upward labour mobility with a combination of a levy and an upfront amount of reparations. Existing organisations such as the Independent Development Trust (which had capacity in this field) could have been used to immediately disseminate these funds. This would have accelerated socio-economic mobility of the majority of poor people. Given the expected time lag between re-training and employment opportunity creation, there can be no doubt that this time lag had a massive opportunity cost for the whole economy. In addition, many SETAs were saddled with corruption, inefficiency and misallocation of funds, while quite a few returned unspent funds to treasury year after year.

An illuminating example of the effective use of vocational schools in empowering citizens by equipping them with knowledge and skills relevant to private sector areas of demand can be found in a comparative study of Singapore, Finland and Ireland (called the Sifire Group) which highlights four common attributes in the design of their vocational schools.

> First, the quality of the instructors sets the tone. The ability to recruit better and experienced teachers is a hallmark of quality. Second, vocational schools need to be well furnished with adequate, up to date equipment so that students are trained on machines and software reasonably similar to the equipment they would encounter on the job... Third, financing vocational training and structuring the system to deliver the mix of skills that could be readily absorbed require close collaboration with potential employers... Fourth the efforts of governments would have come to naught if they had failed to convince parents and students of the value of vocational qualifications and how these burnished their job prospects.[11]

This group of countries was able to apply this training system for the benefit of between one third and one half of post-primary school students, proving that unemployment is not associated with a lack of degrees but rather a lack of marketable skills.[12]

In addition to the private sector skils shortage there is a severe lack of appropriate and applicable civil sector expertise in South Africa. It is therefore time to invest in creating an efficient and effective government bureaucracy. To do so the government should finance on a massive scale the continuing education of all government employees in appropriate areas. Government employees should be actively encouraged to take night school classes at select tertiary institutions on a funded basis that should come out of funds generated by the profits of the Public Investment Corporation (PIC). Currently the PIC manages over R1 trillion of government employees' funds, which generate healthy returns every year. There can be no better investment than one furthering the efficiency with which government officials manage the economic development initiatives designed to accelerate poverty-alleviation programmes. The funding of this training should work like most corporate bursary schemes: the employee gets financed to study and the loan or just the interest accruing can get written off should the employee pass the course and serve a minimum term of service. If the employee moves outside of government then the new employer should be obliged to repay the scheme with interest. Employees who fail their programme of study should be compelled to pay back the cost through salary deductions over a set period. In this way a motivated civil service can be created and strengthened.

Constraints of conservatism

The second major unintended consequence of the 1994 settlement is the acute fiscal and budgetary constraints that post-apartheid finance ministers had to work within. Managing a finance ministry towards a balanced national budget is difficult enough in developed countries with unemployment under or around 4.8 per cent and Gini coefficient ratios of 0.23, like Sweden. But for South Africa, with its unique development challenges, this non-deficit funding, non-development loan financing policy meant that the country was literally tying itself into an economic straitjacket. Pippa Green counted the cost in her biography of Trevor Manuel:

> The Budget deficit hovered near six per cent of GDP. Net government debt in 1995 was just over R244 billion. It had climbed since 1993 and now reached half of GDP. This situation was aggravated by having to absorb the liabilities of the old Bantustan states and to cover the Reserve bank's forward book. In addition to this burden the new government had to pay nearly R15 billion in 'extraordinary transfers' to the government pension fund to cover early retirements (and double retirement benefits negotiated as part of the settlement)... The difference between expenditure on debt interest and education in the 1995/96 budget was a mere R4 billion.[13]

Just so we are clear about what a major sacrifice it was to accept this debt without negotiating to reschedule, refinance or cancel it, we have to appreciate that in 1997 the budgeted education spending was R40 billion and expenditure on debt service was R39 billion.[14] South Africa could have doubled its education spending throughout the period; instead, it chose to service apartheid debt. The opportunity cost of this is evidenced by current skills development failures.

Another inherited issue that further aggravated the budget constraints was the Reserve Bank's foreign exchange forward book. Instead of embracing the opportunity to change the Reserve Bank strategy from one of a strong rand to one of a weak rand, Presidents Mandela and Mbeki's successive governments continued to support the strong rand. This meant relying on the personality of Governor Stals to 'calm the markets' through the transition from apartheid leadership to democratic government. It also meant trusting the Governor to make a transition from protecting minority interests in the apartheid business community, to that of protecting aggregate interests in a country now dominated by poor people, as Hirsch explains:

> When South Africa ran short of foreign capital, as during South Africa's debt crises from 1985-93, the SARB offered preferential long term interest rates to encourage South African borrowers to seek funds abroad... Because SARB had to settle its accounts in foreign exchange, it may have had an interest in further propping up domestic currency so that the final settlement was not too expensive... Some commentators suggested that the use of the forward market to stabilise a falling rand might have led to a vicious circle, where the SARB was forced to expend more and more resources protecting the rand and its position.[15]

This policy had the perverse effect of extending the apartheid-era subsidised development model well into the late 1990s, at great cost to the poor majority.

As if this was not enough, the SARB did not anticipate that the liberalisation policies undertaken by the Finance Ministry (to which the Governor ultimately was at least in some way accountable), would result in a gush of short-term inflows of capital, which had the effect of overvaluing the currency. 'Indeed, its interest rate policies almost seemed to be designed to exacerbate the effects of the adjustment to the removal of the external credit constraint, rather than ameliorate them – perhaps because of a conflict between the inflation target and the exchange rate target in the context of capital inflows.'[16]

These unnecessary policy errors dealt a heavy blow to the economy by starving it of capital (by keeping the interest rates high through a low-GDP growth period) and making its debt repayment problem even worse (because the high interest rates meant a high debt service coupon), at a time that the country could least afford it. Though these policy failures are often acknowledged by officials from this era, what is rarely acknowledged is the knock-on effects that this acute budget shortage had on policy makers' decisions. Would the government have continued to turn a blind eye to the chronic HIV/AIDS crisis had it felt that it had more budgetary breathing room? Could it not have made a much more concerted effort to tackle the housing crisis (as did countries as varied as China, Chile, South Korea and Ghana) if it had accepted concessionary and donor financing from the World Bank? How many black business people did this interest rate policy put out of business? South Africa would have looked very different if its leaders had had the self-confidence and far-sightedness to confront its socio-economic problems head-on and not leave them to be dealt with by the next generation.

Centres of influence

A third, less-well-understood consequence of the settlement is the development of a special-interest-based democratic system. Labour unions under the Cosatu umbrella negotiate in the interest of the marginalised work force. Most of business has organised itself into various groupings under the South African Chamber of Commerce. The interests of black previously oppressed people are deemed to be represented under the umbrella of the ANC. Traditional leaders have a forum that represents all the traditional authority structures around the country. Almost every group one can possibly think of has some sort of representative body that has organised itself around a particular interest group. This was necessary to make sure that there was adequate buy-in from all constituency groups during the final stages of the negotiated settlement.

The consequence of this special-interest-based approach to democracy is that government officials, business people and visiting foreign donors only need to meet with the heads of these groups in order to interface with their constituency base. Repeated across regions, provinces, municipalities and districts, this has had the effect of slowly driving South Africa's leadership away from meeting directly with poor people and instead dealing with their represent-atives. This practice has acutely reduced the normal feedback loops that usually exist in democratic societies, where people get to tell leaders directly through voting, polling or tweeting, what they feel about certain key decisions taken by leadership. Many countries have problems keeping special interests out of politics: what makes the problem more acute in South Africa is that special interests influence politicians in an environment where the direct account-ability that these politicians have to their constituency is curtailed by a proportional representation system that operates with closed party lists.

People have been reduced to lobbying their own representatives for change, as opposed to effecting change by directly electing their leadership at all levels of society. This has influenced and been influenced by the leadership style of the liberation movement as a whole and of the ANC in particular. The unsavoury effect of this trend when superimposed on an economy that is marred by structural unemployment and poverty is to promote abuse of these organisational structures by individuals for their own benefit. The ANC calls it careerism, whilst the public sees it as corruption and abuse of power. This trend of special interest-based democracy has the potential to badly damage the fabric of South Africa's democracy by putting in positions of power people who speak the loudest as opposed to those who work the most effectively or care the most. If left unchecked, this trend will lead to more and more corruption in organisations that will become less and less representative of their constituencies. A society that aspires to greatness should acknowledge that taking away barriers between leadership and its electorate at all levels is in the interest of not only basic democratic principles but also developmental efficiency. Failure to recognise this will result in the repeat patterns of corruption and ineffectiveness. The presence of this deficiency is evidenced in types of leadership chosen by various major organisations reflecting a fundamental lack of core democratic principles.

Cadres in crisis

In Chapter 4 on the Great Fraud I mentioned how the presidencies of both Mandela and Mbeki came to embrace a perverse sense of self-sufficiency that attempted to compensate for the weak hand they were dealt (or dealt themselves, depending on how you look at it). An example of this tendency is the pervasive culture of deployment of ANC cadres – placing them into positions in public institutions in an effort to dominate South Africa with men and women who can be trusted to dutifully engage in transformation.

The premise behind the ANC's insistence on self-sufficiency at all costs was based on two parallel sets of logic. One way of asserting the independence of the new government was to show that the ANC was ready to govern with its own people in key positions. Showing a quick transformation of government personnel was in itself *the* transformation of society. It was to be valued as much as the process of using those offices to transform the lives of ordinary people. This novel idea has to be placed against the backdrop of post-apartheid realities. Very few ANC deployees had been practically trained to the level required to perform their new functions. Many qualified and able South Africans failed to live up to the new (unofficial) primary criterion of loyalty to the party (which had to have been demonstrated prior to one's deployment). Many of the new deployees were men and women who out of loyal service to the country had spent many years abroad and therefore were not familiar with the local dynamics. Many of these cadres were financially destitute because of their long service to the struggle.

With hindsight, this was a recipe for disaster. There are many cases where deployees have performed ably, using raw intelligence, moral rectitude and street smarts, to compensate for lack of experience. In many cases the new cadres were overwhelmed by their jobs, resulting in the type of on-the-job training that required trial and error. The trials unfortunately were too long and the errors too expensive. Budgets went unspent. Billions of rands were spent on consultants. Departmental audits were qualified. Policies were

not implemented and inefficiencies were built up in many government processes. This trend has unfortunately been accelerated by
the Zuma administration, which insisted on a wholesale change of
civil servants as part of its consolidation of power. The effect has
been to lose the meaningful number of skilful civil servants who
had been trained on the job only to be replaced by new cadres who
themselves need to get up to speed with the demands of the tasks
at hand.

So in spite of the incredible successes of the post-apartheid government, its performance would have been many times better had
it had the right management and bureaucratic skills in all – or at
least the majority – of needed government posts. Apart from some
of these innocent mistakes, an insidious practice of systemic corruption, particularly in local and provincial government procurement practices, became par for the course. Carol Paton estimates
that the state is losing 20 per cent a year of its procurement budget
to corruption: with total government procurement in 2010 standing at roughly R150 billion, this means that South Africa loses as
much as R30 billion per annum on illicit payments.[17] The societal
loss of faith in elected officials is more difficult to get one's head
around. The principle that individuals seek higher office to make a
difference in society for the benefit of those less fortunate has been
completely undermined.

Tragically the worst blunders were reserved for the education
sector. Apartheid-era teachers (the same teachers that had bridged
the gap between Afrikaner children and English-speaking children
over a 20-year period) were encouraged to make way in public
schools for African teachers, many of whom were themselves products of the dreaded Bantu Education system. With this decimation
of the fabric of public school education, the Mandela/Mbeki presidencies managed to perpetuate unequal access to education for another generation of African children. As testimony to the drop in
the quality of these schools, many government bureaucrats send
their children to private schools.

Fear and mistrust

A fifth set of unintended consequences of South Africa's settlement relate to the unresolved psychological effects stemming from living in an unequal society. South Africa's Gini coefficient measure of income inequality stood at 0.672 in 1993 and 0.666 in 2008, indicating the relatively consistent statistical level of inequality that has defied all of government's efforts to create a more equal society over this period.[18]

Driving around South Africa, one can easily see that despite all the money that has gone into alleviating poverty, inequality is in fact more pronounced today than it has ever been. The combination of British imperialism then apartheid and an unfair settlement has created a society that allows those with good education and wide networks to flourish, but has failed to extend the education and access to those networks to more than a small portion of the population. The Theil inequality matrix within race groupings shows that inequality has doubled from 0.350 in 1993 to 0.618 in 2008.[19]

Statistics do not tell the real story of how people are affected at a psychological level by inequality. These effects can be put into six generic categories:

❑ **Trust deficit:** Individuals participate in millions of active and passive transactions that require one thing above all others to make society work efficiently – trust. South Africa represents a society built on years of mistrust – fear of people with another skin colour, fear of the abuse of institutional power, fear of the police, fear of the army, fear of informants dominated its existence for many years. On top of these basic fears, the proxy used by the Afrikaners to justify their subsidised development was racism. This deep-seated hate and disregard for other human beings cripples South Africans in their current day-to-day interactions. This societal trust deficit, despite the best efforts of former presidents as well as those of the current one, manifests itself in many forms of South Africa's society.

If one considers that South Africans are all continuously interacting, the combination of residual racism and a trust deficit cannot but lead to massive inefficiencies and lost opportunities. The obsession that has developed within some spheres of the media to prove that most successful black people owe their status to corruption or at the very least impropriety has done more to erode hard-won inter-racial group trust than many other forms of institutional or individual prejudice. It has had the additional negative effect of desensitising black people to the many real cases of corruption as they become unable to distinguish between smear campaigns and real reporting.

❏ **Institutional subversion:** People can behave in unimaginably irresponsible ways when they are not in a space which they feel they own. Many South African people do not feel ownership of aspects of their society and consequently abuse their custodianship when they operate in these spaces. Indeed even some of South Africa's biggest institutions are run by people who feel the need to subvert the institutional agenda to their own personal needs and wants. Abuse of power by black figures of authority is a symptom of this subversive instinct. So is corruption by politicians. Or gross and selective underpaying by white figures of authority with regard to some of their staff, whilst themselves engaging in the practice of jobs for pals. Police who abuse their power to rob helpless people exhibit a similar symptom, as do members of parliament who abuse their travel allowances, and ministers who unnecessarily stay in expensive hotels at the expense of the taxpayer. Consultants who consistently overcharge the government for services rendered or sometimes not rendered at all are part of the same syndrome, as are bankers who do whatever they can to extract an extra pound of flesh from vulnerable BEE groups, and tender winners who don't even bother to perform the service they were paid for.

Across the racial divide this institutional subversion is gradually making the country more and more uncompetitive and simultaneously destroying billions in value in the economy. It comes from an acute lack of a feeling of co-ownership in the post-1994 South Africa. Basic regulating principles such as shame, pride in one's work, morality, are overrun by a need to undermine one's own institution as part of an exercising of one's individual power. 'Institutions provide a matrix of rules and organizations to guide the accumulation of resources along with their allocation and use. With stronger, better-designed institutions, countries can derive superior outcomes... [I]neffective or missing institutions or ones that lead to dysfunctional behaviour are difficult to rectify and erase, thereby making it harder for organizations and individuals to engage in activities requiring complex and long-term contracts underpinned by mechanisms for effective enforcement.'[20] What South Africa needs is to stop creating new institutions as a knee-jerk solution to the challenges of delivery, but rather to focus on the necessary change in the culture within existing institutions, starting from the top.

❏ **Lack of self-confidence:** Core self-confidence is one of the most empowering of all characteristics a human being can have. It is the reason why the way someone is brought up (who their parents were, how much time they spent together, how much encouragement they got) matters in determining their success or failure. In discussions about the unemployment problem or lack of entrepreneurs to drive the economy forward, or lack of competitiveness versus other nations, South Africans often ignore the fact that one of apartheid's chief aims was to shake at its core the confidence of black people. Many people like to say that they survived apartheid – but in practice, many have not survived the system's assault on their core self-confidence.

The majority of black South Africans carry a deep-seated

inferiority complex that plays itself out in unhealthy ways through their conduct. It is a crippling disability that holds back the development of many. It is not a problem restricted to poor or rural people. It permeates class barriers. It is not talked about within many circles of society. If it were measurable it would shock most people to find out how profound its effect is on the country's performance. Confidence is crucial in an era in which psychometric tests determine pay increases, when learning new technology is a make-or-break in the work force, or just when making the right first impression leads to a job opportunity. People with confidence have a massive economic advantage over those who do not.

❏ **Direct link between hard work and results:** One of the facets of growing up in an unfair society is that one is not hard-wired to anticipate reward from hard work. The mind has a wonderful way of defending human beings from the pain of disappointment. One of the protective mechanisms is in the calibration of how much one puts into something if one is unsure of the results. This is one of post-apartheid South Africa's biggest afflictions. The inability to maximise performance because of deep-seated uncertainty about the reward system is a major impediment to excellence. Donna Hicks ties the responses of humans to others to the basic issue of dignity. She observes that 'What seems to be of utmost importance to humans is how we feel about who we are. We long to look good in the eyes of others, to feel good about ourselves, to be worthy of others' care and attention. We share a longing for dignity – the feeling of inherent value and worth.'[21]

This uncertainty affects the way companies perform and the way government departments carry out their institutional agenda. Its effects permeate every aspect of the South African society. It is particularly debilitating when you take into account the lack of a genuine performance culture in government. What has developed in place of a performance culture is a culture of patronage (both political and economic) and centralisation. This may explain why so many of our civil servants cling to their identity as cadres, which in turn creates a dynamic where they judge themselves and their self-worth by the way their political superiors feel about who they are.

Uncertainty is a difficult force against which to motivate in established companies that have a culture of success, but it is also potentially debilitating to new ones that do not. South Africans need to be 'rewired' through a process that resets the understanding of the relationship between performance and reward. Individuals and teams need to be assured that excellence will be rewarded and that mediocrity will be discouraged.

❏ **Capacity for empathy**: Traumatic events of any kind lead to varying reactions from victims. Some are inclined to group healing; others prefer to be alone. Some like to talk about their trauma; others don't. It is one of the curious aspects of the psychology of pain management that people who prosper from adversity tend not to be the most empathetic. Something deep inside tells the person that 'if I went through this horrific event and came away the better for it because of hard work and determination, those who have not succeeded have not worked hard or were not determined enough'. South Africa is a society with a decreasing sense of community as her citizens learn to deal with the interactions between the winners and the losers from a brutal past. Instead of becoming towering symbols within their communities, those (particularly successful black people) who succeed assimilate into new communities to escape the psychological burdens that come from engaging with the reality of their relative success.

In a society that is trying to bridge the inequality gap, empathy is the precondition of good policy making, good community outreach programmes, good citizenship and creative entrepreneurship. Many white people are hardwired by years of denial into believing that if black people worked harder they would be able to overcome their poverty-related issues. The truth about how the apartheid system unfairly accumulated resources in these same white people's favour has been denied to them by the nature of the settlement, resulting in embedded feelings of self-righteousness and prejudice that are perpetuated by the reality of inequality in South Africa today.

❑ **Lack of self-worth**: Whether we like it or not, most human beings base their own value of themselves on how others treat them – and, more importantly, the expectations that fellow human beings have of them. Years and years of low expectations built on prejudice have destroyed the self-worth of many black people. Just as importantly, years of black males being unable to fulfil their two most basic gender roles, to provide for one's family and to protect one's family, have destroyed the self-worth of many black men. The systematic emasculation of black men in order to play to the guilty conscience of white men has destroyed some black people's ability to look at themselves in the mirror. To understand the way this emasculation happened one need only think about the manifestation of *swart gevaar* through insulting and demeaning laws categorised as 'petty apartheid'. The fear of black men was managed by the facilitation of their constant humiliation by white men of all ages.

Post-apartheid materialism accompanied by intra-racial group inequality has added to the sense of shame of those who have not managed to prosper. The prosperity of some people close to them mocks their own inability to join the ranks of the rich. For those not strengthened by faith in a higher power, alcoholism, drugs and sexual conquests are the only available outlets. Crime, AIDS and violence against women and children are testimony to this problem.

'Evolutionary psychologists Margo Wilson and Martin Daly were interested in whether adopting more impulsive and risky strategies was an evolved response to more stressful circumstances in which life is likely to be shorter. In more threatening circumstances, then, more reckless strategies are perhaps necessary to gain status, maximize sexual opportunities, and enjoy at least some short-term gratifications... To test this hypothesis, they collected data on the murder rates for seventy-seven community areas of Chicago, and then they collected data on death rates for those same areas, subtracting all of the deaths caused by homicide. When they put the two together, they showed a remarkably close relationship, neighbourhoods with high homicide rates were also neighbourhoods where people were dying younger from other causes as well.'[22] In other words, lack of self-worth caused by living in dire economic circumstances alters one's ability to correctly modify risk-taking behaviour. This may help explain why high-risk sexual behaviour is so rampant amongst poorer South Africans despite the HIV pandemic.

The lasting cost of injustice

Perhaps the worst of all the unintended consequences of the 1994 settlement is the feeling of societal injustice that has turned some people off capitalism as a way to allocate resources and democracy as a way to elect leadership. Driven by a sense that the current system is not fair, some South Africans have turned in defiance to populism, xenophobia, corruption and crime. Each of these outlets is dangerous by itself, but when they exist in parallel, they become particularly dangerous. It is possible that these various instincts will conspire to create a lowest common denominator outcome that will lead the country down a very dangerous road, following a corrupt populist who uses xenophobia and residual racist feelings against white South Africans as a rallying cry to move the society away from both democracy and capitalism.

It is up to those who are in possession of the means to redistribute wealth in this society in a fairer manner to ensure that these underlying impulses do not get the better of all South Africans. The difficulty is that, historically, societies tend to wait until it is too late before rich people understand that their wealth can only be secured in a more just society. Already there are calls for nationalisation and allowing the government to take over the commanding heights of the economy. So far business has not drawn a line connecting the dots between its own approach to redistribution and where society is in its development.

The question many people are asking is whether government can lean on business to contribute more. In other words, is the overarching philosophy upon which the South African system is built one of unbridled capitalism with unfettered pursuit of self-interest? Most established businesses have offered only cynical compliance as their contribution to transformation. To date, business has relied on the 'commonsense leadership' of ANC centrists to mitigate the calls for more left-leaning policies.

The question is – do business leaders want to leave to fate the durability of the ANC centrists or do they want to enter the debate today and participate in fortifying their resolve? The battle between the left and the right of the ANC is going to decide South Africa's fate as a country, one way or the other.

6

An Imperfect Democracy

The type of liberty attained after many years of struggle is conditioned by the degree of freedom enjoyed before liberation. People sometimes assume that freedom means the same thing for everyone experiencing it. This is simply not true. The concept of being liberated does not have to be accompanied by transformation from one's previous state of existence to another. In other words, freedom often fails to fundamentally transform one's state of being. In very rare cases do liberation movements manage the feat of facilitating simultaneously both liberation and transformation in the lives of the majority of people. Usually there is a trade-off of one for the other. Typically the trade-off is that attaining power and thus claiming the successful liberation of a people comes at the cost of the capacity to create or retain, post liberation, meritocratic institutions free of the negative influence of the cadres of these same liberation movements. This trade-off is usually followed by a political party usurping the spoils of freedom, making liberation the beginning of a demoralising downward spiral for those not in a position to benefit from the new patronage networks.

Take the case of a man falsely accused of a crime and jailed for a long period. Let's say for argument's sake that man was jailed for 36 years. He went to jail as a young man just starting his life, had a new job, was in love with a woman and intended to get married. He was poor, lived in a shanty town and worked as a labourer because he was not educated. Freeing that man after half his term in jail restores his liberty. He is free to go wherever he likes; theoretically he is free to do anything he pleases within the confines of the law. He would be free to exercise all the available constitutional freedoms such as freedom of speech, a right to protest publicly against any action he feels is unjust. Except in reality, that man is hardly free. He will soon need shelter, food and a means to earn a living. This man will have to live the life of freedom accompanied by hopelessness. He will not be able to get a job because there are many people competing for the manual labour positions that he is restricted to. He will soon go hungry. In all likelihood he may end up right back where he started, in jail and feeling no less free than he was on the outside.

Advanced societies would compensate the victim of wrongful imprisonment financially and provide him with counselling and gainful employment. Not because such compensatory measures will make up for what has been taken away from the individual, but because it's the right thing to do in a just society. Such restorative justice sits at the heart of the constitutional concepts of equality.

In South Africa many people have confused the concepts of freedom, liberty and economic transformation in ways that are convenient for elites and debilitating for poor people. For many white people liberty is about rights – a right to vote, freedom of speech, the protection of one's property rights, and so on. They have taken for granted the fact that transformation needs to accompany this freedom because, by and large, they were not in need of an economic transformational mechanism post-1994. Many of their lives had been premised on a simple, enviable principle: if they worked hard and saved enough money they and their children would be better off.

The faulty settlement, which has created a zero-sum game between rich and poor South Africans, induces white elites to typically vote in the direction where they think that this set of privileged rights can be defended at the very least or even further extended. What has been appealing to this part of the electorate is a free-market-centric set of policies that offer protection for the status quo (and their savings), with policies that focus on low inflation even at the expense of GDP growth (and more importantly job creation), and a strong rand even at the expense of the competitiveness of South African exports. The poor majority with no savings to protect had to forego policies that would have generated jobs for them so that this minority can be protected by undue macro-economic prudence.

For the black elite who (with a few notable exceptions) at the point of liberation represented people who were connected to the liberation movement's leadership, the two concepts of liberty and transformation were quite literally linked. To have been part of the delivery of liberty to the masses of African people was trans-formational in the form of the new opportunities that were now available to the new elite. Literally tens of thousands of job op-portunities got opened up by and for this elite group. This allowed those chosen few not just the opportunity for high-paying jobs but the added power of being able to decide who gets what. This led to an immediate and fundamental transformation for a core of the black elite, which had positive impacts on the rest of the black elite class in the form of business opportunities, consultancies, job op-portunities indirectly related to government and access to power. Like any other rational human beings, their attention soon shifted from gaining this new-found freedom and experiencing the trans-formation that came with it, to the grand old question: What do I have to do to keep this?

As it turned out, for those in the new black elite the answer to that question was elementary. They simply had to convince the masses of people that represent the black electorate that their in-terests were aligned and that with a little patience, good things would come to those who wait. The story I have told in this book so far serves as a description of why those good things, nearly 18 years after the advent of South Africa's democracy, haven't come to the majority of people. The tragic thing is that in exercising their rights in this fashion, both white and black elites have, without much effort, temporarily taken away the remaining right of the marginalised to vote them out of power and influence. As Nigel Gibson puts it: 'In other words, whether framed by neo-Keynesian or neoliberal policies, post-apartheid politics was reduced to an elite project of capturing the state and the means of governance, in contrast to creating an expansive and inclusive democracy based in the activity of the mass movements.'[1]

The freedom to vote for the political representative of your choosing is something South Africans are supposed to still have as an inalienable right – but even this basic right has been alienated in the current political landscape by the effective use of patronage, and the constitutional mechanism of closed party lists as a bastardisation of the direct representation voting system.

Democracy SA-style

The South African Constitution provided for 400 members of the National Assembly and the National Council of Provinces to be elected by universal adult franchise in accordance with a system of proportional representation. This system is structured as a mixed proportional system with at least half the representatives elected from the nine provinces (which are in effect constituencies that have representatives elected from separate regional lists). The other half of the representatives are allocated from compensatory national lists in an effort to restore overall proportionality. This imperfect system was constitutionally intended to exist for the 1994 elections and after some modest alterations also the 1999 elections, after which it was envisioned that a new more permanent system would be put in place. It was against this backdrop that with some instigation by people such as Chief Mangosuthu Buthelezi, President Thabo Mbeki put together a task team with the mandate to propose a new long-term solution.

The Electoral Task Team acknowledged in its 2003 report that South Africa's electoral system, though not perfect, had some enduring advantages that needed to be retained – namely fairness, inclusiveness and simplicity.[2] The task team members all agreed on the need to introduce greater accountability into the electoral system. Research done by the task team found that: 'Not only was there a great extent of satisfaction with the inclusiveness and fairness of the current system, but results showed a high degree of political literacy... What was also clear is that a significant majority of voters wanted closer interaction with the politicians who represent them. Thus 71% said they wanted to vote for a candidate from the area where they lived, 64% that MPs should live closer to the people they represent and 53% that party candidates should be chosen by party members rather than party leaders.'[3]

So why was the people's will not adhered to? Why were the results of this extensive and consultative body of work not implemented? The simple answer is that the poor majority of South African voters were victims of one of the rare South African cases where black and white elite interests intersected. Poor people are not wanted as directors of policy through their direct ability to choose policy makers; they are expected to be willing sheep led by the elite shepherds towards greener pastures. The question that is relevant for poor, unemployed and working-class people in South Africa is – what can be done to socialise freedom in the new South Africa?

The answer to this question lies in Lord Acton's prescient saying: 'Power tends to corrupt and absolute power corrupts absolutely.' Having enjoyed tremendous success in the elections of 1994 and 1999, the ANC did not have an incentive to follow through on its constitutional obligation to put a more permanent, less flawed system in place. The Electoral Task Team made some recommendations to President Mbeki that could have gone a long way towards yielding to voter demands for more political accountability. As they put it:

Collective accountability occurs at each general election when a party is subjected to the opinion of the electorate. Is it, however, in any way possible to complement collective accountability with some form of individual accountability? The only way to increase individual accountability significantly would be to create the possibility for a candidate to be rejected *without concomitant rejection of a party* [their emphasis]. This could be achieved using open rather than closed party lists, with voters influencing the order of candidates. They would do this either by ranking candidates or by selecting a number of preferred candidates listed next to the emblems of their respective parties. Should the candidates as decided by the party be acceptable to a voter, however, then a mark need merely be made against the name of the party. Open lists would not only improve accountability of individual candidates dramatically but would also substantially increase voter participation in the democratic process.[4]

The ANC will continue to be a major influence on the political landscape for many years to come. Looking at how democracy works within the organisation is instructive in identifying where and how voter power gets diluted by political patronage. There are four critical trends that are impacting democracy within the ANC with consequential impact on the ability of the ANC-led society to deliver transformation of the lives of the majority of South Africans.

❏ The first is the use of the ANC branch networks to **aggregate power** in the hands of a few people. The ANC has hundreds of branches across the country. These branches are supposed to be support networks and aggregators of local constituency interests. When ANC conferences on either leadership or policy positions take place, the branches send delegates to represent their interests. Delegates are also chosen to vote on behalf of these constituencies in leadership contests. The delegates are typically lobbied and marshalled by provincial party chairmen (or others in the ANC provincial party machinery) who are meant to canvass branch delegates' views on leadership and policy so that voting is 'harmonised' on a provincial level for individual leaders and individual policy decisions.

The principle of consensus seeking through both lobbying and debate at this level creates the first opportunity for those who have the power of patronage to wield their influence. When delegates arrive at party conferences, more lobbying takes place across provincial structures to try and win votes for certain policy positions or particular candidates for leadership. This process dilutes whatever mandate branch members gave their delegates. Nigel Gibson is pointed in his analysis that 'Decentralisation is, therefore not simply an administrative or technical issue, it is a social issue attached to the goal of deepening national consciousness into humanism and connected with the work of involving masses of people in the day to day running of their lives.'[5] Decentralisation is therefore central to fulfilling the ANC's core liberation promise, which says that the people must govern.

There is plenty of anecdotal evidence to suggest that poorer members of the party are manipulated by those with the capital to provide the extravagant entertainment for ANC-mandated gatherings at which arm-twisting for votes can happen. The age-old ANC tradition of substantive debate based on issues of principle affecting the movement has given way to a new environment that is dominated by a cult of personality and individual fiefdoms that serves to bastardise what was in the past a pragmatic system of opinion formation.

❑ Second, the use of **campaign funding** within the ANC deserves further exploration. The ANC has typically managed its party donations through the office of the Treasury. During the days of apartheid this position was crucial to using the ANC's moral authority in order to raise money for the just cause of the liberation struggle. The main donors in the pre-liberation days were the Scandinavian countries, particularly Sweden and Denmark, and of course communist supporters such as Cuba, China and most prominently Russia. This all changed after the fall of the Berlin Wall, when the ANC began to raise money primarily from corporate interests, a policy that has escalated from 1994 until today. Some numbers are probably a better indication of the scale of the problem: 'The ANC spent an estimated R300 million on the 2004 election, whereas in 2009 it spent R100 million on one advertising agency, Ogilvy Group SA, alone... If ANC spending for election campaigns is already R400 million or R500 million, opposition parties will face growing pressure to increase their own expenditure or face effective marginalization.'[6] This is by no means just an ANC problem, of course; the increased cost of getting elected affects all citizens in that it encourages more desperate and/ or unscrupulous behaviour by all parties. The DA had its own problems, for instance, when it accepted funding from international fugitive Jurgen Harksen.

South Africa does not have regulations that force all parties to be completely transparent with the electorate about where their funds come from. Consequently voters have no idea who funds the ANC's or the opposition parties' annual operating budget or election budget. What they do know is that corporate interests do not give money without expecting something in return. The problem of a lack of transparency in the handling of campaign donations has dogged all political parties: a few months after contesting its first election, the newly formed Congress of the People (Cope) was mired in a scandal escalated by allegations of fraud relating to the management of donor funds. One of the main clouds surrounding the DA in the eyes of black voters relates to the identity of the constituent interests behind that party (many black South Africans rightly or wrongly suspect a white business agenda). These concerns will not be resolved satisfactorily until light is shed on who the major donors are behind each political party, and what amounts they have contributed.

❏ The third trend is the use of the ANC's **deployment committee** as a method of rewarding loyal party members with positions of influence. The committee meets to make decisions on key appointments in government and in the wider state-owned enterprise network. It has consequently served card-carrying members of the ANC well to be in the good books of influential members of this committee. Though the intentions of this committee may be noble, the effect is to centralise power in Luthuli House, draining political talent away from rural areas towards urban centres where the branch infrastructure is more pronounced, and the likelihood of being noticed by senior party members is increased. Though President Zuma has said he would like to stop cadre deployment (at least at the level of local government), it is very difficult to see this behaviour shifting without a drastic culture change within the party. The source of pressure to change the ANC culture has to come from the top. Without a displayed shift in the incentivisation and accountability of government officials who are senior ANC members, civil servants will continue to be beholden to party bosses.

❏ The fourth trend is a form of **'othering discourse'** that has been used to distinguish between party loyalists and holders of dissenting views both in and outside the ANC. In Chapter 3, I mentioned how Afrikaner nationalism was preceded by a form of this discourse that later served to justify the policy of apartheid. If one listens to the way in which dissenting opinion both from inside and outside the party is treated today by some ANC leaders, one cannot help but be alarmed at the harshness of the tone. Dissenters are called counter-revolutionaries, sell-outs, ill-disciplined cadres, coconuts and racists. This serves to demonise critics and take the oxygen out of public debate spaces. It starves the broader population of genuine political debate that is necessary to generate an inclusive democratic decision-making process. It also starves the ANC of good transparent criticism from within the party which is necessary to create organisational accountability and enrich discussions around leadership choices. The generation of unity within the party at all costs results in the ANC's best and brightest being muzzled in times of crisis when strong voices need to speak truth to power. This trend will be to the long-term detriment of both the party and the country.

If one considers the implications of these four major factors affecting how democracy works within the ANC for the country, it becomes easy to see how freedom has been monopolised by these interest groups and away from ordinary people. Over 60 per cent of the voting population supports the ANC, but the people actually influencing decision making and policy trade-offs are a very small group indeed. The interests of this group have increasingly diverged from those of the poor majority of South Africans as the country has suffered widening inequality. More principled internal leaders who have attempted to steer the ANC back towards its democratic roots tend to be shouted down at national conferences, drowned out in public debates and slandered in the newspapers through the use of 'othering discourse'.

The practice within provincial ANC leadership of pressurising delegates' voting positions – and in so doing, taking away their responsibility to vote the positions mandated by their branches – is fundamentally undemocratic. It contributes to the further centralisation of power in the hands of a few at the expense of many. It relegates concerns of the majority of the people to election slogans and not fundamental principles around which party policies are built.

Finally, the political patronage capabilities of the deployment committee can be a stronger force in shaping the decision making of delegates and other representatives than the will of their constituents. For many members of the party seeking promotion into higher office, the backroom deals cut by members of the deployment committee are all-important in determining their future. This places a premium on opportunities where these ambitious party members can ingratiate themselves with deployment committee members as opposed to a direct representation system which would force them to be accountable to their local constituencies. South Africans should welcome President Zuma's efforts to lead the ANC's own efforts to remove deployment at the local government level, and encourage it towards a wider ban on deployment in general. Let the people deploy individual party members by direct elections at all levels of the political system.

The importance of reforming these practices cannot be overestimated. South Africa needs a transparent policy for campaign and party funding. Voters need to know who is funding both the governing party and the opposition parties and what the interests of these donors are. More than that, voters need to put a ceiling on the amount that each corporate entity or individual donor can contribute to each party. Particularly strict transparency laws need to be applied to foreign donors, because national interests cannot be compromised by party funding needs. Doing so will force all political parties to cast their net wider towards the ordinary man or woman on the street for small contributions to their parties. This will change the accountability base of individual parties.

The great South African opposition

Given that these reforms will not happen without more political competition against the ANC, it is useful to survey the political landscape in South Africa today.

It is widely believed that the great opposition party will come from a split in the ANC. After Thabo Mbeki's dismissal in 2008 through a process referred to as 'recalling', a splinter group of Mbeki supporters formed the Congress of the People (Cope). The breakaway group comprised members from all the ANC alliance structures but chose to position itself to the right of the ANC. It agreed with the ANC on macro- and micro-economic policy but was highly critical of its leadership quality, which it referred to at various times as morally corrupt and criminal.

It was clear from the outset that Cope thought it could capture the imagination of the black middle class. The party must have thought that members of the ANC had shorter memories than their own leadership did; they clearly forgot the emotional attachment people have to the ANC as the vanguard of the National Democratic Revolution. Additionally Cope greatly underestimated the value of patronage networks to their targeted electorate. Through these patronage networks, and an enormous amount of sentimentality towards the liberation party, the ANC was able to win away the black middle-class vote. It may also be true to say that Cope was too early in its attempt to canvass support on the basis that black people were ready to turn their back on the ANC en masse.

The ANC was able to remodel itself as the driving force at the centre of a newly refined emphasis on using the state apparatus for the purposes of delivery of basic services to poor people. It placed a huge emphasis on the importance of a developmental state as an essential platform for such a drive. It also ran a frenetic and cleverly targeted campaign led by talented politician Fikile Mbalula, which painted Cope as cry-babies, counter-revolutionaries and sell-outs.

The amalgamated Independent Democrats/Democratic Alliance led by Helen Zille has slowly gained momentum, moving from a regional political coalition to one that is beginning to establish a genuine national footprint. Their message is characterised by moral leadership, superior bureaucratic management capability and incorruptibility. The aspirations of this opposition party in the short to medium term have progressed from retaining the Western Cape and trying to win the Northern Cape, in what can be described as a provincial opposition strategy, towards the prospects of national popularity powered by first-time voters who are less interested in parties' liberation credentials. Their strategy actually aims to show qualitative differences in the lives of those living in the DA-controlled areas versus those living in the rest of the country. This coalition is slowly beginning to eat into the black electoral support base of the ANC. According to the DA, nationally it increased its vote in absolute terms from 16 per cent (or 1 611 131 votes) in 2006 to 24.3 per cent (or at least 3 047 649) in 2011.[7] This is by its very nature a long-term strategy that will play out over many election cycles.

All signs point to the fact that the vast majority of the population still attaches political baggage to the roots of the DA in its previous incarnations as the Progressive, Progressive Federal, Progressive Reform and Democratic parties, and its complicity with aspects of the old regime. Furthermore, the fact that the party is deemed to be controlled by white leadership and financially supported by a narrow set of white corporate interests makes it difficult for black voters to support it. But its tremendous performance in the 2011 municipal elections may indicate the beginning of an accelerated growth phase of the DA as its leadership becomes more representative of the demographics of the country and its management credentials overwhelm voter ambivalence based on its political legacy. It could become a formidable competitor to the ANC.

The second biggest variable in South African politics, after the internal contest between left-leaning nationalists in the ANC and more centrist believers in an open, regulated free-market economy, is the political risk appetite of the DA to collapse their party in a broader opposition party led by credentialed black people. To the extent that Helen Zille can avoid the allure of remaining at the helm of the party, and her leadership team can open themselves up to the possibility of working with a cohort of senior black leaders on bases of equality, a giant opposition party may be born. Such a party must by definition have some of the broad church features of the ANC to cater for the myriad political views held by unsatisfied voters. To the extent that voters perceive the amalgamation to represent not just a cosmetic change, but a genuine paradigm shift in post-liberation politics, they will be responsive. If the public believes that a new leadership will genuinely lead to more left-leaning policy positions taken up by such an opposition, success in the near to medium term is possible.

Cosatu and the SACP remain uncomfortable bedfellows with the free-market-centric politicians who aspire to control key aspects of the ANC's economic policy direction. Belying the awkward annual displays of solidarity (often involving ministers putting on union 'hats' and marching against state-owned enterprises or the government itself) that take place every time there are wage negotiations and unions strike against public and private sector employers, is a fundamental difference as to how redistribution should occur. The more left-leaning alliance members feel compelled to arm-twist employers into paying the highest possible increases, believing this to be part of the compensation for what the union bosses see as the historically disadvantaged constituency of union members in general. This has resulted in wage increases that consistently come above inflation.

The free-market-centric politicians worry about the inflationary consequences of such actions. They would rather keep wages lower so as to allow businesses to remain competitive, grow faster and generate higher GDP growth – and with it more employment. The trouble is that while these two sets of groups perform what is becoming a monotonous back-and-forth balancing act, workers have lost patience and decided to support more militant union groupings with a higher risk tolerance for the method through which they exact their desired result. These new union bosses have nothing to lose politically by asking for double-digit increases, sometimes as high as 30 per cent. In fact they have everything to gain. They are seen as delivering real value to a marginalised national work force (particularly the mining industry), which has been receiving what they view as meagre increases off a low base.

The correct solution may be somewhere in between these positions. Australia has proven throughout a Labor Government's term in office during the 1980s that it is possible to achieve higher wages for union members while facilitating the growth of a more competitive private sector. 'Wage negotiations were geared to productivity increases, unions reviewed their members' work processes for improved industrial efficiency, this information allowed more effective enterprise level bargaining.'[8] For this to be effective, workers have to be incorporated in the drive to create an alignment of interest between owners, managers and broader stakeholders of corporations. This requires a mindset shift for some chief executives who view workers as tools through which to extract profits.

This battle of wills is likely to play itself out in the policy arena where two sets of economic planning documents are to be implemented, one written by the National Planning Commission (NPC) led by Minister Trevor Manuel (with the inclusion of comments from the public), and the other put forward by the Economic Development Ministry, headed by Minister Ebrahim Patel. Minister Manuel has come out with a refined, more nuanced version of the current free-market-centric policies, now more balanced in favour of poor people. The state-centric socialists place their hopes and aspirations on the policy positions of the New Growth Path released at the end of 2010 by the Ministry of Economic Development, espousing a more muscular state intervention in the economy.

It will be interesting to see which of the two policies ultimately wins as the blueprint for economic growth. Early indicators pointed to a cabinet-wide adoption of Minister Patel's new growth path principles. The diagnostic portion of Minister Manuel's NPC exercise received a very cold reception from government. In many quarters, particularly the Presidency, it hardly warranted a mention. However, as Mangaung looms closer and the incidences of socio-economic tension become more frequent and violent, some ministers are showing signs of giving Minister Manuel's diagnostic report a second look (and therefore paying more attention to his commission's recommendations). It seems that the truth is too glaring to ignore, except for the most hardened denialists within the party. One can only speculate that the losers of this policy war will rally behind new leadership in and post the 2012 ANC leadership contest.

Curiously the ANC Youth League has stolen a march on a visibly flat-footed SACP with regard to nationalisation and land redistribution debates, which serve as the only transformational redistributive policy proposals. Through relentless arm-twisting by the league and a lack of a credible paradigm shifting redistributive agenda by ANC policy centrists, both these policies (much to the dismay of the local and international business community) are firmly back on the policy discussion table. In contrast to the proposals in ANC corridors of power to tinker with the current free-market allocation of wealth, the ANC Youth League is either being bold or reckless, depending on your perspective of the underlying issues under debate. It is interesting that the Youth League under the fearless leadership of expelled ANC member Julius Malema should be the only proponents for radically pro-poor policies within the alliance. Many brush aside these policy proposals as a proxy for a leadership battle between the old guard and the young lions, but what commentators are missing is that nationalisation and land redistribution resonate with the very core of many people's feelings of economic marginalisation.

Faced with a choice between something radical and more of the same, it seems only natural that many would favour something to shake up the currently unequal system. In discussions about how all this would be paid for, commentators miss the fact that if a referendum were to be held today, more than two thirds of South Africans would probably vote in favour of nationalisation without compensation, based on the simplistic view that in the hands of the state such assets can be translated into economic benefit for the masses. Similarly with the issue of land reform: the overwhelming majority of South Africans would vote for a Zimbabwe-style solution through which they would get the land now and worry about the practicalities of owning and farming it later. Such is the suppressed sentiment of resentment towards the current glacial progress on land reform and economic redistribution policies.

Some cynical members of the business community are betting, perhaps correctly, that the ANC is too divided to undertake radical reform. They bet that the two proposals will get wrapped up in endless discussion groups while the status quo prevails. This may prove an expensive wager against the interests and aspirations of marginalised South Africans. Without significant concessions, poor people are likely to vote with their hearts. Political opportunism will dictate that one of the current popular leaders offers him or herself up to be the representative of such aspirations. The consequences for business interests in the short term could be devastating. Former President Mbeki presciently warned that 'Our nights cannot but be nights of nightmares while millions of our people live in conditions of denigrating poverty. Sleep cannot come easily when children get permanently disabled, both physically and mentally, because of lack of food. No night can be restful when millions have no jobs, and some are forced to beg, rob and murder to ensure that they and their own do not perish from hunger.'[9]

The great South African opposition will be led by someone who is able to put a giant mirror up in front of the country for average South Africans to see that the special-interest-based model does not have their best interests at heart. Someone will draw a line in the sand between the domination of special interests, the unfair settlement, widespread structural unemployment and the economic conditions of the men and women on the street. Someone will tell the inconvenient truth, which is that the elite pact of 1994 can only trickle down small percentages of the country's economic gain to poor people while both absolute inequality and intra-racial group inequality grow.

The unemployed, particularly rural unemployed, have no political representation. South Africa's labour unions worked it out early in their formation that it makes short-term political and financial sense to put paid-up, employed workers' interests above those of unpaid, unemployed workers. Indeed the unemployment situation in South Africa is a faceless killjoy to even the biggest optimists in the country. Not having a seat at the table has cost the millions of unemployed dearly. One can only imagine the effect of a party built around the political interests of this large a number on the political landscape of the country.

The marginalised in South Africa have been paralysed by the twin instruments of political patronage and the 'delivery state'. Most, knowingly or not, have given over their self-determination to the safe pair of hands that sit at Luthuli House, because the majority of poor people were convinced in 1994 that their freedom had been delivered to them by the leadership of the ANC – as opposed to acknowledging their own agency as individual actors in the struggle. It was expected by this constituency that the ANC would deliver economic transformation to accompany the political freedom acquired in 1994 – as promised every election season since then.

South Africans are at their best as a nation when they are activated. That is the way the fragmented, warring country became a nation. Young South Africans need to embrace a no-short-cuts approach to personal development. The introduction of BEE, ready access to the state tender system, deployment and the social welfare system have created an incredibly short-term, quick fix – but passive – outlook for the youth. Young people need an attitude that is focused on the long term but infused in the short term with activism and impatience to spur on political leadership to generate tangible results. Leadership that appeals to young people's drive to gain control over their own future by mobilising themselves around the creation of a more meritocratic society will prosper politically over the long term. Needless to say, it is a source of great frustration to many of the unemployed youth that through the culture of deployment they are being denied both an efficient local and provincial government and opportunities to join government as change agents.

One of the weakest aspects of South Africa's post-liberation political culture is the continuous centralisation of power in Pretoria (and by inference Luthuli House). As a result motivation in the public sector is low, particularly among young professionals who dread the intolerable interference of incompetent government officials who represent a large proportion of dead wood in the civil service, standing in the way of good ideas and applying political pressure to do favours for the political elite at the expense of poor people. South Africa's public sector is a shambles, with rampant corruption as a result of this institutional subversion, gross inefficiency and many instances of unspent funds being returned to treasury as testimony to these challenges.

Only in a political monopoly where a single party has dominated the political landscape for the last 18 years, can the majority of the voting public continue to support a governing party in getting away with such rampant inefficiency. For as long as the ANC's deployment committee is responsible for the majority of South Africa's public sector hiring, this situation will not change. Not because the members of the deployment committee have any ill intent, but because it is impossible to deploy people whose primary motivation is party loyalty and expect them to miraculously get motivated by any other set of incentives. People respond to the predominant incentive structures set within whatever paradigm they work. Until the ANC has a better record of responding to public pressure to dismiss loyal but incompetent civil servants as opposed to defending or redeploying them, civil servants' behaviour won't change. In the current context competent civil servants thrive in spite of the system, not because of it.

Promises, promises ...

To date South Africa's post-1994 elections have been about campaign promises made to different constituencies by the ANC and finger pointing by the opposition about corruption and crime. There have been very few substantive or transformational proposals from opposition parties on concrete policy issues which are relevant to change in the lives of poor people. To raise the level of scrutiny on policy makers and get the best out of ANC leadership, there has to be a marked improvement in the content of political debates.

Opposition parties should take the lead in making policy suggestions and not just criticise from the sidelines. To be sure, the DA has been making an increasing effort to enter the public policy environment as an opinion former. It has also released its own national economic policy document which it will use to seek an election mandate. The trouble is that besides a promise to spend money more efficiently, drastically improving the education system and focusing on service delivery, very little in their policy proposal offers a palatable difference from what the ANC has also promised.

The more astute opposition party leaders will finally figure out that the route to a national electoral victory over the ANC is to come up with economic development programmes to the left of what the ANC is proposing.

One can only hope that the following five key issues of interest are more intensely debated in elections to come.

❏ **Is the experiment with proportional representation working?** The best test for this is in asking the question, do members of the electorate feel they have the power to remove leadership that they think is not up to scratch in the current political system? And if the consensus is no, then what constitutional reforms can be made towards direct representation. Particular attention should be paid to issues of leadership accountability, feedback on local versus national differences in generating different policy outcomes and rural versus urban bias in the current system.

❏ **Should there be redistribution of any kind, and who should pay for it?** This issue has already been put on the table by the ANC in the form of nationalisation as a redistributive policy. Instead of reacting with shock and dismay, or dismissing these proposals as a capitulation to populism, opposition parties need to look at what is behind the demands for nationalisation. It would be more useful for the national debate to have a broader conversation on the issue of redistribution of wealth or restorative justice. It seems that there is a broad consensus across all political parties that Black Economic Empowerment has not been a success in its desired objective of broad-based

116

redistribution of wealth. The more interesting question to ask South Africans is whether they believe that there should be redistribution of any kind and who they think should pay for it. What form should this payment take? How should this payment work? Who should administer the funds, and why has business taken a back seat in this debate?

❏ **Why has South Africa's economy been unable to generate jobs?** Economists can disagree on the general role that our Labour Relations Act has played in the level of unemployment remaining so stubbornly high. What cannot be contested is that on aggregate over the last 10 years, South Africa has been sliding down the list on most available global competitiveness measurements (with the notable exception of those indexes related to the soundness of South Africa's accounting profession and the stability of its financial sector). The issue that should exercise the minds of the electorate is why this is so. What is it that makes this nation produce workers that the economy can't absorb? Why is it that its workers are unable to compete with workers from other parts of the world? Is it the education system, and if it is, then which part of it? What is Sadtu's role in the current poor performance of South Africa's teachers? Is it the rigidity created by the Labour Relations Act? Why can't these issues be translated into policy changes?

❏ **All voters, regardless of what political party they support, should refuse to take part in elections funded without transparency.** Who is funding the opposition parties? What financial interests are behind the governing ANC? How much have individual contributions made up overall donations versus corporate contributions? Should there be a law to put a cap on these contributions? What should that cap be? Which parties are for or against transparency? These are questions that political parties, regardless of who their leaders are, rarely bring to the public's attention. It is certainly a matter of public interest to get this issue firmly on the table so that the public vote is not diminished by the interests of the powerful.

❏ **What can the country do to establish a more professional government?** South Africans disagree on how much corruption takes place in their government, but almost all agree that whatever the current level is, it is unacceptable. It is time citizens discuss the introduction of a meritocracy in the selection of all civil servants. Should South Africa consider the introduction of a process where major government appointments go through a parliamentary confirmation hearing where the financial and professional history of the candidates for office is subject to public scrutiny? How can the country's electorate push for changes in the criminal justice system that will make sure that politicians who are guilty of corruption can be brought to justice swiftly? What can be done to put an end to the idea that these public officials can get away with it?

South Africans should all be keenly interested in the answers that their politicians have to these questions – and, more importantly, what they do to promote solutions around the somewhat uncomfortable (for politicians) implications raised by the answers. The two worst things those who feel marginalised in the current society can do is to lose interest in the political system and not participate in debates going forward. Their voices can change the shape of South Africa for the better. Unemployed people need to focus on how they can make themselves into a constituency that cannot be ignored. They need to shout the loudest, vote in the largest numbers and if necessary toyi-toyi the most, lest they risk remaining off the bargaining table. In fact, as a nation South Africa needs to pray that marginalised members of their communities use democratic outlets for their frustration with the system. Any other type of outlet is too ghastly to contemplate. It is often said that every country gets the leadership it deserves; let this be said as a compliment and not an insult to South Africa.

We should be striving for the creation of a people-centric society, where individual liberties are not protected through special-interest politics against the interests of the people. This should be a society where those masses of people get individual faces and their interests get dealt with on an equal basis with everyone else's, regardless of how wealthy or how powerful they are in this society. The future leaders of this people-centric society should strive to be popular without being populist, by socialising freedom to cover all South Africans and not just the privileged. Popular opinion in a society governed through a set of democratic institutions that provide checks and balances should never be mistaken for populism, because prudence and people-centricity are mutually inclusive principles. South Africans are a collection of equal citizens who have participated in liberating each other so that they can live freely amongst their fellow countrymen and women and exercise these freedoms in non-mutually exclusive ways. If that is not what freedom looks like, then it will not have been worth the fight.

7

Are We Capitalists or Communists?

The battle lines of current South African economic policy follow the contours of an age-old war of ideologies under the generic banner of capitalism versus communism. Here in particular, the heavy influence of the Russian revolutionary model has made it fashionable and at certain times politically correct for politicians to refer to themselves as communists. The fall of Soviet Russia represented a key ideological turning point. Many of the hard-liners who were pupils of communism under Joe Slovo were shaken to their core by the meaning of the failure of communism. Apart from seeming to prove that the communist model was unworkable, the fall of Soviet Russia delivered a crippling blow to the financial well-being of the ANC as a liberation movement. The timing of this loss of support could not have been worse. More than ever the ANC needed the institutional support to create think tanks and policy papers in preparation for its return. The process of moving its infrastructure and personnel back home was both logistically challenging and expensive.

Paradoxically, the history of the South African Communist Party provides context to how the ANC came to be dominated by liberal free-market economic views around the time of South Africa's transition to democracy. It also provides context to the long-running ideological battles between the left-leaning members of the party and those who were influenced by free-market economic policy beliefs.

The Communist Party of South Africa (CPSA) first came to prominence during the armed 'Rand Rebellion' led by white mineworkers in 1922. The large mining concerns, facing labour shortages and wage pressures, had announced their intention of liberalising the rigid colour bar within the mines and elevating some blacks to minor supervisory positions. White miners held the monopoly of supervisory positions over the labouring black miners, who were denied any possibility of promotion. Despite having nominally opposed racism from its inception, the CPSA supported the white miners in their call to preserve wages and the colour bar with the slogan *'Workers of the world, unite and fight for a white South Africa'*. This inauspicious start to the organisation actually coincided with some of the very impulses that would drive Afrikaner nationalism in the late 1920s.

The early relationship between the ANC and the communists was troublesome, to say the least. One of the early manifestations of this conflict arose between the two organisations' budding youth movements. The charismatic and articulate Anton Lembede, leader of the ANC's Youth League, told Ruth First, secretary of the Young Communist League at the time, that rather than choosing to join a class struggle in South Africa, 'We are devoting our energies to the preparation of the greatest national struggle of all time, the struggle for national liberation... Our stupendous task is to organise, galvanise and consolidate the numerous African tribes into one homogeneous nation.'[1]

Lembede was not alone in his distrust of the Communist Party. As Luli Callinicos notes, 'Like Lembede, Tambo distrusted the dialectical materialism of Marxism, and was indeed, Walter Sisulu remembered, a sharp nationalist.'[2] So began a rocky relationship that was to be tested many times by the point of emphasis put on the apex of the battle against apartheid. Was apartheid a policy driven

by Afrikaner racism, as ANC nationalists believed, or was it a manifestation of class warfare, as the Marxists believed?

The Suppression of Communism Act, No 44 of 1955 was used
against all those dedicated to ending apartheid, but was obviously
particularly targeted at the SACP.[3] Given the global anti-commu-
nist sentiment, which was already high in the 1950s, the apartheid
government's branding the ANC and its leadership as communist
threats had the effect of creating a self-fulfilling prophecy: cutting off most Western sources of fundraising capital for the liberation movement forced the ANC into the arms of pro-communist
countries.

The effect of going underground was to force the party to develop efficient organisational structures that could withstand a
constant barrage from apartheid secret police. The party operated
in cells, which emphasised a need-to-know basis for information
sharing. It also learned to penetrate the membership of other organisations and to recruit their top leadership so that the agenda
of the party could be run by proxies. It quickly gained currency for
having as its members the best of the best, as Mark Gevisser notes:
'Many young activists would have classed themselves as socialists,
but only a selected few – a vanguard hand picked by the Party leadership – would be card-carrying Party members, recruited through
a highly secretive process that protected the "vanguard elite" status of the Party within the liberation movement.'[4]

The alliance between the two parties was accelerated by the
ANC's own banning in 1960. The SACP was to have an increasingly
dominant role in the leadership selection and policy formation of
the ANC. 'Joe Slovo later claimed that "there was perhaps no other
period in our history when the Party played such a seminal role in
the unfolding of the struggle": the now banned ANC's "structures
as a mass organisation made it more difficult for it to swing into
underground activity at a grassroots level", so it became very reli-
ant on the SACP. The key effect of this influence was undoubtedly
the move from non-violence into armed struggle.'[5]

The influence of the Communist Party on the ANC's policies

started in earnest with the party's role in the formulation of the Freedom Charter. Professor ZK Matthews proposed holding a Congress of the People in order for the ANC to seek a mandate from the masses that would be the guiding set of principles in the Anti-Apartheid Movement. The Congress Alliance, with the Congress of Democrats (a front for the banned SACP) much in the fore, was formed in 1954.[6] 'Behind the scenes, the influence of Congress of Democrats members was even more crucial. A subcommittee formed to sort out all the bits of paper (submitted by the delegates) and to prepare a draft version of the Freedom Charter for debate by delegates to the Congress of the People included Joe Slovo and Rusty Bernstein. It was Bernstein, a member of the Communist Party's central committee and its chief propaganda expert, who bore most of the burden of writing the draft version of the Freedom Charter.'[7] The principles entrenched in the Freedom Charter with respect to the restoration of the country's wealth and land to the people represented not only the wishes of ordinary people on the streets but also those of the communist-influenced drafters of the Freedom Charter.

With the move to armed struggle the leadership of Umkhonto we Sizwe had to go abroad for military training. Given the back-drop of the Cold War, these training centres were almost always in communist countries. More importantly the ANC alliance struc-tures had to function like an integrated organisational entity which necessarily meant that their cultures became merged through this process. 'The resolution, when it came, was a compromise, but one that smoothed over some of the contradictions inherent in the Alliance. The new body, Umkhonto we Sizwe (MK), would embark on "armed struggle" and, nominally at least would be separated from the ANC – "a necessary fiction", commented SACP member Joe Slovo. MK would also welcome members from all groups. In practice, this meant that whites could join MK through their mem-bership of the SACP. The deliberate ambiguity of the origins of Umkhonto gave the ANC several advantages.'[8]

The necessary fiction that Joe Slovo was alluding to has haunted the alliance movement in many forms throughout its history. The strategic ambiguity that was so necessary for the survival of both the ANC and the SACP has at times led to a counterproductive ideological battle that occasionally bubbles over in bitter leadership contests. Indeed this necessary fiction is at the heart of the question: is the ANC a communist, socialist or capitalist-leaning institution? The often repeated response that the ANC is an ideological broad church only serves to mask the fundamental trade-offs made at the policy level, sometimes to the detriment of poor people.

Leadership battles within the SACP and the ANC were persistently influenced by support for divergent ideological positions among members of both parties.

> Moses Kotane led the SACP for four decades... When he finally died in 1978 after spending most of the decade in a Moscow sanatorium, he was replaced by Moses Mabhida, a man who shared his 'first a native and then a communist' ethos. But by the early 1980s, both Mabhida and the long-serving chairman, Yusuf Dadoo, were over seventy...
>
> ...when Slovo declared his candidacy to replace Dadoo within the Party, Thabo Mbeki made no bones that he disapproved. 'Is it correct to have a white leader?' he asked his Party confidants...
>
> Slovo was so exercised upon reading the draft Mbeki circulated among his fellow Politburo members that he called an immediate meeting of the body. The Mbeki thesis, he declared, was so dangerously racist, so inflammatory, that it should not even be circulated. Mbeki remained silent, but Mabhida defended him, and the meeting ended inconclusively. [Mbeki was never to attend another Politburo meeting.][9]

These leadership tussles would go on right through until the end of apartheid, with the Thabo Mbeki–Joe Slovo axis being a particularly important one. The ultimate leadership contest was in the selection of deputy president of the ANC after Nelson Mandela rose to the rank of president.

Controversy, however, surrounded the remaining offices. Delegates were looking to the future, and contemplating the likely successors to the ageing generation of Mandela, Tambo and Sisulu. Two relative youngsters were clearly in the succession frame, at least in the eyes of exiles: Chris Hani, charismatic leftist firebrand and head of the ANC's armed wing (who had been groomed for leadership by Joe Slovo); and Thabo Mbeki, protégé of Oliver Tambo... Fearing a divisive contest, the movement's elders characteristically persuaded Thabo Mbeki and Chris Hani not to contest for the senior office of deputy president.[10]

At the same time the party was being steadily lobbied by corporate South Africa to adopt a market-friendly set of policies. Corporate South Africa was only too willing to pick up the slack from Russia as the new ANC benefactor. Having left the day-to-day responsibility of Communist Party work, Thabo Mbeki was free to play a central part in fundraising for the ANC by interfacing with big business leaders from South Africa.

The assassination of Chris Hani (who was a hugely important leader of the school of thought that was still greatly suspicious of the free market, particularly its ability to facilitate poverty alleviation) and the ascension of Thabo Mbeki at the expense of Cyril Ramaphosa (who at the time was secretary-general of the ANC on the heels of his role as a leading trade unionist) to the position of deputy president sealed the economic fate of post-apartheid South Africa. The ANC therefore shifted from an economic development strategy based on a philosophy of state-dominated communism with an eastern orientation towards the capitalist-leaning liberalism with a western orientation.

Well-read leaders like Thabo Mbeki understood that communism had run its course and failed a crucial test in creating alternative incentives that would be as robust as those that existed within capitalist societies in driving human behaviour. Francis Fukuyama casts some light on the problem:

THE GREAT AFRICAN SOCIETY

Based in part on a misreading of anthropologists like Lewis Henry Morgan, Marx and Engels argued that an early stage of 'primitive communism' existed prior to the rise of exploitative class relationships, an idealised state that communism sought to recover. Morgan had described customary property owned by tightly bonded kin groups; real-world Communist regimes in the former USSR and China forced millions of unrelated peasants into collective farms. By breaking the link between individual effort and reward, collectivisation undermined incentives to work, leading to mass famines in Russia and China and severely reducing agricultural productivity.[11]

In reality the recent discussions on nationalisation of mines (which intensified in 2011) and potentially banks, and the restitution of land, have displayed the meaninglessness of the communist versus capitalist title in determining the ideological positions of various senior ANC members. Though the dual membership policy between the SACP and the ANC still existed, many senior ANC leaders had let their Communist Party membership expire in the early 1990s. There are very few real communists left in the ANC. Nowhere was this more evident than at the September 2010 National General Council meetings in Durban, with so-called capitalists within the ANC like Minister Tokyo Sexwale and successful businesswoman Bridgette Radebe arguing in favour of nationalisation while the head of the Communist Party, Minister Blade Nzimande, urged caution and circumspection.

The actual battle within the ANC today is between state-centric socialists and free-market-centric capitalists. The latter emerged victorious in the post-1994 period as winners of a ferocious battle for the soul of the ANC that had begun nearly a decade earlier. This was not an ANC-specific battle: all around the developing world economic policy makers were trying to make sense of the failure of Marxism and what it meant to their aspirations for poverty alleviation in their countries. In 1989 John Williamson invented the term 'the Washington Consensus' to describe a form of neoclassical economics (because it was a modern application of Adam Smith's 'invisible hand of the market' theory) which had 10 basic prescriptions: impose fiscal discipline; reform taxation; liberalise interest rates; raise spending on health and education; secure property rights; privatise state-run subsidiaries; deregulate markets; adopt a competitive exchange rate; remove trade barriers; and remove barriers to foreign direct investment.[12]

Developing countries the world over were given this one-size-fits-all laundry list of policy measures by institutions such as the World Bank and the IMF as preconditions for concessionary loans. South Africa's economic policy makers were convinced by their own independent advisors to follow this same policy mix. As outlined in Chapter 4, South Africa instituted many of these policies, resulting in moderate jobless growth and what many scholars would recognise as de-industrialisation (which in South Africa's case has manifested itself in the severe reduction on a relative basis of industrial capacity, with growth of the service sector and retraction of the manufacturing sector).

The presence of left-leaning leaders in the party necessitated some policy concessions in their direction. The RDP policy represented the last stand of the state-centric socialists championed passionately at the time by former Minister Jay Naidoo. The RDP office was dismantled by then Deputy President Mbeki and replaced by the market-friendly GEAR programme along with elements of a welfare state rolled out as pro-poor concessions. Gradually, under pressure from the increasingly impatient black constituency, the free-market-centric capitalists increased the scale and scope of the welfare state, appeasing some representatives of the marginalised constituency. According to a 2009-2010 survey released by the South African Institute for Race Relations, South Africa had 14 million people living on government grants (child support, old age and disability).[13] At the time of writing this number has jumped to over 16 million.

Crucially, through a generous use of the patronage networks and a genuine desire to spread competent people across the landscape of the political economy, the free-market capitalists were to co-opt able union leaders and strong communist intellectuals such as Mbhazima Shilowa, Kgalema Motlanthe, Marcel Golding, Johnny Copelyn and Alec Erwin into senior government positions or through irresistible business opportunities. These redeployments left a few lonely and at that time less well-known voices (all SACP members) to carry the cause for the poor and marginalised people, namely Blade Nzimande, Gwede Mantashe and Zwelinzima Vavi.

Ironically, the enduring major concession that the free-market-centric capitalists made was in facilitating, under the leadership of then Labour Minister Tito Mboweni, a pro-worker Labour Relations Act which added rigidity to the labour markets just as South Africa was suffering from the textbook definition of structural unemployment. It became increasingly difficult for small businesses to hire workers in line with their expansionary growth plans for fear of not being able to fire redundant staff if expansion efforts fell short. The Small and Medium Enterprise (SME) sector was forced to downscale its cost structure in a hurry, often using temporary staff or outsourcing labour-intensive work to remain competitive. Given the fact that SMEs are by far the largest employment generator in the country, this robbed South Africa of the opportunity for these enterprises to pick up the slack from large corporations that were actually shedding jobs faster than they were creating them in their efforts to become globally competitive.

The massive amounts of foreign direct investment (FDI) that the success of the GEAR policies was hinged on did not come. Annual FDI inflows averaged less than 1.5 per cent of GDP during the 1994-2002 period compared with averages of 2-5 per cent of GDP for peer group countries.[14] Instead there was a relatively large amount of 'hot money', in the form of short-term portfolio inflows of capital that were to take advantage of the 'carry trade' South Africa was to offer as a result of the macro-economic policies of the free-market-centric capitalists, characterised by high interest rates and relatively low inflation.

The lack of local private sector investment was not compensated for by a more free-spending government (given the Finance

Ministry's determination to keep government deficits to a bare minimum by aggressively paying down debt), and therefore foreigners refused to be the only long-term investors in the economy. To quote Nattrass and Seekings: 'The problem with this macroeconomic strategy was that one of the most important determinants of whether a firm invests is whether it expects to be able to sell its products. A high level of demand thus encourages higher investment. If the government holds back on spending, and if private-sector incomes are growing slowly, then firms will worry about poor market conditions. They will lack the confidence to invest, no matter what signals the Minister of Finance tries to send them about sound fiscal policy.'[15]

In truth there was a perfect storm descending on South Africa's labour markets. A domestic political transformation was draining effort away from necessary macro- and micro-economic trade-offs between labour, business and government. Just as this was happening, competitors like Brazil, Australia, Singapore and Chile were starting to reap the benefits of reforms undertaken in the 1980s. All the while, developed countries were deciding which emerging markets to outsource business processes to and which of these markets would warrant their FDI. In a time when the margin for error could not be narrower, South Africa was making both unforced (through policy mistakes) and forced (through a rebalancing of the relationship between capital and labour) errors.

Economic achievements under President Mbeki's administration were nevertheless impressive, given the challenges the administration faced. It is impossible to tell where South Africa would have been had Chris Hani lived to become president instead of Thabo Mbeki. It is difficult to see when the tide turned against the remaining communists in the ANC in the run-up to the 1994 election. It would not be unfair to say that even during Chris Hani's last living year his ability to impact the ANC's economic policy positions was limited by its strong leaning towards a market-based set of policies.

Several micro-economic initiatives, such as the Motor Industry Development Programme, whose intention was to induce private sector spending in targeted aspects of the motor industry through the use of incentives, had great success: '... tariffs were cut, but steadily and slowly; auto manufacturers were encouraged to streamline their production, so as to produce higher volumes of fewer models... In return for chipping away at the tariff wall, motor manufacturers who exported their goods would be able to import other models duty free.'[16] The automotive sector is highly efficient, contributing 7.5 per cent of GDP in 2008 and employing around 36 000 people. In 2010 South Africa managed to provide 0.61 per cent of total production of vehicle manufacturing worldwide, which gives it a ranking of 24th in terms of world market share.[17] As of 2010 a broader analysis of the multiplier effect created by this policy shows that approximately 200 000 jobs have been created by automotive assemblers, automotive component manufacturers, the tyre industry and motor trade and servicing.[18] The success of this policy has heartened many believers in state-led growth and prompted calls for more micro-economic interventions by the state as a way of targeting high-growth job-creating sectors. More balanced observers would view it as a shining example of how public–private partnerships can work.

There was a genuine effort led by the Department of Trade and Industry (DTI) to support SME development, through the support of the government to the Small Business Development Corporation (which eventually became known as Business Partners). Business Partners has become a tremendously successful organisation investing in over a hundred SMEs a year. The policy framework around BEE started generating transactions in big volumes in the late 2000s. Through this policy close to R500 billion was invested over the last 15 years in the acquisition of shares by previously disadvantaged investors.[19]

In addition, all of the apartheid-era debt was repaid. This allowed the government to start boosting public sector spending on infrastructure including the construction of close to 2 million low-income houses, sanitation facilities and rural electricity provision. As a result of the aggregate of these efforts, GDP growth between

2000 and 2005 averaged just below 5 per cent. Free-market-centric capitalism had reached its zenith at the end of 2005.

The Polokwane ANC conference of December 2007 thus represented a shock (for some) defeat of everything that the free-market-centric capitalists stood for. The press ran the story as a victory and political redemption for the then embattled deputy president of the ANC, Jacob Zuma. But JZ was a symbol for 35 million South Africans who had been economically excluded from the free-market-centric project and left literally to stand in the welfare queue.

The creation of a welfare state alongside a free-market-based economy was a confession that the society South Africa was becoming was neither politically nor economically sustainable. 'This is precisely the trap into which the ANC government has fallen. At least a quarter of the population receives social grants... Grants also add and/or accentuate the humiliation that unemployed people feel about being dependent and unproductive and therefore unable to look after themselves and their families.'[20] To add insult to injury, the Education Department, between 1994 and 2007, went from one disaster to the next, squandering big portions of the resources being allocated every year on ineffective education, leaving another generation of mostly African children unprepared for the twenty-first century.

Since 1994 South Africa's corporate sector has significantly developed to play an important catalytic role in the South African economy, just as the *sagoodnews* newsletter claims:

> In a relatively short space of time, South African business has emerged from the isolated laager of apartheid South Africa to become a significant and influential player in the global business arena. As highlighted by Stephan Malherbe and Nick Segal in their report on corporate governance in South Africa, many of South Africa's corporations in the late 1980s were bloated, unfocused and run by entrenched and complacent managers. With local business operating in isolation from the rest of the world and shielded from international competition, our business practices, laws and regulations

fell behind international norms. In the past two decades, much has changed: South African business has been exposed to a changing political environment; rapid integration into the global marketplace; the stringent demands of international investors; an emerging market crisis; and changing regulatory reform. Cumbersome conglomerates have been unbundled and businesses have become more streamlined, focussed and competitive. Legislation, regulations and corporate governance has converged to international standards. As a result, South African firms have been able to compete internationally and we have witnessed the emergence of world-class industries, such as the oil-from-coal, offshore oil-from-gas, health care, deep mining, armaments, information technology, forestry products and food processing. South African companies are playing an important role in mobilising private capital flows in Africa, both for new investment within South Africa and as an important source of foreign direct investment in other African countries.[21]

More astute corporate leaders have joined in a chorus of voices asking for the leadership of the country to do a better job of facilitating more investment in the training of currently unemployed South Africans. The more cynical private sector lobby has succeeded in getting away with a profit-maximising outlook that has led them to outsource jobs overseas, find creative ways of avoiding taxes and anger union leaders by paying large bonuses and salaries to senior management whilst resisting 8-12 per cent salary increases for workers who are coming off a low wage base.

A significant number of corporate leaders believe that the country is being held back by the Labour Relations Act and that it hampers the workings of free-market capitalism. These corporate leaders have to balance criticism of government policies with the knowledge that South Africa's apartheid legacy has denied the majority of the population a level playing field to participate in the competition that a normal free-market economy would provide. These corporate leaders have failed to offer either the unions, government or workers a significant grand bargain to replace the elements of the Labour Relations Act that they believe are holding the country back. This private sector paralysis with regard to net employment creation is facilitated by a failure of leadership within the three major constituencies, labour unions, corporate CEOs and government. Unfortunately this paralysis has not resolved itself between the Polokwane and Mangaung ANC conferences.

It is important to realise that the developments leading to the adoption of an economic set of policies that rely on a muscular state are significantly influenced by the presence of newly formed economic development orthodoxy. Cambridge University professor Stefan Halper has coined the phrase 'the Beijing Consensus' to describe a new phenomenon encouraged by China for nations to adopt what he calls market authoritarianism.[22] This new orthodoxy allows some countries to liberalise economically without surrendering to domestic or international calls for a liberalised political environment. In countries that have liberalised politically – South Africa among them – the threat is a roll-back of civil liberties as the state assumes the role of a provider at the political cost of the citizen's right to call the state and its officials to account.

The New Growth Path

The state-centric socialist project in South Africa is at an early stage of its development, but it seems that the Zuma administration – having drafted and adopted a new economic policy document called the New Growth Path – is a firm believer in the 'Beijing Consensus'. Accompanying the adoption of this policy are early calls to relax inflation targets and for the government to intervene to weaken the rand in support of export competitiveness. The Economic Transformation Discussion Document for the ANC's 2010 National General Council calls for:

> In the short and medium term, industrial policy [that] would emphasise labour-absorbing sectors geared largely to domestic and

regional demand, with consistent but much more gradual encouragement of high-tech and dynamic industries as a more long term aim... Requirements for narrow BEE would be more limited, while incentives and support for employment equity, collective ownership, small and micro enterprise and local procurement would increase... Training and education systems would have to increase the emphasis on improving basic education in poor communities combined with measures to improve social mobility and legitimacy by ensuring more merit based access to Model C and tertiary education. Access to quality further education and training and internships to improve employability would have to be dramatically expanded.[23]

An exploration of the policy document that outlines the basis for the Zuma administration's New Growth Path reveals eight important differences between the NGP and policies of the free-market-centric capitalists.

❏ The entire national policy focus has shifted towards the stimulation and state direction of **domestic investment.**

❏ The NGP is explicitly opposed to a strong rand policy, and instead uses the nuanced language of creating a **competitive currency** to signal its preference for the rand to weaken over time relative to major currencies.

❏ The thinking behind the state's role has moved from passive participant in a market-based economy towards a more **muscular state** that seeks to actively lead the charge in picking key sectors that it deems likely to stimulate growth and investing ahead of the private sector to crowd in commercial investment.

❏ The state will provide active support to ensure that future South African **exports are value-added.**

❑ Government's efforts are to be driven by a **single-minded focus on job creation**: importantly new job creation will be the acknowledged measure of success or failure of all government programmes.

❑ There will be an explicit **openness towards partnering with NGOs** that are doing creative work to solve national priority challenges.

❑ Use of **state-owned enterprises as tools for coordinated industrial development** will be more focused, explicitly removing any ambiguity created by the BEE mandate that drove the previous administration.

❑ The final change is a simple statement: '**Government has adopted the position that black economic empowerment (BEE) should seek to empower all historically disadvantaged people rather than only a small group of investors.**'[24]

These eight changes underpin the future policy direction of South Africa. The success or failure of the New Growth Path is of critical significance to at least 5 million South Africans hoping to be among the newly employed.

At face value, these aims sound consistent with what most South Africans should be wanting for their country. The points of emphasis are also fair and reasonable. The question is: does the state have the capacity to deliver on the scale imagined, given some of the immediately apparent service delivery constraints? The ANC's Economic Transformation discussion document categorises government's role in the following way. 'Government fulfils core state functions that are required for sustained economic growth, especially through supportive fiscal and monetary policy, adequate infrastructure and social services and efficient regulation.'[25]

The ideological battle between capitalists, socialists and communists has of course been raging since the nineteenth century, with the writings of Marx, Engels and later Lenin and Trotsky. Since the publication of these seminal works economists have been grappling with the best way to label and predict the evolving economic systems that govern socio-economic behaviour, set prices and create long-term incentive structures for large-scale capital investments. What is clear is that labels hide the grey areas. In 2010 Fidel Castro told *The Atlantic* magazine's national correspondent, Jeffrey Goldberg, that 'The Cuban model doesn't even work for us anymore.'[26] Cubans are now trying to introduce free markets in aspects of their economy. The Chinese refer to socialism with Chinese characteristics, which is the socialist market economy blend that they have used to lift hundreds of millions of Chinese out of poverty. Their system started with a strict state-controlled form of communism, followed by the creation of special economic zones where capitalism was experimented with. Gradually they have taken working models from within these special economic zones and applied them to the rest of the country with a healthy dose of not just provincial but also local government autonomy.

What is becoming clear, no matter where one goes in the world, is that the state is being supplanted by the market with respect to setting prices and creating incentive structures. In some countries state-owned companies (SOEs) have effectively competed with private sector companies (largely because they successfully mimicked their incentive structures); in many more, SOEs have survived only because of their access to cheap capital (ultimately paid for by the taxpayer). The state has a crucial role to play in intervening where market inefficiencies exist; this is especially true in states that are undertaking economic development against the backdrop of huge wealth disparities. But the nature of state intervention needs to be to induce market participants to correct these imbalances using all the policy levers it has in its control. Successful development outcomes have been achieved when equilibrium has been reached between incentives for both private and public sector investment programmes.

What South African policy makers are in danger of doing is

over-correcting the state management of the economy from one extreme to another. Moving away from over-confidence in the free market and its ability to stimulate growth led by FDI, towards a form of state-directed socialism that requires scientific precision by government policy makers poses a risk – specifically in picking the winning industries and backing the national champions in these industries through funding by the IDC and DBSA. Policy makers have acknowledged this risk by stating in the policy document introducing the New Growth Path that: 'In South Africa, no tech-nocratic solution – if it existed – could be imposed from above. We must develop this New Growth Path in conditions of active, noisy democracy. The deep inequalities that rend our society complicate efforts to reach consensus.'[27] Indeed this societal consensus on a set of redistributive policies that will accompany the type of mas-sive government investment being envisioned by the Zuma presi-dency is dependent on receiving both private sector and labour union commitment in a genuine three-way compromise.

I believe that the South African state is not capable of the scale and scope of the expansion in service delivery envisioned by the New Growth Path without partnership with the private sector. State-directed capitalism works when those states have a large number of experienced, dedicated and well-trained civil servants marshalled by a well-oiled bureaucracy. This is usually coupled with a large, isolated (from international retailers) set of consum-ers who serve as a drawcard for large foreign direct investments. In countries like China and India, their populations of more than a billion people each and large domestic markets, combined with their long history during which the systems have been slowly im-proved (China, for example, was a unified state run by profession-al bureaucrats over 100 years before the birth of Christ), provide them with enormous competitive advantages. Different approach-es to decentralised decision making have evolved in each country, making their systems both robust and balanced.

It is difficult not to categorise India as a market-based society today. As recently as the early 1990s India was a state-dominated socialist economy complete with detailed consecutive five-year planning. The country has, since 1991, reformed and developed a more free-market economy with a dynamic, competitive labour force. India used its healthy dose of federalism to decentralise regulation and economic developmental decision making to the level of the state (the equivalent of South Africa's provinces). This has unlocked creativity and helped address hidden inefficiencies that were holding the economy back.

A World Bank study explains: 'Following liberalization in 1991, the Indian economy grew rapidly, with the service sector leading the way. The share of service value added in gross domestic product (GDP) increased from 44 percent in 1990 to 55 percent in 2009. Service exports grew even faster, and their share in service value added increased from 3.6 percent in 1990 to 17.0 percent in 2009... India's experience differs from the typical development of other countries because services, rather than manufacturing, are playing a leading role.'[28] India has shown the benefits of investment in human capital and the high return on investing in globally competitive higher education institutions. These have produced a highly skilled labour force able to take advantage of the decentralised business process outsourcing by western firms.

Another necessary condition for successful state-directed capitalism is a culturally subservient population that is willing to take its direction from the state. In many ways it is this particular trait that has allowed the Chinese Communist Party to organise China in the manner that allows it to dominate every aspect of its society from business to family planning. It is important to note, however, that there are 600 000 villages in China where democracy is allowed to thrive and in which the Chinese Communist Party is not at all active. The absence of any other significant democratic rights in China, combined with the authoritarian characteristics of the state, enable it to use coercive means to suppress dissidents and to make developmental decisions that are sometimes bad for the environment without challenge.

China has used a very single-minded approach to public sector skills development for its government bureaucracy, run by its Central Organisation Department. This department keeps statistics on the performance of every bureaucrat throughout China's sprawling government infrastructure.[29] This is a feat that requires not only a military precision in management, but also a dogged adherence to rules set in Beijing by government employees. Equally important is a responsive and pliable corporate leadership whose agenda is synchronised with that of the state.

None of these conditions exist in South Africa, which will have to forge its own future drawing on lessons from the last 18 years as well as global models. A genuine grand bargain has to be struck between government, labour and business that will allow the hard economic trade-offs to be made that will overcome the impediments to economic growth today.

This grand bargain can find a middle ground between economic development perspectives by championing **people-centric capitalism** informed by a national strategy for human capital development. The South African approach has to be rooted in an understanding of both its strengths and its weaknesses.

A people-centric version of capitalism

South Africa has a free-spirited population that cherishes its hard-fought individual liberties and wants to exercise them in all walks of life. That this population believes in capitalism is evident everywhere one goes, from the poorest neighbourhoods to the richest. There is an aspiration for prosperity and a belief in the liberating effect of financial independence (however modestly defined) that is irrepressible. What is needed is a process to socialise South Africa's new-found political freedoms through massive investments in the equalisation of high-quality education and training opportunities for black South Africans. The balancing of urban versus rural economic development to help correct historical imbalances and create national shared prosperity and sustainable growth needs to be vigorously pursued. To be successful, this form of capitalism needs to supplement and in the long term replace the welfare state by stimulating GDP growth through domestic demand created by massive upfront private sector-driven investment in the upliftment of the poorest citizens.

The country's corporate leadership should propose the creation of a fund (which I will describe in more detail in Chapter 12) that would benefit from redirecting the existing BEE commitments, not scrapping past deals but redirecting money earmarked for new ones, towards an initiative managed by the presidency. Despite disputed figures there is roughly R500 billion in outstanding BEE equity transfers (see Chapter 8 for further explanation as to how this figure is derived). Redirecting these commitments in exchange for full BEE equity credits would allow South Africa to start from a clean slate without the baggage of history that has been a crutch for some and a kill-joy for others.

These investments should be directed at the key areas of need outlined by a detailed diagnostic along the lines of the report produced by the National Planning Commission. This report identified the key socio-economic challenges facing South Africa as poor educational outcomes, high disease burden, underperforming public service and spatial patterns that marginalise the poor.[30] This initiative should be focused on making marginalised South Africans more secure today, and at the same time preparing for a more competitive future. It is imperative that these investments be direct ones made by corporations in initiatives that affect the lives of South Africans today and not indirect investments through government agencies. To achieve this goal a standard form of Public Private Partnership (PPP) would have to be created to allow private sector firms to invest in these social initiatives and manage the roll-out of such investment as part of their corporate social responsibility.

To supplement this programme on a voluntary basis, corporations and individuals need to drastically increase their corporate and individual giving. This practice should be encouraged by using tax legislation to increase donations to support social entrepreneurs in their development initiatives. South Africa needs to actively engage the extensive network of social entrepreneurs by supporting their programmes through direct cash contributions. This initiative should encourage individuals and corporations, through a combination of moral persuasion, a social contract and tax policy, to unleash a culture of giving that speaks to some of South Africa's most fundamental challenges. Greater empathy needs to be fostered between rich and poor South Africans through shared recognition of the mutually assured destructive path of economic development with persistent income inequalities.

The government needs to use some of the reduction in public sector spending to be generated from these programmes by redirecting funds towards investment in rural infrastructure. South Africa has an acute urban-rural inequality problem that has led to imbalanced economic development. Rural infrastructure development will open up new opportunities for corporate South Africa. Within this area of focus, government needs to facilitate the development of both commercial and subsistence farming. Unemployment in the rural areas is at a shocking level and more urbanisation increases economic pressure in the cities, which are already cracking under the burden of massive squatter areas on their margins. By creating job opportunities through commercial farming operations and enhancing food security through the promotion of subsistence farming, government could significantly reduce rural unemployment.

The common denominator in successful global experiments in **land redistribution** schemes is related to government playing the role of the guarantor for parts or all of the land redistribution funds, which are then widely disseminated by private sector distribution networks (usually government guarantees come in the form of a first loss provision). The government should incentivise financial institutions to take advantage of new agricultural loan guarantee programmes to create sustainable skills transfer plans in the areas of farming management expertise. The key to successful land redistribution programmes is not to forget the fact that the family unit is central to successful farming in any part of the world.

In South Africa the conversation tends to be about whether the country should focus on small-scale farming or commercial farming. This is not the most important determinant of success. 'The main reason why family-scale farms are more efficient is that their owners operate them primarily using family labour. Owners live on the farm, manage the farm themselves, and are aided by other family members who do not need a lot of supervision to work well because they care about their own property.'[31] South African policy makers should encourage the replication of this time-tested family ownership model in the way that land is redistributed in country by facilitating financing for families that are not in possession of equity capital or collateral for cheap access to long-term capital.

From a macro-economic point of view, in keeping with recommendations from the New Growth Path, government needs to increase its inflation targeting band from the current 3-5 per cent to one that is between 5 and 8 per cent, creating more head-room for pro-growth policies. It is nearly impossible to stimulate GDP growth without the cooperation of the Reserve Bank Governor. For this set of policies to work, the Reserve Bank needs to create a better balance between targeting growth and targeting inflation and to ensure that South Africa has a more competitive currency. More importantly, the Reserve Bank needs to reprioritise away from a business-first approach, to one that more inclusively considers the well-being of middle-class consumers as well as poor South African citizens.

Unions need to agree to a five-year freeze in above-inflation wage increases, agreeing upfront to strictly inflation-linked increases. This should be supplemented by an agreement that industry-specific collective bargaining agreements facilitate future above-inflation wage increases on a basis that rewards workers for quantifiable productivity gains. This measure was instrumental in creating less friction between labour and business in Australia in the 1980s. Unions need to agree to use at least 30 per cent of their union investment funds for skills development. The Government Employees Pension Fund, through the PIC, should make a 5 per cent (which would be close to R50 billion) pledge to a programme of measurable skills development through soft loan finance for public sector employees, public school teachers, police officers and clerks in the criminal justice system.

A large investment in **improving the quality of teaching public policy** for future practitioners in the civil service is needed to train the policy makers of tomorrow. Equally important is the immediate **upgrade of teachers' training facilities** to allow more night school training and education of existing and prospective teachers so that the aggregate teaching skills base can be drastically improved. This capacity-building exercise is the key to enhancing the quality of the education system by enabling teachers to function at the levels required to produce globally competitive students from the public school system.

Police officers need to be taught holistic law enforcement techniques at police academies and not (as is the case currently) in shoddy training rooms at the back of police stations. The country also needs to train its legal clerks and state prosecution personnel to a higher level of legal proficiency to allow for improved prosecution rates. These measures would do a lot to decrease crime rates and increase both arrests and convictions. The key spin-off from a well-functioning criminal justice system is its deterrent effect on prospective criminals. In administering the skills development funds, emphasis should be placed on generating a return on the investment by using first-rate training institutions. South Africa is more than adequately supplied with training institutions that can be improved and scaled up to accommodate an influx of new trainees. Inventing new untested training centres is an opportunity for waste and corruption. Money should flow directly from the Government Employees Pension Fund (administered by the PIC) into these initiatives so as to avoid delay or corruption.

To facilitate the dynamism of the economy and create an incentive for more competition, government needs to adopt a carrot-and-stick approach to business in South Africa. Because of the country's legacy of imperialism and apartheid's subsidised development model, South Africa has an oligopoly-dominated business community. In almost any industry one can point to, it is likely that one will find that it is dominated by only three or four players. All of these players are typically well established and have strong bargaining power in their purchasing arrangements with myriad small and medium enterprises that service them. Ironically it is these small enterprises that have generated the job growth in South Africa and not their larger corporate partners.

The first stick that the government should use would be a stronger, bolder and more assertive Competition Commission (Minister Patel is already pushing for this in line with the goals of the New Growth Path) which should be better resourced to explore unfair barriers to entry into certain industries, and not merely focus on cartel behaviour or predatory pricing. The second stick should be the breaking-up of oligopolies by inducing pan-African companies to come and compete in certain oligopoly-dominated sectors. South Africa's government has to embrace its role as a facilitator rather than a generator of growth. The more industries it can exit as a player through the stimulation of increased private sector competition, the more it can use its role as a referee to increase competition, bring down prices and increase dynamism in the economy.

The biggest beneficiaries from a more competitive, less oligopolistic corporate landscape will be SMEs who will have the ability to serve more clients and therefore be forced to hire more South Africans. The state should simultaneously invest at least R10 billion a year above and beyond current commitments in the SME sector through a combination of National Empowerment Fund (NEF), IDC, Khula, Business Partners and through the increased use of incentives for corporate investments in SMEs. It is important that the emphasis when investing in SMEs is on ensuring the growth and progression of these firms from small to medium to large companies. This means some venture capital invested at

144

an early stage but most of the money going towards medium-size companies looking for expansion capital.

It is only in the progression of SMEs from small to medium to large that they can create economic dynamism and job growth. If they remain small it is to the economy's detriment. In this regard the Reserve Bank needs to encourage more SME-orientated corporate banking licences, preferably for African (outside of South Africa) banking groups, to encourage the introduction of more expansion capital, which is sorely lacking in the economy. Pan-African banks have been developing sophisticated SME corporate banking support models that could go a long way towards solving working capital challenges for local SMEs looking to grow. These banks should be supported by state-owned enterprises keeping significant deposits with them so as to facilitate liquidity that can be passed on into the highest job-creating firms in the country.

Outside of the mining sector the post-apartheid economy is structurally, for better or worse, geared towards the service sector. South Africa is in a neighbourhood of fast-growing African economies, home to nearly a billion people, creating a massive set of commercial opportunities. It is unlikely, given the high base the country is coming from, that it can grow faster than its neighbouring states. Further out, countries such as Nigeria, Angola, Ghana and Kenya offer not just high growth but markets with high population densities. The South African government has to use its full diplomatic arsenal to offer opportunities for South African banks, law firms, accounting, construction, architecture and engineering firms to prosper from the growth of its neighbours.

Government has to focus on increasing the size of the economic pie so that there is more to go around for everyone. At present there is a distinct feeling of a zero-sum game between the government-based mandate for redistribution and corporate interests in maximising profits. In moving towards a great society South Africa should encourage a more comprehensive ownership of all aspects of society. Corporations should 'own' the bad elements of society as well as the good. If the country wants to encourage more buy-in from currently marginalised members of its society, corporate South Africa should partner government by investing in the country's future to show that the capitalist system can be made fair for more than just rich people.

A people-centric version of capitalism will not materialise in this lifetime if business continues to ask for and receive protection from government against genuinely contributing to redistribution. Neither will South Africa achieve its potential if it opts for a state-directed capitalist model whilst the country is mired by corruption, lack of political accountability and inefficiency. The existence of what Zwelinzima Vavi has termed a 'parasitic state' is incongruent with the well-oiled bureaucratic machine necessary to deliver efficient state-led growth. Leaders of business, government and labour unions need to critically explore their participation in South Africa's democratic system and consider changes in their approach that will help socialise freedom in order to catalyse genuine economic transformation for those previously marginalised. Through these compromises enshrined in the form of a financially binding social compact South Africa can create the conditions for a new growth path towards shared prosperity.

8

Economic Freedom and the Comrades Marathon

Since 1921 South African athletes from all walks of life have had an opportunity to run a race called the Comrades Marathon. The symbolism of this race, as a living memorial to the spirit of the soldiers of the Great War, their trials, tribulations and camaraderie, has always been more important than prize money or position attained at the finish line. It is a 90 km race between Pietermaritzburg and Durban that tests the stamina and endurance of all participants. At the same time the length of the race challenges the spirit of the athletes to motivate themselves to perform well above their normal capacity. The romanticism of the event was such that it was viewed as possible for a poor mine worker who had not participated in any other event that year, to put on running shoes and out-duel seasoned athletes. For some lucky mine workers who were able to get into the event, the race became an outlet for their frustrations endured in the stifling working environment underground.

Over time however the race has lost its sentimentality and ultimately its altruistic image. Modern families, unlike those who used to gather around the television to watch the entire day as a celebration of human endurance, have significantly shorter attention spans. The romanticism of amateur athletes outlasting professional athletes in a race of this length, has given way to the more realistic view that amateurs should be content with enduring the long race, not aiming to win it. The nature of the race's competitive dynamics has been a stark reminder that in athletics as in real life, repetition, preparation and training get you further than raw untrained talent. In reality the race has been dominated by talented athletes like Bruce Fordyce and a handful of international long-distance specialists.

Like post-apartheid South Africa, the race has been unable to bridge the gap between vision and lived reality in interesting ways, perhaps because the vision of a utopian South Africa, where no one is a loser and everyone is a winner was always impossible to attain. Equally difficult to come to grips with is the reality that though we are all able to run and theoretically win the race to financial success in South Africa, in reality not all of us will. We all have to be content with the unobstructed opportunity to participate in the competition for scarce resources and perform according to the best of our natural abilities. As in the Comrades Marathon, the spirit of competition should enable those South Africans leading the race to help those less fortunate to the finish line.

Nearly a decade before 1921, comrades of a different sort had entered another endurance event, the struggle for independence. The liberation movement has been the focal point of tens of thousands of families that participated in political organisations led by the ANC (this is quite distinct from the millions of South Africans who participated in all aspects of the Anti-Apartheid Movement outside of formal party structures). The political liberation achieved in 1994 came with a deferred promise of economic liberation at a future date for many of these families and their extended offspring. The question that has not been overtly raised in the debate on shaping society for the future is: Is it not absolutely logical and fair for families with struggle credentials to expect their justice in the form of economic patronage in a post-liberation South Africa?

Are constitutional and legal requirements governing anti-corrupt behaviour robbing the comrades of their opportunity to recoup what they have sacrificed? A senior ANC leader, Smuts Ngonyama, when confronted about getting a large up-front advisory fee related to the Elephant Consortium's acquisition of a stake in fixed-line company Telkom (which at that time still owned 50 per cent of Vodacom), famously stated that he did not join the struggle to be poor. By saying this he was implying that it was not only fair for him and other comrades to utilise their relationships to their financial benefit but also that it is indeed the just thing to do. At the time that he made that statement most mainstream media treated its sentiment with ridicule and contempt. Was it really such an outlandish thing to say, or was Mr Ngonyama merely capturing the sentiment of the day with a level of honesty that society was not ready for? Without a formal mechanism for repaying hundreds of thousands of loyal party cadres for their years of service, was it not rational for the ANC to come up with informal ways through the guise of BEE of recognising such contributions as were made by people like Smuts Ngonyama?

Such a line of inquiry may be uncomfortable for some people to deal with on many levels. Where does the line get drawn in terms of what is permissible behaviour when it comes to wealth creation by party comrades? Which families should be allowed to benefit? How much should they be allowed to accumulate before they are deemed to have been adequately compensated? Should meritocratic rules of engagement be suspended to deal with these historical imbalances? How should private sector organisations account for payments made to these individuals? Do these individuals pay tax on these income streams?

Such questions have not been asked or answered when it comes to dealing with the peculiarity of South Africa's past and how it should affect its future as a country. The pillars on which great societies are built usually include social justice, freedom from repression of any kind and a meritocratic labour market together with a facilitative and responsive government. These pillars require a unified view of the type of society the collective citizenship is striving to achieve. In the South African context, there is a gap between what is aspired to in the constitution and what is signalled as the overarching set of aspirations by the actions of the elite class and its sub-groups. This gap is made murkier by the lack of clarity on where each subgroup of the elite stands on the questions raised in the previous paragraphs, and how they relate to the interests of the underprivileged members of society.

Elite subgroups comprise the black business elite, white business elite, labour union representatives (by virtue of their seat at the highest decision making tables of the land), ANC National Executive Committee members, civil servants, members of civil society and leaders of opposition parties. The challenge of this current leadership is to facilitate intergenerational, public to private, interracial and cross-party discussions on the country's future before South Africa moves from low-intensity class conflict to high-intensity and potentially violent class warfare.

The prescience of former president Thabo Mbeki in creating the Black Economic Empowerment framework (later revised to become Broad Based Black Economic Empowerment) was in allowing for the framework to be set by government and in requiring that private citizens independently (either as individuals or through the organisations that they represent) negotiate their contribution to national economic redistribution. A major weakness of this structure was in not equipping the new black empowerment entrants with substantive leverage for negotiating strong and sustainable transactions. The genius of the equity aspect of BBBEE was in creating societal buy-in behind the principle of black empowerment.

Having received this societal buy-in, the flexible nature of BBBEE has facilitated a gradual refinement and in some cases material redrafting of the key principles, like with the narrow ownership of holding companies which has now been broadened by popular demand. The other intelligent aspect of this policy making was to create industry-specific codes that forced business, labour and civil servants to engage on substantive and quantitative aspects of social redress in a commercial manner. This was facilitated by a carrot-and-stick approach created by the government which rewarded early adopters (through the state tender system) and punished late adopters (through the loss of government business).

The key challenge for BBBEE as a policy is precisely the fact that the framework allows for market-based, gradual transfer of wealth financed within normal commercial rules. Appetite by financiers and sellers for subsidisation has gradually decreased as the premium generated by being an early adopter of BBBEE has been outweighed by the cost of providing discounted share sales, making the willing-buyer willing-seller paradigm identical in some instances to normal commercial transactions between two white-owned entities. This has decreased sophisticated black buyers' appetites. Broad-based schemes led by employee trusts have become the new preferred route. The identity and indeed the number of owners behind the schemes do not mask the diminishing economic wealth-creation prospects of such transactions. There is typically simply not enough equity net of debt left over after paying financiers to spread the proceeds to initiatives that make a significant dent in poverty alleviation challenges. This leaves mostly the banks, accounting companies and law firms as the chief beneficiaries of the high transaction costs involved in executing these deals.

As a result of this reduction in the attractiveness of the equity aspect of BBBEE from an economic point of view, and the pent-up frustration within poor black communities because of the failure of BBBEE to meet the impossible expectation of being a silver bullet for poverty reduction in South Africa, the ruling party has started to entertain alternative redistributive mechanisms.

Currently South Africans are struggling to place inter-racial group wealth transfer in the context of their collective societal aspirations. Conservative white citizens do not agree at all on the need for a national redistributive mechanism, while at the other end of the spectrum staunch black nationalists view nationalisation without any compensation as the only fair basis for redressing the past. The majority of the population are less extreme than either end, but united in their lack of clarity on the mechanism that would most fairly redistribute wealth. To achieve this national clarity requires disciplined analysis of the form and content of these social aspirations and how they accommodate aggregate interests.

An indicator of the country's conflicting societal aspirations lies in the voting patterns of South Africans: specifically who the majority puts in power and what agenda is tabled to this majority at election time. Of course the practical problem is that collective interests cannot be expressed at the polls alone. Voting patterns are racially delineated, leading democrats and libertarians to make a strong case for minority protection rights which do exist in many forms in the constitution. Collective interests have to find expression in the form of modified social contracts that more accurately reflect the will of the people.

> Based on estimates using inter alia AMPS data from different years, the number of blacks in households with a per capita income greater than R40 000 per capita in 2000 Rand-values tripled – approximately half the increase within this income decile – between 1994 and 2004. There was a significant movement of blacks into the per capita income group above R250 000 per annum, with blacks making up a third of the population in this category in 2004 compared to only 21% 10 years earlier... This pace and extent of economic progress thus allows for higher consumption levels, which should be reflected in both increased expenditure and a change in the goods mix.[1]

What is interesting about the analysis done by Nieftagodien and Van der Berg is that they identify what they term as a historical 'asset deficit' generating artificial demand amongst the emerging middle class as they make purchases of assets that other more established middle-class groups already have. They identify these asset deficits as home ownership, telephone lines, vehicle ownership and other luxury items. The trendy category used by marketing firms, 'black diamonds', refers to this population segment of mainly African emerging middle-class consumers who are acquiring consumer goods at a faster clip than the rest of the population, relative to their income. What Nieftagodien and Van der Berg do is to temper the excitement about the sustainability of this trend, and caution economists and public policy makers against using consumption-based statistics to make inferences about the extent of wealth creation by these so-called 'black diamonds'.

There is disagreement amongst industry experts as to the exact level of transformation of the ownership of public equities in South Africa. According to a recently released study by the Johannesburg Stock Exchange, black South Africans hold at least 17 per cent of the top 100 listed companies.[2] This same study breaks down the ownership patterns into two categories, 8 per cent held directly mostly through empowerment stakes and 9 per cent of so-called mandated investments held through third-party structures such as pension funds and asset managers.[3] The JSE has also noted that if one excludes (as they believe one has to in order to get a more accurate basis for comparison) shares held on behalf of policy holders, shares held by government or unit trusts, which account for 40 per cent of the total equity pool, then this amplifies the total black ownership to 28 per cent.[4]

The Black Management Forum (BMF) has come out very critically against the current study and previous JSE surveys, implying that the JSE was deliberately obscuring the facts to try and overstate black ownership as part of an agenda to indicate that BEE should be deemed a mission accomplished and business as usual should resume. '[Then BMF President Jimmy] Manyi pointed out that BEE shareholding is not always synonymous with Black shareholding, the former could have a white component and thus a distortion of what is effectively in black hands.'[5] Well-respected rating agency Empowerdex backs this BMF view up with numbers indicating that black South Africans owned a meagre 1.6 per cent or R81 billion of JSE value.[6] Empowerdex credits this 1.6 per cent as the debt-free portion of the total 5.75 per cent black ownership of the JSE.[7] Even though the JSE has the most updated view, many members of the black business community remain suspicious of just how much actual improvement there has been on the transformation front.

These distinctions have resulted in an increasingly uncivil

public conversation on the form and content of a new redistribu-tive methodology in South Africa. So far there seem to be two nar-ratives that are competing for airspace in the quest for popular opinion making. The first narrative is of an emerging black middle class that is a small group of 'usual suspects', who are accumulat-ing wealth through both corruption and nepotism all the while displaying incompetence and/or a lack of diligence in the way they manage their personal financial affairs. The second narra-tive competing for the same airspace is that of 'ungrateful, greedy white capitalists who have accumulated extraordinary amounts of wealth off the back of the blacks, yet are too greedy and/or short-sighted to cut the new black elites a slice of the wealth'.

The first narrative has largely been carried into the living rooms and workplaces of most news readers in South Africa by the popu-lar newspapers, representing a disturbingly high proportion of all stories covered. It has shaped many neutral perceptions of how the emerging black middle class is conducting itself. In reality many of these articles focus on a handful of individuals from different ele-ments within society, conflating socialites, criminals, entertainers, entrepreneurial business people and those involved in the state tender system. People in these groups who happen to qualify as being both rich and black are depicted in the same light, as if the newspaper writers are describing a monolithic emerging culture. The net effect of this unfortunate attitude to covering what should otherwise be a celebrated social phenomenon (black wealth crea-tion), has been to demean the black South African aspirations to progress from poverty to prosperity in a single generation.

The second narrative is equally disturbing in the way that politi-cians and black business people cop out of rigorous debates by play-ing the race card, removing in the process a key cog in South Africa's makeup, genuine white patriotism. It is entirely possible that many well-meaning, good-natured white business people and committed professionals have been turned off by this attitude, which is mani-festing itself in a number of ways, occasionally by younger black government officials, who perhaps not having participated in the most intense elements of the struggle suffer from a 'hangover combativeness' that is out of place in an environment where all race groups need to do their part in working together to build a more equally shared prosperity. There are also those 'hard-core' black nationalists who would read the previous sentence as a sell-out of the so-called 'black agenda'. To their way of thinking, white people have had their turn; now it is the turn of black people to generate wealth in a way that benefits them first and foremost.

The trouble with such nouveau radicalism is its lack of consistency: a logical step would be to call for full egalitarianism, foregoing all luxurious aspects of the modern South African lifestyle in the quest for true equality of all citizens. Instead, it envisages continued sacrifices by the masses as subjects catered for by the welfare system rather than citizens operating in the mainstream of the economy, while these radicals enjoy the new-found spoils of victory. These spoils come on the back of a protracted majority subsidy of a minority, only this time the minority elite is of a darker hue. Such attitudes discourage public accountability and are the breeding ground for corrupt practices that unfortunately feed into promoters of the first narrative.

Statistically one may be surprised that both local and international research views South Africa as being at the low end of global corruption scores – for example, 'WorldAudit.org ranks South Africa as 47th least corrupt nation out of 150 nations surveyed in 2011, ahead of Italy and Greece.'[8] However a local survey conducted by the Human Sciences Research Council found that 74 per cent of all South Africans believe the incidences of corruption have increased in the last three years.[9] Perhaps the gap between actual (low) and perceived (high) corruption lies in the fact that South Africa's opinion leaders are privy to many of the informal arrangements struck under the guise of BBBEE that amplify the rumoured versus reported cases of corruption. Or that the lived reality of corruption is hard to measure so the surveys are misleading because of the varying ways of measuring, defining and categorising acts of corruption.[10]

155

Bryan Evans describes corruption as the act by which insiders profit at the expense of outsiders.[11] By this simple definition members of all elite sub-groups in South Africa are participating in illicit transactions that happen under the veil of secrecy, hidden by blind trusts, warehoused shares, offshore bank accounts and proxies. 'Any policy that creates an artificial gap between demand and supply creates a profitable opportunity for opportunistic middlemen... With an armoury of rules and regulations behind them public officials can use rigid application requirements to create delays, and take bribes to bend their own rules.'[12] This more specific criterion for corruption is a fairly accurate description of the South African state tender environment, which has bred a new culture of tenderpreneurship based on (typically) black power brokers of transactions that usually facilitate the successful participation of (largely white-owned) corporations. Whenever any of these scandals break through the comfortable veil of silence surrounding corruption in South Africa, the warring elites are quick to point fingers at each other, using either of the two dominant story lines to either blame black individuals' corruption and their incompetence and largesse, or white greed-driven opportunism. The reality is that members of all race groups are benefiting from their position as insiders to wealth-creation opportunities generated through the state tender system.

These sub-groups of elites presenting variations of the story lines above make up a combined total of fewer than 5 million South Africans. The real question is how these 5 million people can expect to have this debate without adequately considering the interests of the other 45 million? The inability of the elite pact of 1994 to produce policy that can generate a solution that works to eradicate poverty for the 45 million leads to the fundamental unsustainability of the status quo.

Two leaders have offered to fill the breach and speak for the interests of the marginalised. First, Zwelinzima Vavi, general secretary of Cosatu, has spoken articulately about the danger of the new black elite representing a predatory state bureaucracy which exists first and foremost to feed the increasing appetites of party cronies, who influence-peddle their way into state tenders by abusing the system and corrupting the bureaucrats. This analysis has wrongly been interpreted by the opponents of the opulent black middle class as an endorsement of their chief concerns. Far from saying that it is wrong for South Africa to be rapidly creating a black middle class with overt state preference for black entrepreneurs, what Vavi is opposed to is the abuse of political power as a means to that end. In other contexts he has been very strong in his opposition to the maintenance of wealth in the minority interests of the white elite. As general secretary of Cosatu, his chief mandate is to wrestle power away from both elites into the hands of workers. The method that Cosatu has chosen so far is to transfer this wealth through incremental reforms in labour conditions, including a welfare structure that takes care of the short-term effects of temporary unemployment through the provision of unemployment insurance. The payment of an increasing minimum wage to shift the balance of power between workers and their employers, using militant strike action when necessary, is another strong thrust of the method of redistribution.

His description of South Africa as a predatory state signals Vavi's belief that the country has moved from incidental corruption (bribes to junior officials) or systematic corruption (which affects specific areas of government) towards the much more perilous realm of systemic corruption. In this realm honesty becomes irrational because the entire government procurement environment is entangled in corruption at multiple levels.[13] Given that Vavi is part of the leadership of the alliance that governs the country, this is a very profound rebuke – a break in the silent treatment.

What was previously acknowledged by government was that there were rogue officials engaged in incidental corruption. Given Vavi's stature, his contention that what is in fact happening in South Africa is a more insidious, far-reaching form of systemic corruption might call into question the mechanism that has so far served as the most effective method of wealth transfer to

ANC-affiliated comrades with struggle credentials. The effects of this disturbance of what was previously seen as a sacrosanct channel of wealth creation on the greater debate on redistribution will be profound. More important still is the effect of the inevitable disgust that the largely poor supporters of the ANC will feel as they read more stories of their struggle heroes engaged in corruption at the highest levels of government.

The second vocal supporter of the 45 million voiceless South Africans is Julius Malema. In his former role as head of the ANC Youth League he took up the cause of the marginalised by advocating a programme of nationalisation of both mines and banks, and also called for the restitution of land. In making this point Mr Malema cites the following passage of the Freedom Charter: 'The national wealth of our country, the heritage of all South Africans, shall be restored to the people; the mineral wealth beneath the soil, the banks and monopoly industry shall be transferred to the ownership of the people as a whole; all other industry and trade shall be controlled to assist the well-being of the people; all people shall have equal rights to trade where they choose, to manufacture and to enter all trades, crafts and professions.'[14]

By using the Freedom Charter as the basis of this argument, Malema and the ANC Youth League claimed democratic and popular legitimacy behind the nationalisation policy and the redistributive demands it places on those charged with its implementation. It is very difficult to argue with the source of legitimacy at a technical level because the ANC has not publicly distanced itself from those views expressed in the Freedom Charter and has continued to carry majority support. So would it not follow that, given the popular majority that the ANC holds, the people's will is behind the policy of nationalisation?

So far Malema's opponents have used various tactics to attempt to reduce the momentum that might build behind this policy proposal. Firstly they have alleged that the proposal of nationalisation is a way to generate exits out of bankrupt BBBEE deals in the mining sector for the black elite who have existing mining investments. Secondly they have accused Malema of being corrupt and guilty of hypocrisy by representing poor people in public but living a lavish private lifestyle. The third charge is the subterranean innuendo that Malema is not himself intelligent enough to come up with a cogent rational mechanism to manage the very complex processes demanded by a redistributive system of the magnitude that he proposes.

All three forms of rebuke miss the central issue. They trivialise what is a very legitimate set of concerns and by focusing on the messenger and not the message they miss the obvious point that the messenger will change over time because the core concern is gross inequality which will continue to be a chief source of long-term instability. They also assume that nationalisation is something that will have to be forced on poor people or that poor people will vote for a platform that supports nationalisation out of ignorance, thereby unwittingly sealing their fate to a future of economic depression as investment in South Africa dries up and GDP slows down.

The truth is much more complex than that. Firstly, it is not clear that given a referendum two thirds of South Africa will not vote for nationalisation. Secondly, given the current state of destitution that most South Africans live in it may be difficult for them to become any worse off in economic terms. Lastly, there have been examples in both Brazil and Botswana of successful and largely pain-free renegotiations of mining interests facilitated in no small measure by threats of nationalisation. These two countries have gone on to enjoy rapid GDP growth as they reaped the additional benefits of increased mining royalties that were invested successfully in the long-term future of their respective citizens.

What cannot be ignored by the protagonists of nationalisation is the long list of failed attempts at state ownership as a wealth transfer to poor people. There is no guarantee that the process of nationalisation can be executed without economic disruption to the entities that are being nationalised. Often the process of nationalisation, particularly in countries with high existing corruption, will lead to oligarchy in the form of insider deals to attain management contracts, dubious procurement practices and sometimes whole-sale theft of assets through sub-economic deals done under the pretext of asset sales for fundraising.

It is also difficult for supporters of nationalisation to argue that the government – which has at best a mixed management track record when it comes to state-owned enterprises – will be in a posi-tion to run entities such as Anglo American, Goldfields, Northam Platinum and African Rainbow Minerals in more efficient ways than their current owners. More to the point, there is no real con-nection between ownership and value creation if one supposes that there will be fair value compensation for the existing opera-tions; the government has to out-perform the previous owner to reap the rewards of ownership. Given the likely trade-off between spending on infrastructure (for which government has over R600 billion earmarked) and payment to private owners for nationalisa-tion, it would be impossible to justify the risk-reward relationship to the South African taxpayer. If the objective is nationalisation without compensation then the government will have to develop the fortitude to withstand years of local and international retribu-tion through sanctions and disinvestments. Little evidence of such collective fortitude has so far been displayed.

What people are asking government to do is not to gain owner-ship over yet more assets. Service delivery protestors are asking offi-cials to use their current resources, including the ability to regulate and tax corporate South Africa more effectively, in order to deliver better quality jobs and services on an accelerated timeline. The ability to create an income stream for ordinary South Africans has nothing to do with how big an asset base the state has. The state has to find ways of increasing its revenue base – and nationalisation is theoretically one of those, but far from the only one. According to Annabel Bishop, fewer than 6 million South Africans pay 95 per cent of the total income taxes; 90 per cent of all company tax comes from just 2 000 companies.[15] Surely the government has to be focused on policies and regulations that increase the number of operating profitable companies so as to expand both the corporate tax base and increase the number of income tax-paying employees in the country. At the same time, profitable non-tax-paying entities should be forced, through closing tax loopholes, to contribute to state coffers.

Perhaps this would be an appropriate time to remind ourselves why the normal electoral system is not adequately producing sufficient feedback loops to allow for elected officials to act in the best interest of the majority of the population. Why is it that South Africa finds itself in a situation where pro-poor policies are confused with populist policy options while fiscally conservative economic policies that protect the existing monopolies stay in place? Why is it possible for systemic corruption involving tens of billions of rands to go on without senior party members being called to justice? Why is it that inept civil servants drain the system of valuable resources while detracting from the hard work of their more competent colleagues and closing opportunities for better qualified, well-intentioned members of society to step into these jobs?

Some of the previous chapters have dealt with the basic factors that facilitate this status quo. A faulty settlement in the form of an elite pact in 1994 (Chapter 4), insufficient attention to people-centricity in the make-up of South African society (Chapter 5), and a special-interest-based democratic dispensation that protects the minority at the expense of the majority (Chapter 6). But more attention needs to be paid to why South Africa is headed nowhere fast in its aspirations to journey towards meritocracy.

Political and government failure

'Let us define a thorough-going meritocracy by means of two characteristics... They are, first, the allocation of power, prestige and wealth in society largely on the basis of the educational credentials with which one enters the labour market and second, a high degree of formal equality of the opportunity to acquire those credentials.'[16] Strangely enough, in South Africa the absence of the second principle – that is, the low degree of formal equality of the opportunity to acquire credentials – has been used as an excuse to nullify the first principle, namely the allocation of power, prestige and wealth on the basis of educational credentials. While what I have termed the attempt at the intellectual genocide of African people by the apartheid regime (see Chapter 9) may have justified government interference in the normal allocation of skills across the economy in the form of legislated employment equity standards, nothing can justify the current assault on both core principles of meritocracy in South Africa.

If the aim is to create a sustainable society set on pillars of social justice, freedom from repression, a meritocracy together with a facilitative and responsive government, then the status quo has to be broken down systematically. Principled leadership is necessary to break the deadlock between the warring classes. As Amartya Sen eloquently points out: 'Freedom to choose gives us the opportunity to decide what we should do, but with that opportunity comes the responsibility for what we do – to the extent that they are chosen actions. Since a capability is the power to do something, the accountability that emanates from that ability – that power – is part of the capability perspective and this can make room for demands of duty – what can broadly be called deontological demands.'[17] These 'deontological demands' represent a dual obligation to leadership and the electorate to exercise their respective power, to elect officials who will exercise their duty to fulfil the needs of the electorate. It is worth breaking down into more detail the ways in which this relationship can function sub-optimally so that we can understand in more detail the structural challenges faced by South Africa in the resolution of its inter-class stand-off.

Somewhere along the way between 1994 and today, government officials have lost sight of where they are in the spectrum between 'principals' and 'agents', which has resulted in some officials acting as principals representing their own interests within business transactions and abusing their roles as insiders within the decision-making structures. 'At the heart of the political agency model is the principal–agent relationship between citizens and government; the principals are the citizens/voters while the agents are the politicians/bureaucrats... In the political agency approach, the incentive problem arises because citizens have delegated authority to policy makers who enjoy an informational advantage.'[18]

The lack of clarity between the roles of government officials, specifically their failure to act as agents to the principals who are the voters, occurs because the South African system of closed party lists does not facilitate a direct relationship between government officials and the voting public (as discussed in Chapter 6). This problem manifests itself in two ways: '**Monitoring**... The policy maker may act opportunistically. There is a need to establish whether this has happened and to reward/punish behaviour accordingly in order to minimize opportunism... **Selection**...There is a need to select the most competent policy makers and/or those whose motivations are most likely to be in tune with the public interests.'[19]

Given the fact that most public officials are in jobs as a result of a decision made by the deployment committee of the ANC, these bureaucrats correctly calculate that they are agents of the party within government and therefore are chiefly beholden to party bosses. As a result their accountability is to individuals who will measure them first and foremost by virtue of their adherence to party discipline displayed by strict compliance with party instructions. The interests of the actual principals – the voting public – are consigned to the bottom of a long list of special interests. This system facilitates the insidious practice of corruption as long as one has a senior party member as a source of political security.

The damage that this system does to society is multi-faceted. It creates a lack of public accountability of public servants. It creates adverse incentives for anti-corruption whistle-blowers within the party. It creates a selection bias in the leadership profile, given that backroom dealing and skulduggery are as useful in advancing one's political fortunes as popularity. It creates mistrust by the public

of civil servants and their agenda in office. It cuts valuable information feedback loops on voter policy preferences. Most damag-
ingly, it opens up opportunity for incompetent leadership to creep
into power through the political back door, robbing the public of
better-qualified leadership at all levels of the political structure,
resulting in suboptimal policy making and implementation.

It is possible in light of these entangled systemic problems to
characterise South Africa as experiencing both government failure
and political failure:

> Government failure refers to problems that arise when one actor in the
> economy (the state) monopolises the legitimate use of force. Political
> failure refers to the narrower idea of problems that arise when power
> to control this monopoly is allocated in democratic political systems.
> Political problems as described here are therefore a subset of govern-
> ment failures... A government failure might then arise either because
> the policies selected are poor or because the means of picking (even
> good) policies is very costly. A system of government free from gov-
> ernment failure will pick good policies and policy processes. It will
> also encourage efficient private actions to affect policy outcomes.[20]

The opportunity cost of political and government failure at this
juncture of South Africa's development is unquantifiable. Just
15 years ago South Africa was roughly the same size economy as
Brazil. Now the Brazilian economy has left South Africa far behind. Nigeria is slated to surpass South Africa in 2025 as the largest
economy in Africa. Given the relative sizes of both economies in
1994, this is an amazing feat. The external factors that impact this
comparative analysis, relative differential in resource allocation between these three countries, differentials in the relative size of each
country's populations, commodity price booms, etc, should not
distract us from the central issue, which is that South Africa has
become less competitive over the past 15 years.

Another example of the level of political and government failure is the level of chronic under-spending of local government

budgets due to a lack of capacity at the bureaucratic level. 'Local government in South Africa consists of 295 metros, municipalities and district councils and is an important government interface with delivery. However, it is also a tier of government that is faced with significant capacity constraints. This is illustrated by the fact that in 2007/2008 95 local authorities spent less than 40% of their capital budgets, 44 spent between 40% and 60% of their budgets, 9 spent between 60% and 80% of their capital budgets.'[21] On top of the fact that the budgets went unspent one has to account for the wasted expenditure at all three levels of government. According to reports from the Auditor General, over R8.7 billion in wasted expenditure was recorded in the financial year 2009-2010.[22]

According to a study produced by the World Bank Group, South Africa has three key economic challenges. Firstly, it is exporting far less industrial output and attracting less FDI than other middle-income countries in its peer group. Second, it has low levels of manufactured exports relative to its peers, not because its manufacturers are inherently less productive, but because the country has low industrial allocative efficiency, which is largely caused by high concentration in its industries. Third, improving allocative efficiency requires more than just sharpening the Competition Commission's legislation and its functionality; attention has to be paid to increasing and maintaining current infrastructure capacity, skills shortages, crime and small business access to finance.[23]

These three challenges would be difficult to overcome when tackled by a vibrant, highly skilled public sector bureaucracy trying to keep unemployment below 10 per cent. But in the context of a South Africa that is encountering both government and political failure as well as reeling from high unemployment and the effects of multi-level class warfare, it may be a bridge too far.

Dealing with the political challenges enabling and facilitating corruption will allow for a more meritocratic process of selecting civil servants, which in turn will create the possibility that these civil servants will be less beholden to corporate lobbyists, as well as political pressure from party bosses (who may themselves be compromised by oligopoly lobbyists). These civil servants could then begin to look at breaking oligopolies by legislating for genuine competition in the private sector, removing a major impediment to foreign investment, and facilitating lower price outcomes for consumers, as well as job opportunities for the unemployed. The status quo will not facilitate such a process. Corruption facilitates regulatory capture which results in lower FDI (as well as low levels of domestic investment because of low incentives to compete in oligopolistic industries), reducing GDP growth and the prospects for significant job creation. The same regulatory capture makes the support of SMEs uneven, often hampering their growth through the continued support of unfair competition by big corporates which stifles the country's biggest job-creating sector.

This creates the real possibility of social unrest of the kind that will make the August 2011 British riots look like a picnic. The economic and political agents operating at the highest level in both the private and public sectors have to be more forward-thinking in their approach to allocation of talent in the country so that the new talent can invest (private sector) and regulate these investments (civil servants), in more nationally responsible ways.

It seems that leadership in government has heard the message. In the annual Ruth First lecture in August 2011, Deputy President Kgalema Motlanthe made the following statement: 'The pestilence of corruption menacing the soul of our democracy is a life-and-death matter on which our future depends.'[24] The challenge that the deputy president has to face up to is the fact that the political Comrades Marathon has created a culture of 'takers' who view power as a proxy for money making at the expense of poor South Africans. As the head of the deployment committee within the ANC, Motlanthe has a unique opportunity to bring to an end the era where politicians see themselves as agents of the party and not of the electorate that voted them into power.

The Deputy President raised another important issue during the same speech: 'We may need to begin exploring creative ways of introducing subjects related to ethics into our school curriculum very early in the development of the learner.'[25] The key issues raised by these comments relate to the culture of entitlement, loss of the connection between hard work and progress and the values that are normally reinforced by society relating to honest conduct. These are all cherished aspects of meritocratic societies.

'It seems fairly safe to say that the basic idea of meritocracy is rooted in principles of exchange and reciprocity that lie at the heart of all social systems, and that enjoy high levels of acceptance in all cultures. What you put into society directly determines what you can legitimately take out of it – and within this broad rule, inequality of rewards does not seem to be a problem.'[26] South Africa has a historical imbalance in that corporations have a tendency to replicate their current leadership in terms of their educational backgrounds, hobbies and socialisation patterns, making it difficult for largely white executive teams to hire outside of this comfort zone. The fact that it normally takes 10 to 15 years' experience to qualify someone for entry into executive management has also presented challenges in the transformation of the South African corporate landscape.

Diligent, thoughtful and persistent policy making and implementation led by the Department of Trade and Industry in the form of employment equity, and the codes of good practice embedded into the BBBEE legislation, have helped to significantly transform corporate middle management. It is up to the current corporate leadership to have the foresight to convert this middle-management group into the corporate leaders of the future. Corporate self-interest is leading to the increasing adoption of meritocratic principles in corporate South Africa, helping to ensure its long-term sustainability. As Peter Marris articulately puts it: 'The market will trump institutionalised power of occupational privilege, if supply and demand diverge too widely.'[27]

In the civil service the prospects for meritocracy have been limited by two factors. The fact that all senior positions in government are essentially political appointments via the process of deployment from the ruling party, limits the universe of talent.

Party loyalty is a key criterion that often eliminates large numbers of people from that limited talent pool. Secondly, the culture that is encouraged by political appointees is one of 'bureaucratic fiefdoms' that function on the basis of loyalty to that individual, meaning that accountability is reduced and talent displacement and opportunism are encouraged.

In South Africa two key constituencies feel particularly offended by the lack of meritocracy in the public sector. One is the young, energetic and committed South African who wants to give back to her/his country by working as a civil servant. The second is experienced and committed South Africans who want to spend their final active working years using management and professional skills developed in the private sector for national benefit. Neither can succeed in an environment that currently does not place a premium on education levels, core professional skills and management talent above their connection to the ruling party.

This is not a problem unique to South Africa: most great societies go through a period where their civil servants start off being extremely politicised, dependent on the aristocracy or ethnically stratified. The societies that went on to achieve greatness found a way to customise meritocratic principles in the public sector that facilitated accountability. 'The British civil service's adherence to the principle of merit came after a hard-fought battle. Essentially, the struggle began in 1853 when Sir Charles Trevelyan, Permanent Secretary to the Treasury, and Sir Stafford Northcote MP were asked by then Chancellor of the Exchequer, William Gladstone, to conduct an investigation into its recruitment and promotion... The Northcote-Trevelyan Report, which has since become synonymous with upholding the almost uniquely un-politicised nature of the permanent side of British government, was short, pithy and punchy... The report went on to unambiguously support the principle of competitive examinations for recruitment to the Civil Service, much on the basis of Macaulay's (Trevelyan's brother-in-law) reforms to the Indian Civil Service.'[28]

The Japanese used the 'new economy' (the manufacturing of microchips and semi-conductors) as a catalyst to break away from talent allocation that functioned roughly like a feudal system towards a ruthless meritocracy that powered their growth model for three generations.

> The other distinguishing feature was that, in Japan's 'new economy' – in 1900, say, the one-fifth of the population not engaged in family-based peasant agriculture, artisan production and commerce-educational credentials became the passport to career success in a much more definitive way than in Britain. One reason was that underlying the 'national utilitarianism' of the new economy, the old samurai values, which rated governing and fighting as much more prestigious occupations than producing and trading, still informed ambitions of the young. The 'aristocracy' that had produced these values was now genuinely open to this talent… And precisely because that educational competition served as an elaborate IQ test, the large merchant houses were happy to recruit their managers from those who didn't quite make it on the road to that most glittering prize (civil service).[29]

Key to the process of moving from a relationship and hereditary-based talent allocation system towards a more meritocratic talent allocation paradigm, is the acceptance of the basic principle that competent management of South Africa's private and public sectors will lead to shared prosperity. The fairness principle instilled into the economy has to 'grandfather' (a legal term that refers to the entrenchment of old rights in a new or changing agreement) a mechanism to address imbalances created by South Africa's legacy of apartheid. Long-term investment into the economy, both domestic and international, requires a meritocratic paradigm shift so that South Africa can put its best people in charge of key institutions that can be globally competitive.

Fortunately countries in South East Asia have led the way in showing that investment in education institutions that produce top graduates who are allowed to lead key institutions in both the public and private sectors has a crowding-in effect for FDI. This is especially the case if the talent is enabled by a local infrastructure that facilitates smooth commerce and is supported by a facilitative government that regulates in favour of competition. More than a billion people have worked themselves out of poverty as a result of these policies; there is no reason South Africa can't do the same for its 20 per cent or just under 10 million of its population currently living off less than $2 a day.

South Africa is in a unique position on the African continent to become the example of a great African society that accomplishes such a feat. Doubling the middle class will have an astronomic impact on all companies in South Africa as they begin to enjoy the benefits of an expanded set of consumers and savers. This accomplishment has to be led by some tough political decision making accompanied by give-and-take between the elite sub-groups.

9

The Original Sin

The crime of Bantu Education can be likened to Adam's biblical sin in eating from the Tree of Knowledge of Good and Evil, as a result of which all of humanity was exiled in perpetuity from the Garden of Eden. All South Africans suffer the effects of this 'original sin' both directly and indirectly. The process of social engineering implemented by Dr Verwoerd in the Bantu Education Act of 1953 has scarred the South African consciousness so deeply that it can only be termed an attempt at intellectual genocide of indigenous South African people. As Cynthia Kros puts it:

> I have taught many students battling to overcome the treacherous legacy of Bantu Education. What this means, I think, from my work with them, is that they have been deprived of essential language skills: their reading and writing abilities have been almost irredeemably stunted by the time they come to the university. They have been so conditioned to rote learning and authoritarian styles of teaching that, at first, they can make no sense of a question that asks for critical evaluation or an argued response. And this continues to be the case for many black students, despite the advent of Outcomes-Based Education, which is aligned to the democratic principles of our fabled constitution. For those children obliged to go on attending township

schools – for the most part (though there are some honourable exceptions) – Bantu Education continues to exercise its brain-numbing potency, transmitted to new generations by helpless teachers.[1]

Effective education policy requires an unwavering belief that, all things being equal, learners from all walks of life will perform up to the maximum levels of their ability. To take this rather simple rule of thumb one step further, educators and policy makers must believe that learners from all walks of life, different race groups and religious groups produce in equal quantities brilliant students, ordinary students and those who are academically challenged. Intellectual talent is randomly distributed in every society. Having said this, very few societies achieve the momentous task of making all things equal for their intellectual talent to thrive. All great societies are trying to achieve that very difficult task as we speak. To the extent that progress is made, bigotry is quickly identified as the enemy of success, based on its inherent propensity to protect mediocrity and suppress the normal talent aggregation process that takes place in meritocratic societies.

In South Africa the original sin committed by successive governments after 1953 institutionalised the underdevelopment of African children. This underdevelopment was rooted in the fear that there were not going to be enough resources to allow Afrikaner children to catch up to their more educated English counterparts and at the same time help their parents compete for jobs in a rapidly industrialising and urbanising South Africa. 'In the words of an NP member of parliament in 1945, the natives will be powerful competitors with the Europeans in every sphere. They are given the same education as the whites and it will not be long before they dominate on account of their tremendous majority.'[2]

The resulting Bantu Education policy, executed against the backdrop of so-called 'separate development', entrenched into the legal framework of South Africa a structural under-funding of the development of African, coloured and Indian learners as well as their teachers. It cemented the economic model of subsidised development, all for the sake of ensuring that Afrikaner farmers were protected from the 'tragedy' of African migration to the cities (especially of women), which starved the farmers of the cheap labour they had been accustomed to and created competition in semi-skilled urban jobs for poor white (mostly Afrikaner) labourers.

Implementing Bantu Education required a centralisation of all institutions that had anything to do with the education of indigenous South Africans in the Department of Native Affairs. 'Furthermore the legislation recognised only three types of schools as legitimate: Bantu community schools, government schools, and other state-aided schools, including mission schools. The significant proviso was that financial grants would only be made to the state-aided schools where the existence of such schools would not preclude or retard the establishment of government-run schools.'[3] This financial coercion had the effect of making it impossible for non-authorised schools to be adequately funded: just in case they managed, the government made it illegal to operate an unregistered school.[4] For many children this meant a sea change in the way that they were educated, a change that was instituted at the stroke of a bureaucrat's pen. Their economic future immediately looked vastly different from that of their elder peers who managed to complete their high school education under the relative privilege of missionary education.

> The effects were far reaching. Of 7000 (in South Africa) schools, over 5000 had been missionary-run prior to Bantu Education. By 1959, virtually all black schools except the 700 Catholic schools had been brought under the central control of the Native Affairs Department. Finance had been pegged to a set (non-correlated to needs) figure. All teachers were being trained in government training colleges and all syllabuses were to be those emanating from the government and imbued with the ideas of racial inferiority.[5]

There is no way of fully coming to grips with the enormity of the reduction in quality of education resulting from this restructuring of how schools and teacher training colleges functioned.

Missionary schools were far from perfect but they had to date produced a disproportionate share of great South African black talent: one need only look at the ANC's nearly 100-year pipeline of excellent leaders at all levels of the organisation as an example of the outsized contribution of missionary schools – and the subsequent opportunity cost of Bantu Education.

The year 1953 was a landmark year for teacher training as well.

> As teachers came under State (as opposed to Mission) control through the new Bantu Authorities and School Boards which were largely government nominated, so the freedom of teachers to protest against any of the new provisions was inhibited. Teachers, syllabi and language medium were among the nineteen specified areas over which the Minister had discretion. This meant that adjustments to the system of Bantu Education could be easily introduced over time and that it could be effectively extended on a planned and uniform basis.[6]

Thus began a long process in the reduction of accountability of African teachers as they felt belittled by a system that treated them as conduits through which a 'dumbed-down' curriculum could be passed on to successive generations of indigenous South African children. This soul-destroying process transformed the teaching profession from a calling to a job like any other in apartheid's stifling workplace environment. Critically the standards for entering the teaching profession were also lowered, in the case of lower primary teachers from Standard 8 to Standard 6.

Understanding the impulses that led to the Bantu Education policy being enacted illuminates the commercial nature of the decision making by the apartheid government. Between 1930 and 1945 the percentage of black students receiving education had been on a dramatic rise. In 1930 about 284 250 black people, representing 4.9 per cent of the population, were being educated. This number shot up to 587 586 in 1945, representing 7.7 per cent of the population.[7] This newly educated black labour force felt the need to seek jobs in the city as opposed to the rural areas where they had served as cheap farm labourers for many years. During these same years an emerging 'poor white problem' was creating social tension and political fault lines within the Afrikaner establishment. Dan O'Meara gives some background:

> By September 1933, approximately 22 percent of all white and coloured males (188 000 men) were officially registered as unemployed... The ranks of the unemployed were swollen by the thousands of white farmers driven off the land and into acute poverty by the Depression. In December 1932 it was conservatively estimated that one-sixth of the white population was 'very poor'. A further 30 percent of all white families were classified as 'poor'... so poor that they cannot adequately feed or house their children.[8]

This competitive environment for jobs created a need to 'rig' the system by incapacitating the black labour force and removing it as a source of competition for poor whites.

> Both the expansion of African unemployment in operative positions and the emerging organisation of Africans in militant unions, presented the potential of undercutting white operatives. Indeed, during the war years, the earnings gap between white and African industrial employees actually closed slightly... Particularly during the war, specific strata of the white workers began to perceive themselves as threatened by the influx of African labour and by the continuing ambivalence of the UP (United Party) government on issues such as migrant labour, pass laws and influx control.[9]

So it became apparent that a political solution was necessary to protect white labour from black competition before the poor white problem got further out of hand. Interestingly enough, Afrikaner intellectuals both in and out of the Broederbond took the lead in demanding a solution to the poor white problem. One such individual was a Broederbond member and became a named author of the report produced by the commission that created the framework for Bantu Education – namely Dr Eiselen.

> Eiselen expanded on the dangers as well as the inhumanity of relying on coerced, exploited African Labour. Cheap African labour also eliminated the poor white, already the victim of 'economic revolutions of the last thirty years' from competition in the urban labour market. The other side of the 'Native Question', he observed (by no means originally), was the poor white question. ... [A]nticipating the 'Homeland' solution of the future, Eiselen argued that relief from all these problems could only be obtained when the 'reserves' were transformed into more viable areas.[10]

From a macro-economic point of view, pressures were building that shifted a large proportion of wage earners away from the traditional areas of mining and agriculture towards servicing increasingly rapid industrial growth.

> Although gold mining continued to form the base of the economy, by the end of the 1940s its contribution to the national income was to be overshadowed by manufacturing. Throughout this decade the profit margins of gold mining were shrinking conspicuously, and there was considerable anxiety over the long-term future of gold as well as this industry's more immediate difficulty in attracting labour in the face of competition from better paying secondary industries. The sharp decline in the absolute numbers of 'non-Europeans' employed in mining from 1943 onwards reflected the closure of some of the low-paying mines, but is also indicative of labour shortages on the working mines.[11]

Thus the mining industry also felt that it was in danger of losing its subsidy of cheap African labour. This threat was made all that much more troubling by the reduction in the number of migrant workers from neighbouring countries as the forces of liberation struggles for national independence in Southern Africa gathered steam.

It would seem that whites had little confidence in the ability of schools (pre-Bantu Education) to reproduce black labour in the form they desired; it is possible that they themselves, believing in the ideology of mobility through education, feared that schooling would operate in the same way for blacks, and thus impede the continuous provision of the lowest level of workers.[12]

This fear of a loss of white supremacy through the education of black people (including coloureds and Indians) was the predominant reason why the policy of Bantu Education was enacted without much public outcry from members of the white community.

The same fear that – other things being equal – it was inevitable that black students would do proportionately just as well as white students led the apartheid government to forecast the extinction of the system of subsidised economic development that they cherished. Bantu Education and separate development allowed them to buy enough time to eradicate the poor white problem and establish the Afrikaner as an economic force that could withstand any type of future competition.

The economic condition of Afrikaners improved drastically between the 1950s and 1980s, powered by a huge investment by all South Africans both directly and indirectly in the education of the Afrikaner child. The investment in Afrikaner education bridged the gap to the point where the education levels of white English-speaking and Afrikaner children were almost indistinguishable by the late 1970s.

Education was important because it ensured that white South Africans were given huge advantages in the labour market, which in turn meant higher incomes and enhanced capacity to pay privately for healthcare and to save for retirement. Insofar as whites were already privileged, differential education served to reproduce this privilege. Insofar as some white South Africans had few skills in the 1950s, the disadvantage of one generation was not passed onto the next. The improvement of public education (in white neighbourhoods) was thus an important factor in the rising prosperity of Afrikaans-speaking white people. [...] the differences between Afrikaans- and English-speaking children in aptitude and intelligence test scores narrowed dramatically. In the 1950s the gap was as wide as half of a standard deviation; by the 1970s it had disappeared.[13]

The cost of free education for white children was undoubtedly subsidised by generations of indigenous South African parents and learners who had to pay for the privilege of sending their children to schools with declining quality of teachers and decaying school infrastructure. The discrepancies in education among racial groups were glaring.

By the early 1980s teacher pupil ratios in primary schools averaged 1:18 in white schools, 1:24 in Asian (Indian) schools, 1:29 in coloured schools and 1:39 in black schools. Moreover, whereas 96 percent of all teachers in white schools had teaching certificates, only 15 percent of teachers had teaching certificates [in black, coloured and Indian schools]. The De Lange report released in 1981 highlighted the discrepancies in education spend. In the 1979/80 financial year the government spent R534 per child in primary education and R960 per child in secondary education of every white child. It spent R92 per child on the primary education and R459 per child in secondary education of black children.[14]

The legacy of apartheid education is a combination of lagging education infrastructure in black and coloured communities in particular, unqualified teachers teaching complicated subjects such as maths and science, and a majority of parents who themselves are products of Bantu Education and hence were and are unable to adequately help their children with the day-to-day challenges of modern-day schooling.

On the infrastructure side the disparities in the environments within which students are being taught in South Africa could not be over-emphasised:

In 1996, one in four schools had no water within walking distance, and nearly one in ten had to get their water from dams and rivers. Over half (57%) did not have electricity. Over half (52%) had pit latrines for toilets, and 13% had no ablution facilities at all. There was no learning equipment in 73% of the schools, and 69% had no learning materials. Nationally, 57 499 classrooms were needed. The level of library provisioning was appalling, with 72% of schools having no library collection. Approximately half of the schools in the most rural provinces had no sports facilities.[15]

The current teaching crisis is the greatest legacy of Bantu Education: '50 per cent of mathematics teachers were either unqualified or under-qualified in 1994, while corresponding percentages for biology, physical science and general science teachers were 32 per cent and 64 per cent respectively.'[16] Equally disturbing was an average ratio in 1994 of 47 pupils to one teacher.[17] In 1993 school expenditure on a per capita basis was four times less for black pupils than for white pupils.[18]

On top of that, the formation of the South African Democratic Teachers Union (Sadtu) and its participation in the ANC government of South Africa via Cosatu has protected the majority of teachers from the harsh realities of normal competition and has facilitated the retention of a large cadre of poorly trained, de-motivated teachers.

> Although 98% of white teachers (in 1993) were properly qualified (with at least Grade 12 plus 3 years of professional teacher training), only 37% of African teachers were similarly qualified. Of the remaining 63% of African teachers, 12% had no professional qualification and 51% were under-qualified, having either less than Grade 12 or less than 3 years' training... In addition to the overall shortage of qualified teachers, 72% of mathematics teachers in African schools, and 70% of science teachers were under-qualified.[19]

The teacher crisis

The history of teacher trade unionism in South Africa dates back to prior to the 1900s. 'The first unions were divided along racial and provincial lines. Although they considered themselves as professional unions, there were already some activities that could be described as unionist functions. The first unions could be described as child-centred, with a more professional approach than a worker oriented philosophy. The first black union was established in 1879 and it was called the Native Educational Association.'[20] It was not until October 1990 that a large collection of different teachers organisations, namely Atasa, Utasa, Neusa, Tasa, DTU, Wectu, Edasa, PTU, Ectu and Matu, unified to form the South African Democratic Teachers Union (Sadtu). Today Sadtu has over 240 000 members and is clearly the leading teachers' union in the country. The South African Teachers Union (Satu) and the National Professional Teachers Organisation of South Africa (Naptosa) are two less well known active teachers' unions.

Sadtu articulates its objectives as follows: 'We teachers of South Africa having fully committed ourselves to the transformation of education and dedicated ourselves to the development of an education system which is fully accessible, equal and qualitative, free of apartheid legacy and which is the just expression of the will of the people – as enshrined in the constitution of the country – hereby proclaim the need for a single teachers union in our land.'[21]

One of the worst consequences of any social engineering process is the inevitable over-correction that is driven through the policies of successive governments. The ANC-led government was no different. Lobbied by Sadtu, the focus from 1994 was on transformation of the teaching profession, the school governing bodies and their administrative structures at all costs. 'Sadtu believes that if teachers' working conditions, salaries, facilities in schools and proper functioning of the Department of Education are satisfactory, then they can start talking about professionalism.'[22] The challenge with the approach that Sadtu has taken was the protection of

180

mediocrity in the name of transformation and a culture of ill-discipline in the name of activism as well as a legacy of unaccountability that was facilitated by having a seat at the table of power. The other glaring reality is that Sadtu has a charter that is not leaner-centric, indicating a bias towards the well-being of the teachers ahead of that of their students.

'At the root of the problem is a lack of a profit motif incentive, which has given rise to "managerial slack", inadequate teaching and a general inability on the part of government to ensure that teachers adhere to the terms of their contracts ... in many schools it is estimated that as few as 100 actual teaching days out of a possible 195 are realised.'[23] Under any normal conditions this type of absenteeism would be the source of parental activism and widespread outrage against the unions. However in the South African context the legacy of apartheid provides convenient cover for gross under-performance, and obstructs the majority of parents from a clearer view of what their expectations from their teachers and schools should be.

Under the onslaught of transformation at all costs, many capable and dedicated teachers have found themselves alienated from the profession of teaching. 'Many teachers have voluntarily chosen to quit the profession, often with the help of lucrative severance packages, rather than being re-deployed in disadvantaged schools. In 1994/5, for example, the average rate of attrition (or number of teachers quitting as a percentage of the total) was estimated at 10.3 per cent amongst whites as against 5.7 per cent for Indians, 4.8 per cent for coloureds and 3.7 per cent for blacks.'[24]

Replacing qualified, highly skilled teachers proved easier said than done. 'In practice, it would seem, teacher shortages have been eliminated somewhat artificially by a process of "inferior substitution", rather than by adjusting the price of teachers in accordance with prevailing demand and supply conditions. Inferior substitution refers to the process whereby surplus teachers (e.g. in the arts and social sciences) and temporary substitutes (including early retirees) are appointed to positions for which they are not suitably

181

qualified or do not have the necessary experience.'[25] More than any other factor, South Africa's competitiveness as a nation is being held to ransom by these disturbing trends in the teaching profession.

Nowhere is this pattern of inferior substitution more apparent than in the areas of maths and science. The International Association for the Evaluation of Educational Achievement held its Third International Mathematics and Science Study in 1994. South Africa was one of three African countries amongst 63 to participate. In South Africa alone 194 schools and 8 147 pupils from a cross-section of the country participated in the study.

> South African pupils performed poorly when compared to other participating countries... The mean score of 275 (standard error, SE, 6.8) is well below the international mean of 487(SE 0.7). The result is significantly below the mean scores of all other participating countries, including the two other African countries of Morocco and Tunisia as well as that of other developing or newly developed countries such as Malaysia, the Philippines, Indonesia and Chile... Only 1% of South African pupils reached the International Upper Quarter benchmark – the average score achieved by the top 25% of pupils internationally – which corresponds to a score of 555 (68% of the possible 800) points. This is a great contrast to the Asian countries where the benchmark was reached by more than 60% of pupils from Japan, Hong Kong, Korea and Chinese Taipei and 75% of Singapore pupils.[26]

These mathematics results were perhaps to be expected, given that they were captured in 1994, fresh from 50 years of Bantu Education. Indeed they represent the success story of a policy that was geared to ensuring the un-competitiveness of the majority of South Africans in the local and global economy.

'South African pupils also performed poorly in science when compared to all participating countries... The mean score of 243 (SE 7.8) is well below the international mean of 488 (SE 0.7)... The International Top 10% benchmark corresponds to a score of 616 out of 800 and is the point where the top performing students can be found. Less than 0.5 % of South African pupils reached this benchmark.'[27] Again these results in science can be expected given South Africa's history pre-1994. What is interesting about these two data points is that they reflect a benchmark against which South Africa could have gone on to measure its progress in the eradication of the Bantu Education legacy. Sadly, for reasons that will be explained below, South Africa chose to bury its head in the sand and hope the challenge represented by this poor inter-national performance would wait for it to resolve higher priority domestic challenges such as transformation of the teaching profes-sion and incompetent teachers protected by Sadtu.

It is important not to use the participation of Sadtu through Cosatu in the leadership of the country as an excuse for policy mistakes. Indeed, these are not just policy mistakes, they are politi-cal realities. The majority of our teachers are failing the system but Sadtu's role in Cosatu prevents reform-minded people from taking the necessary steps to fire poorly performing teachers en masse. An interesting set of lessons can be drawn from looking at the experience of the Australian government in the 1980s in tackling tough policy choices under a Labor government in which unions were strongly represented. They viewed the key to their teacher education policy as the recognition that teaching is a performance orientated skill which relies on measurement for improvement. What policy makers in Australia felt was needed was for education to be seen 'by the state, the unions and business interests as one of the key elements of a broader programme for micro-economic reform, human capital and the economic restructuring of the na-tion.'[28] In doing so the Australian government managed to get the following measures right in working with their teachers' unions to improve the profession:[29]

❏   They legitimised the shift from narrow trade-based vocation schools to a broader, more professional approach, moving from accreditations of diplomas to encouraging the attain-ment of degrees in education.

❑   They supported the extension of formal initial teacher educa-
    tion to a minimum of three years with four years for many
    aspiring teachers intending to teach secondary school.

❑   They justified the rapid growth of specialist teaching areas like
    early childhood education, guidance counselling, special edu-
    cation (for children with special needs), physical education
    and maths and science, by supporting higher pay for higher
    skills.

❑   They emphasised the importance of a structured programme
    of continuing professional education for all teachers, making
    sure that there were financial incentives for earning higher
    qualifications.

To be sure, the challenge faced by President Mandela's government
with regard to the reconstruction of the education sector in 1994
was immense:

> One of the first actions of the new government, started in 1994, was
> to amalgamate 19 different departments of education into one na-
> tional and nine provincial departments of education... The fact that
> more than 95% of the Department of Education's budget was be-
> ing spent on teacher salaries (one of the highest proportions in the
> world) meant that there was virtually no money left for resources
> such as textbooks, equipment and building new facilities. This led
> to teacher voluntary retrenchments and redeployments starting in
> 1995. Ultimately, many teachers left the teaching profession, includ-
> ing in critical areas such as mathematics and science. This was ac-
> companied by a nation-wide evaluation of the Colleges of Education
> in South Africa, which resulted in colleges being earmarked for merg-
> ers with higher education institutions, being reconfigured into com-
> munity or technical colleges, or being closed.[30]

It is easy in retrospect to be critical of the government's performance. But it is important to recognise and celebrate the numerous achievements.

> Access to primary and secondary schooling improved significantly, with near universal enrolment in primary schooling and 86% enrolment in secondary schooling by 1998... There was considerable improvement in the qualification of educators, with the proportion of under qualified educators reduced from 36% in 1994 to 26% in 1998... [T]hrough the Reconstruction and Development Programme, R1.4 billion was allocated for school reconstruction and maintenance between 1995-1997. Much progress was made in school electrification, and increased water supply to schools.[31]

In addition, both President Mandela's and President Mbeki's administrations showed an exceptional commitment to the financing of education for all. 'There has been a significant increase in education expenditure under the post-apartheid democratic government, from R31.8 billion in 1994 to R51.1 billion in 2000. At almost 6 percent of GDP, South Africa has one of the highest government investments in education in the world.'[32]

Sadly, despite this hard work and high expenditure, South Africa made no progress in the 1999 version of the International Mathematics and Science Study. 'In science its score actually decreased by 20 points, whilst in maths the results were identical to 1995, less than 0.5% of pupils in South Africa reached the top 10%.'[33] A 1999 Department of Education study unearthed some disturbing trends within the teaching profession in South Africa: '27% of pupils were taught mathematics by teachers with no formal qualification in mathematics... 38% of pupils were taught science by teachers with no formal qualification in science... half the mathematics teachers do not feel confident to teach mathematics and half the science teachers do not feel prepared to teach science to Grade 8 pupils.'[34] These extraordinary statistics speak for a teaching profession that has been in crisis from the moment South Africa became a democracy.

The challenges with regards to maths and science have only become more severe between 1994 and 2011. Some sobering statistics (drawn from a conference held by some of South Africa's leading education practitioners) help put the status quo into context:[35]

❑ 'In 2006 the participation rate calculated as the percentage of students enrolled in higher education institutions relative to the population aged 20-24 was 15%. This figure is much lower than the figure for Latin America and the Caribbean (31%), Central Asia (25%) and East Asia and the Pacific (25%). These overall numbers have improved by 2010 to 16%, but there is a big interracial discrepancy.[36] The participation rate of Africans is 12.1%, while the coloured participation rate is now 14.3%, yet the Indian and white participation rates are 51.2% and 58.5% respectively.'[37]

❑ In 2007 only 126 641 people graduated from public Higher Education Institutions with a higher education qualification out of a population of 48 million.

❑ The mid-year pass rates for the first year engineering students dropped significantly between 2008 and 2009, with some universities reporting a 50 per cent decrease in students passing.

❑ The Department of Education indicates that 136 515 candidates passed mathematics and 207 260 passed mathematical literacy in the senior certificate examinations written in 2008. The number of candidates who passed mathematics with a final mark of more than 50 per cent was just 63 040.

❑ In 2008, the KwaZulu-Natal Department of Education advertised 4 900 posts including mathematics and science teaching positions, but most of these 2 500 posts could not be filled because no suitable candidates were found; 800 of the unfilled positions were for mathematics.

❏ In 2008 there were 49 503 total qualified mathematics, mathematical literacy and physical science teachers. Of these 32 203 were qualified and teaching, 16 956 were qualified and not teaching, 7 597 were non-qualified and teaching. According to the Minister of Basic Education, a survey of the country's public schools indicated a shortage of 2 888 maths teachers and 2 669 science teachers in 2010.[38]

❏ Between 2005 and 2008, 24 750 teachers left either through resignation, ill-health, death or early retirement;[39]

❏ The Department of Education needs 20 000 teachers a year but only 8 000-9 000 are qualifying;[40]

❏ Even though the Department of Education awarded 4 000 quota permits for foreign teachers, only 138 had been utilised by December 2008.[41]

Every one of these statistics screams crisis. When looked at as a universe of data, they indicate a country failing to comprehend, diagnose and cure its biggest national crisis. Yet until the Zuma government came to power it was taboo to say that South Africa's education system was in any crisis. Indeed such was the culture of denialism in President Thabo Mbeki's administration that South Africa refused to participate in International Mathematics and Science Studies post-1999.

Between 1994 and 2008 South Africa made a series of glaring policy errors regarding education, none more so than the combination of what is termed 'inferior substitution' when it comes to teachers and the simultaneous introduction of Outcomes Based Education (OBE). There were bound to be casualties in any substantive reversal of the institutionalised subsidy being received by white children at the expense of their African, coloured and Indian counterparts. But who knew that under a black-led government, the chief casualties of bad policy making would be black children?

The Outcomes fiasco

In 1997, in response to pressure from different quarters of the education community, the government introduced Curriculum 2005, an outcomes-based (OBE) curriculum. The aims of Curriculum 2005 were: to promote the new constitution, rebuild a divided nation, establish and promote a sense of national identity, offer equal education for all, inspire a constituency that had been oppressed by the very nature of the previous education dispensation and policies and lastly to establish a socially valued knowledge set to be transmitted to following generations.[42]

The introduction of OBE was based on international research, which showed that students working in groups, interacting not only with the teacher but each other in an environment that enabled a dynamic curriculum and flexibility in lesson construction, were more stimulated and were likely to be more productive in the work environment. Intuitively the logic underlying the introduction of Curriculum 2005 could not be faulted. Who would not want their children learning to work in groups, interacting with their teachers instead of just listening to the typically boring monologue of a lecture? This seemed like a big improvement on the rote-learning culture that dominated the school environment in the years of Bantu Education. In the information age, it also seemed logical that teachers should move away from a rigid adherence to the use of textbooks and incorporate a more flexible synthesis of all knowledge bases including the internet. 'Coupled with the NQF [National Qualifications Framework] strategy of outcomes-based education the curriculum was to be learner centered... This focus on learner involvement, in turn requires that schools and teachers take major roles in curriculum design: teachers know more closely than anyone else in the system, learners' experiences and needs. They are in a position to decide what is locally relevant, and implement with devotion programmes they have designed and chosen themselves.'[43]

Sadly for most children who go to government schools, OBE

only accelerated a race to the bottom in which there were to be no winners. In most other countries without South Africa's legacy of Bantu Education in particular and apartheid in general, Curriculum 2005 could have been successful. Unfortunately, given the shocking quality of teachers, who by their own admission are not up to the task of teaching courses such as mathematics and science, the additional administrative burdens imposed by Curriculum 2005 proved catastrophic. Very few people could express rational disagreement regarding the necessity of switching from content-focused testing to an outcomes-oriented approach, but many respected academics argued about the impracticality of making the switch within South Africa's teaching and school infrastructure capacity constraints.

To use a soccer analogy, the difference between the 'beautiful game' as it is known and played in Spain, versus 'footie' as it is known and played in England is the way in which players express themselves given their relative skills bases and historical development of the game in both countries. Even more important, however, is how these relative skills and the relative historical developments of the game have impacted the coaching profession in both countries. In Spain one has over a hundred years of the beautiful game played in an expansive and attractive form. The game is generally played at a mid tempo with high degrees of technical skill leading to a form of football that is easy on the eye. The English, on the other hand, play a high-tempo, physical style of soccer that requires more endurance and desire than skill.

Switching the English system from what it is to the Spanish system of playing would be a mammoth task requiring a massive reconstruction particularly of the way that the English youth football system works, the type of players picked and most importantly the type of coaches together with the coaching philosophy they bring. The task could only be achieved if it was combined with the wholesale dismissal and substitution of most if not all English coaches who were raised and trained under the old system.

South Africa attempted the same scale of task in its overhaul of the way schools taught in 1997 without a superior substitution of the incumbent teachers who were trained under an old system. The results have been predictably tragic. As the Task Team charged with reviewing the system after five years reported:

> The current system is almost completely dependent on Subject Advisors (and district staff) to act as intermediaries between curriculum policy and implementation in the classroom. In every province, teachers mentioned that there were several challenges around the role of the district... there are too few subject advisors nationwide to do justice to thorough and qualitative in-class support for teachers. Many do not have sufficient knowledge and skills to offer teachers the support they require to improve learner performance... Teachers across the country complained about the onerous administration requirements and duplication of work... Furthermore, C2005 (Curriculum 2005) discouraged the use of marks and percentages, introducing a number of complicated assessment requirements such as Common Tasks of Assessment, portfolios and research projects as well as related jargon. The country's repeated poor performance in local and international tests has left parents and other stakeholders sceptical of curriculum and related assessment practices.[44]

The South African government has failed over the last 17 years to chip away at the structural inequalities in education provision between public schooling and so-called Model C and private schools. Despite spending over a trillion rand on education during that period, public schools have fallen further behind their private and semi-private counterparts. Particularly worrying is the focus on access to schools for all children at the expense of a focus on the quality of education offered to those already at school. This race to the bottom has been further reinforced under the Zuma administration, which has sought to punish universities who do not take in a set quota of matriculants by giving them a smaller proportion of the annual higher education subsidy.

> Human capital contributes to growth, but educating more people does not cause growth or an increase in jobs, as many countries with legions of unemployed educated youths are discovering... Sifire (Singapore, Finland and Ireland) countries differ from other low and middle income countries that expanded school enrolment in several respects. They were able to raise the average quality of education imparted to ensure that a high percentage of secondary and tertiary level students had good science, technology, engineering, and mathematics (STEM) skills and graduated with science and engineering degrees...[45]

In South Africa, the poorer the family you come from, the worse school you are likely to attend, which ensures that you will be taught by teachers who have poorer maths and science skills, giving you a slimmer chance of being able to pursue higher value skills in the national and global economy. South Africa relies more than most countries on the tenuous outcomes of what Warren Buffett describes as the 'ovarian lottery', meaning that children born to mothers living in more affluent homes where the prospects for a stimulating learning environment are high, are far better off than children born to mothers living in abject poverty.

This is a failure in policy making, but also a failure of successive ANC-led administrations to understand education as a 'competitive world sport' in which all countries are trying to outcompete each other in the preparation of their children for the global workplace of the future. This global labour force knows no boundaries, is not held back by language barriers and is intolerant of inflexibility. In decisions made as to where firms will place their manufacturing facilities, where they will conduct research and development, where capital will be invested, the competitiveness of the local labour market is always under scrutiny. The attempts at increasing South Africa's industrial capacity will by definition be challenged by the country's lack of competitiveness. There is little evidence that the Zuma administration has embraced the connection between the quality of education provided to the majority of South Africans and the competitiveness of the economy.

It is time to finally eradicate the legacy of Bantu Education. To do so requires sober analysis of the economy's structural unemployment problem as being a hostage to the vicious circle of incompetence, in which under-resourced, largely under-qualified teachers working in schools that have deplorable teaching infrastructure produce poorly equipped students. These students arrive in tertiary institutions poorly prepared and intellectually intimidated, only to predictably under-perform and emerge as unemployable members of the work force.

We owe our children more than this. To create a level playing field in the country requires a three-step programme, which will work alongside the various established corporate and government interventions in the education arena. None of the steps are easy, all are fraught with political dangers, but we no longer have the luxury of postponing the hard decisions. First, South Africa has to embark on a **teacher substitution and re-training programme**. Second, the government has to enact legislation permitting the development and functionality of **charter schools**, operated outside of the public school environment, with a massive tax break for corporate donations into these schools. Third, the government has to raise World Bank funding for the immediate **modernisation of the infrastructure of all primary and secondary government-owned schools**.

Class act – confronting the teacher crisis

If Verwoerd's ghost is to be laid to rest once and for all, a certain basic principle has to be accepted: incompetent teachers have to be pensioned off and re-trained to pursue other careers. The best way to do this is to establish a competency examination for all teachers to establish where they fit on a pre-determined scale of competence. The benchmark has to be a common standard of teaching as accepted by independent schools and applied in relation to the competency of public school teachers. Having established this benchmark and designed the examination, adequate time should be allowed for all teachers on the government school payroll to participate in the examination process. Those who get within a certain predetermined percentage of the pass mark should be given the opportunity for intensive training and retesting within a short period of time. Those who pass should be eligible for increased salaries and benefits. Those who fail should be asked to join a voluntary retrenchment programme that will include a reasonable pension and a funded skills development programme.

Qualified teachers who for whatever reason have left the profession should be asked and encouraged through financial incentives to apply to participate in the competency examination process. Should they pass they should be immediately placed in needy schools to plug the gap in areas where there are certain to be teacher shortages. The current Home Affairs allocation of 4 000 for foreign teachers should be tripled to 12 000 and all teachers from all nationalities should be encouraged to apply and given residency on condition they pass the same competency test written across the nation by other teachers.

Huge strike action is likely to be threatened by Sadtu in response to such a policy. Pressure could be placed on teachers to stand in solidarity to not write the test. There may even be strike action to disrupt the testing process as the union seeks to protect those teachers who will anticipate their failure. To combat this likely strike action the government has to be resolute in the belief that Sadtu's 250 000 membership cannot hold to ransom the rights of more than 12 million learners attending over 48 000 schools around the country. Every single one of these learners – regardless of which school they are attending or what level of educational qualification they seek – deserves the protection of quality control: the same protection the government gives to the rest of the population through the insistence that all products sold have to pass a stress test by the South African Bureau of Standards. If necessary a legislative amendment to the Labour Relations Act, No 66 of 1995, should be put forward to parliament in order to facilitate this democratic process.

At a corporate level, firms should be encouraged through tax write-offs and BEE credits to supply staff to be supplementary teachers serving two to three years' national service while new teachers are recruited and trained. This national service should receive the highest social recognition for the role that those men and women would be playing in helping transition the educational system in South Africa out of the bottom quartile in world ranking.

Charter schools – a new way

A third tier of primary and secondary schools needs to be created, resembling what are referred to in the United States as charter schools. These schools would – much in the same way as mission schools did before 1953 – fill the gap between what the government can support in the public schooling environment and the demand by school-going children who cannot afford private school education. These entities should be completely private sector run and owned, following the same general curriculum as other schools but with teachers' salaries and administrative salaries that are unregulated by government.

So as to avoid cherry-picking by the private sector, the government should select the worst-equipped 10 per cent of schools in South Africa, based on the schools with the most teachers failing the competency examination. These schools should then be 'auctioned off' to corporate sponsors who should take them over and run them through regulated section 21 companies. Tuition for all school children should be fully covered. The expenses invested in these schools should be directly offset against BEE requirements of any participating company, on the 'once empowered always empowered' basis, meaning that those credits generated should be permanent, provided that the schools produce a certain minimum level of matric passes. Once this 10 per cent has been converted to charter schools then the legislation should allow for new schools to be created anywhere in the country by any firm willing to invest in the establishment and the operation of a new school.

Establishing unified standards has to include a tracking mechanism on nation-wide student testing that resembles a national synchronised, standardised test that students take to measure maths, science and language skills. Taking this test every year will give the system a one-year national feedback loop as opposed to the panic that is generated by matriculation results testing 12 years of learning, which essentially provide the only standardised measurement at a national level. The test results should (taking a leaf out of the education programme introduced by the Obama administration called Race to the Top) be designed to measure how all students are doing against the very highest standards in the country. President Obama neatly sums up the virtues of such a system in the following way:

> Part of making sure our young people meet these high standards is designing tests that accurately measure whether they are learning. Now, here too there is controversy. When we talk about testing, parents worry that it means more teaching to the test. Some worry that tests are culturally biased. Teachers worry that they'll be evaluated solely on the basis of a single standardized test. Everybody thinks that's unfair. It is unfair. But that's not what Race to the Top is about. What Race to the Top says is, there's nothing wrong with testing – we just need better tests applied in a way that helps teachers and students, instead of stifling what teachers and students do in the classroom. Tests that don't dictate what's taught, but tell us what has been learned. Tests that measure how well our children are mastering essential skills and answering complex questions.[46]

Better schools, better schooling

Nowhere is the issue of inequality within the South African school system more blatantly apparent than the issue of school infrastructure. There are schools in South Africa with facilities that are no different from those in the best schools in Switzerland. These schools offer laptops and tablet computers for all students (in some schools as early as grade R); homework is electronically sent to students; classrooms, computer labs and libraries are integrated, and class lectures are conducted in world-class presentation format. All this makes for a stimulating learning environment that is adequate preparation for the global workplace. Yet often within 10 kilometres of these schools one can find examples of students learning in conditions that can only be described as primitive. These schools have classrooms with no windows, no functional toilets and often far too few desks, if any at all, resulting in students being taught sitting on the ground, writing notes on scruffy notepads on their laps.

These critical infrastructure shortages are replicating poverty at a rate that is much faster than the economy can alleviate it. The result is the formation of an economic barrier to entry into the South African mainstream economy that is insurmountable for most. Yet every year wonderful teachers and exceptionally bright students manage to create examples of scholastic performance that break these barriers, allowing a select group of students from these humble beginnings to attain corporate scholarships and join one of the country's prestigious universities. To its credit, South Africa is excellent at celebrating these successful students from disadvantaged backgrounds and supporting them through the university ranks into the mainstream economy. The country's top companies are filled with leaders who exemplify such success against the odds.

An education policy that is lulled to sleep by occasional exceptions to an otherwise depressing rule of thumb is unsustainable. Its reality is that if you grow up unlucky enough to be sent to the majority of government schools around the country, especially in the rural areas, you will have to do not only with below-par teaching but with a fraction of the basic educational infrastructure enjoyed by peers that you will inevitably compete against for jobs. Today, of the 24 793 ordinary public schools, 3 344 schools have no electricity, 2 402 schools have no water supply, while a further 2 611 have an unreliable water supply. Only 7 per cent of these schools have stocked and functional libraries; only 5 per cent have stocked computer centres. Of these schools 11 450 schools still use pit-latrine toilets while 913 are still without ablution facilities.[47]

Despite tremendous pressure placed on Minister Angie Motshekga she has failed to create national infrastructure standards that were legislated in 2008 in Section 5A of the South African Schools Act. The reason for the failure is political rather than analytical: once these standards are in place the majority of government schools will be below them. Rather than burying their heads in the sand, policy makers need to seize the opportunity to make the case for a major low-interest World Bank loan which should be used to equalise the infrastructure disparities around the country. This action, taken alongside a commitment to supply the necessary learning material and qualified teachers, would signal the welcome end of a national double standard in education. South Africa cannot afford to continue to pat itself on the back about how low its public debt is, while its children needlessly fall further behind. It is time to use the national balance sheet wisely by investing in the very best quality asset, South Africa's children.

10

Societies in Peril

Societies in peril such as Libya, Tunisia, Zimbabwe, Venezuela and Egypt may differ in terms of how they metamorphose from relative socio-economic prosperity and promise to full-blown socio-economic meltdown, but there is a common feature. Somewhere along the way, citizens in these countries lose faith in the prospect of a better life for themselves and their children: all they see is extreme protracted injustice that they believe will be irreversible without some sort of revolution.

The causes of that injustice are varied. They usually involve a political party or individual leader overseeing a parasitic state that doles out patronage in exchange for sustained political power. This often escalates to levels of violence against citizens which were previously unthinkable as the despot becomes more and more brutal in the quest to repress dissent. Sometimes a common enemy is found in the form of an ethnic group, foreigners or a foreign power. At other times a less-defined group of so-called 'counter-revolutionaries' are identified as scapegoats. This targeted enemy is one that focuses the frustration of the masses and usually galvanises support for further divergence from democratic norms that would ordinarily necessitate a rotation of holders of power.

These are societies that are home to talented citizens with

deeply unfulfilled ambitions, to whom at some point the prospect of armed warfare, violent revolt or non-violent populist revolution behind a 'liberating figure' may be more bearable than the perpetuation of a blatantly unjust order. The collateral damage suffered by all during the process of revolution is usually underestimated until the true costs are tallied up in the cold light of day. It is not unusual to hear elites from these societies reflectively wishing they could have actively avoided the meltdowns. The challenge is the degree of difficulty in generating and sustaining societal buy-in to spread fundamental fairness in the current system – for all citizens, and in good time.

All social systems are in a perpetual state of rebalancing competing economic interests. Great societies meet this challenge (often more than once); societies in peril do not. The divide is that simple. As complex as the factors for societal meltdown may seem from the outside, the commonalities can usually be reduced to a monopoly over political and economic power by a small elite that usually sustains this power through corrupt social networks underpinned by military protection. This often results in a centralisation of power that isolates the powerful from the rest of society, creating an 'information bubble' not penetrated by the reality of everyday life in those societies. The slide from normality to peril is often undetectable to many elites living in the country – until things have gone beyond the point of no return.

If one looks at a country like South Africa, for instance, the signs of looming peril are hidden behind a robust economy, producing moderate but consistent growth. These signs of peril are obscured by a dizzying level of infrastructure spend that continues to ensure that the first-world aesthetic quality of South African infrastructure is maintained and further enhanced. Even certain ratios such as the percentage of GDP spent on education or health give analysts a false sense of comfort about the level of social harmony being generated by current government policies. To this day there are many well-informed senior businessmen who continue to believe that South Africa is fundamentally sound in its current social construction. Sure, there could be more done by the government, such businessmen often say, but by and large the country is poised to go from strength to strength, just as long as government sticks to sensible macro-economic fundamentals – meaning keeping inflation low, national debt manageable and instituting pro-business policies that can allow business to generate job growth.

For any society in the midst of relative economic calm, sociopolitical stability and enjoying a functional democratic system, it is difficult to accept a prediction that it is headed towards peril. Moeletsi Mbeki made such a prediction early in 2011 when he said: 'I can predict when SA's "Tunisia Day" will arrive. Tunisia Day is when the masses rise against the powers that be, as happened recently in Tunisia. The year will be 2020, give or take a couple of years.'[1] The governing party naturally went into defensive mode, accusing Mbeki of being a counter-revolutionary, having an agenda or carrying anger towards the ANC. His comments sparked a series of articles around the sustainability of South Africa's development path, but the topic of whether we are headed into peril has not been adequately probed.

The fragility of the South African society lies in a single formula. How long does it take the system to generate economic growth fast enough to get unemployment below or close to 10 per cent and in so doing pull at least another 10 million people out of poverty? Moeletsi Mbeki thinks that the current system does not have the ability to increase manufacturing and industrial capacity to competitive global levels based on structural inefficiencies inherited from the imperial/apartheid model. 'The year 2020 is when China estimates that its current minerals-intensive industrialisation phase will be concluded. For SA this will mean the African National Congress government will have to cut back on social grants, which it uses to placate the black poor and to get their votes.'[2] If one takes this quote at face value, the implication is that South Africa is 'bandaging' the true severity of its 25-40 per cent (depending on whether you believe government sources or independent data) unemployment. The soft underbelly of the country's social fabric therefore lies in its reliance on the continued passivity of the nearly 16 million people supported by the government grant system.

In the National Assembly in 1998, then Deputy President Thabo Mbeki made one of the most profound admissions by a second-in-command of any country, namely that the country he was helping to lead was divided into two nations sharing space within the same borders but essentially living two separate realities:

> A major component part of the issue of reconciliation and nation building is defined by and derives from the material conditions in our society which have divided our country into two nations, the one black and the other white...We therefore make bold to say that South Africa is a country of two nations. One of these nations is white, relatively prosperous, regardless of gender or geographic dispersal. It has ready access to a developed economic, physical, educational and communication infrastructure...The second and larger nation is black and poor, with the worst affected being women in rural areas, the rural black population in general and the disabled. This nation lives under conditions of grossly underdeveloped economic, physical, educational, communication and other infrastructure.[3]

In his two terms in office as President, Thabo Mbeki led a radical restructuring of the country by breaking the racial barrier that separated the two nations. Over 2.5 million black South Africans joined the ranks of the 'first nation' through the generous support of state-led initiatives like BEE and affirmative state procurement policies and social infrastructure spending. For the 'second nation' President Mbeki and his successor President Jacob Zuma have provided temporary comfort in the form of social grants. It is my firm view that this is not a sufficient remedy for the poor majority of South Africans that are either unemployed or who toil in relatively shabby conditions for wages that are scarcely enough to cover living costs in shanty towns around the country. For the last 18 years the majority of elites in South Africa have seen this as the government's problem to solve, arguing that they pay enough tax to be absolved of any guilt that accompanies the obvious inequality between these 'two nations'.

The early years of the Mbeki administration were mired in a debate about whether government should be providing a Basic Income Grant available to all South Africans living below the 'bread line'. An alternative view was for a less comprehensive programme of segmented welfare benefits that should be rolled out. Ultimately the government went with the latter, rolling out segmented welfare benefits to senior citizens, children, the disabled, struggling parents and most recently ill South Africans (in the form of National Health Insurance). 'The South African Social Security Agency (Sassa) has indicated that just less than 14.5 million (this has recently increased to 16 million) people receive grants, with 9.9 million of these recipients receiving the Child Support Grant. The rapid growth of these grants indicates that over a quarter of all South Africans receive some form of social grants.'[4]

South Africa has done an excellent job with very scarce resources in creating a social safety net that seeks to catch those who are unable to provide for themselves, specifically the most vulnerable members of society. In the 2009/2010 financial year approximately R85 billion (or 3.5 per cent of GDP) was spent on government grants.[5] There are seven types of welfare payments made by the South African government: old age grants, disability grants, child support grants, a grant in aid for persons with severe mental disabilities, care dependency to parents and guardians of children with severe mental disabilities between the ages of 1 and 18, foster care grants and war veterans' grants.

According to Sassa, the two biggest contributions to the welfare regime are the child support grants and old age pension payments. Parents or guardians responsible for looking after children who are between the ages of 1 and 18 years of age can get a monthly payment from the government called the Child Support Grant for R250 a month on a means-tested basis.[6] Members of the community who are 60 years or older receive grants of R1 140 per month.[7] These grants are also provided on a means-tested basis to elder citizens with assets that are no more than R792 000 and income of no more than R47 400.[8] These two grants are the direct result of the promulgation of the Children's Act, No 38 of 2005 (which came into effect on 1 April 2010) and the Older Persons Act, No 13 of 2006, which were the brainchild of President Thabo Mbeki and have been enthusiastically carried forward by President Jacob Zuma. These grants serve to protect society's most vulnerable from abject poverty. When one unpacks the extent of help citizens receive from government it amounts to not more than R1 500 per month per recipient, but over 9 million of the 16 million recipients of social services grants get just R250 per month.[9]

Research indicates that the focus on the arbitrary figure of 1 dollar a day as an indicator of the number of citizens living in abject poverty is outdated. Even so, it is shocking to see the contrasts in wealth when they are placed in numeric terms. South Africa has 71 000 dollar millionaires and more than 4 million people living on less than a dollar a day.[10] Research commissioned by the Department of Social Development was based on the following:

In its crudest, most basic form, an individual's ability to satisfy his or her nutritional requirements, one of the most basic of Man's needs, is deemed to indicate whether or not that individual is poor. Poverty lines constructed on the basis of nutritional requirements are known as food poverty lines (FPL) and are classified as absolute poverty lines... Given the structure of expenditure on food and non-alcoholic beverages of the reference group, it was estimated that the daily intake of 2 230 calories per capita would cost between R226 and R273 per month... However, food or caloric intake is only one basic need that individuals should be able to fulfil. There are a number of other basic needs which need to be fulfilled, including shelter, healthcare, clothing and education... This yields a range of lower bound poverty lines between R364 per capita per month (revised total expenditure, original food spending) and R442 per capita per month (total expenditure, adjusted food spending)... These lines provide estimates of poverty rates of between 45.3 percent (total expenditure, original food spending) and 56.9 percent.[11]

What is so shocking about this analysis is the fact that it estimates that 50 per cent of South Africans live below the poverty line according to this modified formula (of roughly R400 per capita, per month). That is close to 25 million people who cannot make ends meet. No society can remain stable, free of repression and peaceful over a long period with these types of statistical realities.

For some of the white elite the notion of becoming a welfare state is unbearable. The first concern is the fact that welfare as a concept is at variance with their interpretation of the principle of meritocracy, which involves picking yourself up (out of poverty) by your bootstraps through hard work and thrift. The second concern is that the country can't afford to subsidise so many poor people. Historically some of these same elite's parents or grandparents were the beneficiaries of subsidised welfare. 'Non-contributory social pensions were instituted in 1928 for Whites and Coloureds that were not covered by occupational retirement insurance. Pensions were subject to age criteria and a means test to ensure that only the poor were targeted. The white population dependent on social pensions remained relatively small despite an increasingly liberal means test, as occupational retirement insurance covered the majority of the white population.'[12]

Others within this same elite group view welfare as a necessary evil that allows them to live guilt-free lives of prosperity, oblivious to the poverty around them. Members of the poor majority view the current level of government support as insufficient, arguing that they deserve more help. South Africa will be a society in peril if the views of these elites temper concerns for the poorest citizens amongst policy makers long enough to shake the patience of poor people and their faith in the willingness of their government to deliver the illusory reality of a 'better life for all'.

At a human level the idea that a fellow citizen suffers only because he or she has been born to the wrong circumstances, to the wrong parents of the wrong skin colour should be offensive to all who believe in genuine equal opportunity. The disparities in resources on the home front; in terms of take-home income; in the community in terms of basic infrastructure; in the schools attended by their children; the hospitals patronised by their loved ones, simply do not allow a basis to claim that South Africa is an equal-opportunity society. The destabilisation of the family unit that results from living in abject poverty yet surrounded by neighbourhoods in which fellow citizens live in prosperity in a consumer-driven society is enormous. All children aspire to own the same toys and access the same recreational facilities, yet poor parents have to admit to the painful fact of their inability to generate enough income to allow them to follow through on these aspirations.

'You have come face to face with the hard reality of South African poverty: a dense forest of shacks, crowds of unemployed people milling on the streets, and attempts by some at small-scale commerce in makeshift shops. Men cluster in groups, throwing dice or playing cards. The place has the dull metal glow of aging zinc housing, the chaos of unpaved roads, the noise of a life lived in packed public areas, the smoke of smouldering braziers and the stench of sewage spilling into the streets.'[13] Anton Harber's description of Diepsloot could be used to describe any of hundreds of informal settlements that have developed on the fringes of South Africa's urban areas.

The majority of poor parents are left with the shame that they are entirely dependent on hand-outs from the government to put food on the table. These communities cannot help but produce two categories of dissatisfied citizens. The first, adults who have a deep-seated resentment of both white and black elites for the injustice that has locked them out of participating in the prosperity of a nation after many years of struggle. The second category is made up of children and adolescents who grow up with a brewing anger about the injustice that led them to be born in poor circumstances with the embarrassment of seeing the daily humiliation of their parents as they fail to make ends meet. The two categories

205

of dissatisfied citizens differ in their temperament and in their degrees of patience.

Societies move from stability to peril when a fuse is lit by a talented leader (or multiple leaders) of a populist movement, usually blessed with great oratorical prowess, but increasingly driven by crowd-sourcing technology that allows mass mobilisation from a decentralised leadership group at short notice. Based on the level of poverty impacting the lived reality of close to 25 million South Africans, one can not but classify the country as a fertile ground for a populist-led political movement.

Crime seems to be an individual protest mechanism against the status quo in South Africa. The Crime Report of 2010/2011 produced by the South Africa Police Service (SAPS) has the following chilling commentary on violent crime in South Africa:

> People will find it difficult and even impossible to change their lifestyle if their living conditions are grim and their present lifestyle represents adaptation to such conditions. If for example, somebody lives in appalling conditions (e.g. cold wet shack); has no work or secure income; possesses low level of education which does not assist in finding a job or creating an own income; and there is nothing in the environment to keep such an individual busy in a positive way (e.g. through recreational activity). This will occur in social conditions already tense because of damaged self-esteem and intense competition for scarce resources.[14]

According to the SAPS, alcohol abuse is behind a large number of the 198 602 cases of assault with intent to inflict grievous bodily harm. This is the third most frequent criminal offence in South Africa behind petty theft (369 095) and burglary at residential premises (which happened a staggering 247 630 times in 2010/11). If one adds up all the reported criminal cases it amounts to South African residents being subjected to just over 1.8 million incidents of crime, most of which have the threat of violence.[15] There is no nation that can be subjected to such a criminal siege for long periods of time without transforming into a violent, suspicious, and in South Africa's case, deeply racially divided society. Though the 2012 Crime Statistics saw a 3.1% decrease in the murder rate, it is more than four and a half times the global average of 6.9 murders per 100 000.[16]

> Among the dominantly social contact crimes committed against children, 51% were sexual offences, while only 18.7% of the social contact crimes committed against adult women were sexual offences. The dominant social contact crime committed against adult women, is common assault (46.9% of cases)... However, it is disturbing to note that in the case of the most prevalent crime against children, namely the 20 141 cases of sexual offences recorded during 2008/2009 in this regard, 60.5% were committed against children below the age of 15 years. It is even more disturbing to note that 29.4% of these sexual offences involved children aged 0-10 years.[17]

Only a truly sick society decaying from within can produce such frightening statistics. Unattended humiliation suffered over decades and passed on from generation to generation is at the root of many of these heinous crimes.

Only the truly cold-hearted can look at these statistics and claim not to be concerned about the direction in which the country is going. Just to put the numbers into context, if the average age of children suffering from these cases of sexual assault was roughly 8 years old in 1998, these children will be young adults roughly 30 years old when Moeletsi Mbkei's predicted 'Tunisia Day' occurs. Given that psychological studies have demonstrated that children suffering violent attacks at a young age are more likely to end up as perpetrators of violence in their adult years, South Africans who ignore Mbeki's warning of looming peril are at best unwise and irresponsible citizens. 'The simple answer is that increased inequality ups the stakes in the competition for status: status matters even more. The impact of inequality on violence is even better established and accepted than the other effects of inequality... A large body of evidence shows a clear relationship between greater inequality and higher homicide rates.'[18]

In late 2006 South Africa started to experience a growing sense of dissatisfaction in many poor communities in the form of violent and non-violent protest marches. A long tradition of civil protests formed the backbone of the Anti-Apartheid Movement over many decades. Not unexpectedly, communities continued with this tradition after the ten-year honeymoon granted to the ANC-dominated government had run its course. What may have taken political commentators and politicians by surprise is the frequency and the increasingly violent nature of these protests. They have mostly been lumped into the innocuous category of service delivery protests which are curable by simply getting government to 'deliver'. The truth is that the reasons behind these protests are more complex. The remedy that is needed goes well beyond 'delivering'.

'South Africa experienced an average of 8.73 protests per month, and 9.83 protests per month in 2007 and 2008 respectively. In 2009, the average number of protests ballooned to 17.75 per month... Protestors often cite the lack of accountability of government officials, along with the absence of public participation as factors that further aggravate their service delivery complaints.'[19] After witnessing a spike in the number of incidences in early 2010, the combination of a more responsive government, the 2010 World Cup and the resumption of economic growth (after a recession) saw the number of protests fall dramatically. It is instructive to look at why they occurred in the first place to make a determination about whether the protests are likely to resurface with the same or greater levels of frequency and intensity.

Four main characteristics of these protests are discernable. The first is that protests are context-specific. They take place largely during winter, increase during periods of economic turmoil, have become increasingly violent in nature and they take place in urban areas.

There are several (potentially mutually reinforcing) explanations for the greater unrest in the winter months. First, the increased need for electricity and power during the colder winter months makes residents more likely to protest electricity shortages, which occur regularly across South Africa. Second, the damage caused by the winter storms and subsequent instances of flooding may contribute to community unrest. Of the 5 instances between 2007 and 2010 participants cited flooding as motivating a particular protest, all occurred during the winter months. Third, the winter weather may amplify concerns residents have about the absence of adequate housing.[20]

These are all infrastructure-related challenges stemming from an inability to deliver acceptable living conditions to people who cannot move to areas that have superior basic facilities because they are too poor. It is perhaps because they are poor that they are being taken for granted by local officials who continue to squander resources through corruption and inefficiency and are not held accountable at a provincial and national level.

The second main characteristic of these protests is that though the level of frequency has subsided, the protests are increasingly violent, leading to clashes with police that result in a vicious cycle of (sometimes brutal) repression and violent reaction from unruly crowds. More than half of the community protests have been violent. 'The death of Andries Tatane in Ficksburg is a tragic example of chaos ensuing when seemingly peaceful protest is met with aggressive police response. Tatane, a schoolteacher and community leader, participated in a demonstration to the Setsoto Municipal offices concerning the community's service delivery grievances. The media has reported that Tatane was beaten and apparently shot by police officers after asking them not to use water canons to disperse elderly bystanders.'[21]

Elites of all race groups find themselves in an invidious situation regarding crime-fighting approaches by police. At one level, elites decry the increasingly violent nature of crime that is characterised by a callous use of force by criminals that goes beyond the pursuit

209

of whatever material asset they are seeking to steal. These elites find themselves inundated with stories of how families and loved ones have been the victims of armed robberies and murders. They therefore applaud robust crime fighting and tacitly support former Police Commissioner Bheki Cele's 'shoot to kill' policy. But in so doing, it must come as somewhat surprising even to these elites that they are now supporting tactics used by the apartheid regime to repress criminal and political violence. In the apartheid days it was white elites who viewed police brutality as a necessary evil to protect a lifestyle that they deemed under siege by unruly blacks. In post-apartheid society it is both whites and the 2.5 million black middle class that seek the protection of the police against the violent crime carried out largely (but by no means exclusively) by 'unruly blacks'. The irony is that the free South African society has higher security gates than apartheid South African suburbs, more armed response guards patrolling their gates and a similar tacit complicity to police brutality.

Making matters more complicated is that criminals are now indiscriminate about the race of the victim, their age or sex. In fact the elderly, children and the disabled are being targeted. The result is public consensus that they are a source of discomfort to the well-to-do that needs to be eradicated by a zero-tolerance policy towards crime. This is interpreted by police as an invitation to take matters into their own hands in the fight against crime or any kind of civil disobedience because law and order is superior to civil liberty as a national imperative. The long-term consequences of this complicity by elites in the escalating police brutality towards civilians is the relaxation of oversight on law enforcement officers, the militarisation of the police force and its chain of command and the advent of vigilantism as citizens adopt their own zero-tolerance approach to alleged criminals. All this further aggravates an already violent society with potentially chaotic long-term consequences.

The third characteristic of the protests is that they increased during a period of economic turmoil: 'Given that the global financial crisis and the subsequent economic recession likely hampered the ability of local governments to adequately provide on behalf of residents with basic services, and independently contributed a negative effect on the financial security of community members (unemployment, reduced savings etc), it is likely that the difficult economic climate impacted the frequency of community protest. The spike in the number of the protests taking place between December 2008 and November 2009 supports this claim.'[22] This is understandable and completely intuitive, but it also supports the notion that the strikes are about more than just basic service delivery. It would be more accurate to say that greater personal hardship, caused by extreme weather, a bad economy, electricity blackouts, and so on, increases the likelihood of protest. This again makes Moeletsi Mbeki's prediction chilling. The thought that exogenous economic factors can compound local socio-economic realities, resulting in uncontrollable unrest and even revolution, should be frightening to all stakeholders in South Africa.

A final characteristic of the community protests is that they occur with far greater frequency in urban as opposed to rural areas. Between February 2007 and May 2010, 49 per cent of all community protests were in the Western Cape and Gauteng.[23] 'Municipal IQ has suggested that Gauteng's striking contribution to the number of community protests nationwide demonstrates that the protests are largely an urban phenomenon, resulting from relative deprivation members of a community feel when compared to their more affluent neighbours.'[24] The prevalence of these protests in urban areas is the main reason why the term 'service delivery protests' is a misnomer, because anyone familiar with the South African realities will tell you that rural areas have greater service delivery challenges than urban areas and should be the hotbed for violent protests if that is all that these protests are about.

It seems far more plausible that the relative discomfort felt by shack dwellers on the fringes of prosperous neighbourhoods drives communities to action. The success of building houses for 11 million people has formed a culture of dependency on RDP housing, creating an additional pull factor away from rural areas towards

211

urban slums as a way to join the national queue for free houses. This has replaced a long-standing tradition within the black community of building one's own house as part of a male rite of passage. This only serves to further emasculate males in poor communities, feeding a vicious cycle of social humiliation and violence.

> Further, the preoccupation with 'formalising' those living in informal housing and reducing the housing backlog – a political imperative for the African National Congress (ANC) – has failed to consider the numerous benefits of aspects of informality for poor individuals and households and various unintended consequences of 'formality' (often involving relocation to underdeveloped dormitory estates or transit areas) that make people worse off in real terms, particularly in relation to access to livelihoods and job opportunities. This is demonstrated by the high percentage of people who sell or relocate from their RDP houses back to informal settlements to be closer to employment.[25]

The irony of current national housing schemes is how closely they resemble apartheid-era town planning and racially segmented development strategies. Poor people are given terrible trade-offs in exchange for RDP houses, often involving moving to far-flung developments which significantly increases their transportation costs to well above one third of their income. They have to reconstitute communities in unfamiliar terrain, destroying the psycho-social benefits that arise from communal familiarity, destroying organically formed social accountability mechanisms.

Reasons for underperformance of the so-called RDP housing schemes are varied. They include lack of co-ordination between local, provincial and national government; corruption and its insidious tendency to lead to misallocation of funds away from competent construction companies towards fly-by-night solutions that often either do not do the job or leave it half-finished despite having being paid; inability to unlock public land; the lack of sufficient quantities of mixed-use housing that would bring employees closer to their workplaces; and inability to coordinate the delivery of sanitation services, electricity and roads to prospective developments, leading to unnecessary delays.

Delays are compounded by shoddy workmanship which leaves inhospitable housing for poor people to move into, only to see these houses fall apart often during bouts of bad weather when shelter is needed most. The inconvenient truth that needs to be admitted by policy makers in general and the ANC in particular is that they cannot keep up with the required number of houses necessitated by rapid urbanisation. More and more people abandon lives in rural areas where unemployment is a virtual certainty, to live in urban areas where only half of them have any chance of finding work.

> Others continued to pour into Diepsloot of their own accord, and the 2001 census counted 49 725 people. By 2005, the official figure was 23 000 families, which would make it more like 90 000 people, but this is undoubtedly undercounting. Official city estimates are now 150 000 to 200 000 but the figures used by NGOs are at the top limit of that rage. Unemployment is of the highest order, officially measured at 54 per cent of the potential labour force in 2007, with 73 per cent of the people living below the poverty line.[26]

Those residents of Diepsloot and other similar urban informal settlements who are fortunate enough to find employment spend every day passing well-to-do neighbouring suburbs such as the immaculately well-kept golfing estate called Dainfern (which is less than a kilometre away from Diepsloot) where many of the residents are dollar millionaires living lives that are incomprehensible in their luxury to poor people. The daily reminder of one's 'station in life' relative to well-to-do black elites, not to mention their white counterparts, must rub salt into the wounds of struggling South Africans.

Looking around the streets of Johannesburg, Durban, Port Elizabeth and Cape Town, the sight of a begging child, a new shack

213

dwelling or the sight of a scavenging vagrant has become the 'new normal', an inconvenient but routine part of the hustle and bustle that all elites have to go through. Perhaps if these elites took time out to learn some hard lessons from other societies in peril, they would have the requisite perspective to try and remedy the situation before it becomes too late. Looking at Zimbabwe, Venezuela, Egypt and Tunisia for lessons learnt may prove instructive to this end.

Zimbabwe and the perils of land reform left unfinished

The Kingdom of Zimbabwe which existed from 1100 to 1450 had as its capital Great Zimbabwe, whose ruins are designated a Unesco World Heritage Site. Following the fall of the Kingdom the numerous Shona tribes unified to create the Rozwi state which sprawled over half of modern Zimbabwe. This state lasted until 1834, when it was invaded by Ndebele warriors and came under the control of Lobengula. Zimbabwe's colonial history is very similar to that of South Africa. The asymmetrical understanding of the concept of land title and the way that title was held and transferred, were used as a proxy for land expropriation from blacks to whites.

> In early 1888, John Moffat, a British official, persuaded Lobengula the Ndebele King to sign a treaty to protect the riches in Matabeleland and Mashonaland. It is alleged that when he signed the treaty, Lobengula claimed to be not only the King of the Ndebele, but also the Shona and Kalanga people. This treaty put all these territories under the British sphere. Lobengula could not sign another treaty with any other European treaty-seeker, and in return, Lobengula hoped to gain British protection from the Transvaal Boers. On October 13, 1888, Lobengula, under the influence of a British official/missionary CD Helm, and his most senior *indunas*, Lotshe and Sikombo, signed the Rudd Concession.[27]

Between 1894 and 1895, 15.8 million acres of land were unlawfully expropriated or fraudulently 'acquired' by Europeans, usually through private companies.[28] This large-scale theft of land laid the foundation for decades of unequal economic development along racial lines that would be accentuated upon the discovery of minerals in Zimbabwe. Land tenure in Zimbabwe was granted to the existing occupants in exchange for newly introduced land taxes which served as the basis for funding the imperial economy. As a result, Europeans owned nearly 49 million acres of land while black people were left with just 28 million of which only 7 million acres was freehold land that could be bought and sold; the balance was held in 'native reserves'.[29]

As in South Africa, part of the ulterior motive behind introducing land taxes was to force the land occupants to become a source of cheap labour for the industrialisation of colonial Zimbabwe. In times of revolt by the native population (these revolts were grouped together under the label the First Chimurenga), as in South Africa, the full wrath of British military force was used to suppress any possibility of victory for the outmatched Africans.

This framework of political control, 'privatisation' of land previously owned by indigenous communities and passage of laws by a white-dominated parliament to force them into providing cheap labour, is a carbon copy of the South African subsidised development model. In this system, tax receipts generated from the black majority's limited economic activity were used to pour money into commercial farming, mining and logistics infrastructure for the benefit largely of the white minority. The participation of a cohort of the black elite was used as a legitimising tool by the system's puppet masters.

The pattern of development in Zimbabwe was greatly affected by similar exogenous factors, as in the rest of the African colonies. British resource constraints led to a reduction of appetite for direct control of the colonies, which was expensive and cumbersome. The local European population failed to create a sustainable symbiosis between themselves and locals. Attempts at qualified suffrage and selective puppet native representation only served to stoke anger at minority rule, leading to the Second Chimurenga, a full-scale armed rebellion, which ultimately forced Ian Smith's government to the negotiating table. This settlement was as fundamentally flawed as the South African compromise of 1994 in its insistence on a delayed land redistribution programme to be funded by Britain on a willing-buyer willing-seller basis in exchange for immediate minority protection laws.

The liberation heroes in Zimbabwe made similar fundamental mistakes to most African liberation leaders (mistakes that would later be duplicated by the ANC) by focusing most of their attention and energy on winning political concessions at the expense of economic concessions. This focus undermined the sustainability of the newly formed state.

> At independence in 1980, Zimbabwe inherited a highly skewed ownership pattern, with around 42% of the country owned by some 6,000 large scale farmers, most of whom were white... This commercial agricultural sector dominated the formal agricultural economy, contributing 75% of total agricultural output and 96% of sales... The commercial sector also employed a significant workforce, about a third of formal sector employment and around 250, 000.[30]

Having secured a funding mechanism from Britain, President Mugabe failed to forcefully pursue land redistribution, choosing instead to focus on building his own version of a rainbow nation of Zimbabweans. Predictably, Britain took any opportunity to avoid footing the bill for land redistribution and local white farmers showed no inclination to back away from the willing-buyer willing-seller principle.

Structural adjustment policies adopted post-independence as part of IMF loan programmes led to mixed results. The economy performed relatively well in the first 15 years, with commercial farming leading to increased production that allowed Zimbabwe to become known as Africa's bread basket. This performance was aided by huge investments in education by President Mugabe's government which made Zimbabweans amongst the best-educated on the continent. The challenges came from a growth model that was highly unequal, leading to a growing dissatisfaction among ordinary Zimbabweans with the prospects of a better life. The formation of a formidable opposition in the Movement for Democratic Change (MDC) and its increasing inroads into the strongholds of the governing party created the impetus for President Mugabe to support land invasions by the masses. Having seen his popularity decline, this opportunistic use of the land issue was his only hope of remaining in power.

White South Africans, by and large, seem to have drawn the wrong conclusions about what went wrong in Zimbabwe. The brief history sketched above is seldom mentioned in the identification of the breakdown point in Zimbabwe's development. Instead commentators go straight to the part of the story where the villain is identified as President Robert Gabriel Mugabe and his clinging to power over more than two decades. The journey he started as a darling of the West because of his uncanny intellect, his urbane demeanour and his moderate policies during the late 1980s and the early 1990s, then becoming a pariah for his so-called 'land grab' policies in the early 2000s, is often simplified. As a result of this selective history, the lesson learnt from the Zimbabwe experience from the perspective of many white South Africans is that land redistribution doesn't work and that commercial farming is the only sustainable form of farming. Countries are, in this view, better off letting go of the past and focusing on the future regardless of present inequalities of wealth. Governments are best suited to looking after poor people and leaving the private sector to get on with the business of doing business. This is an incomplete and largely misleading interpretation of the Zimbabwean story.

Though the land invasions have led to tens of thousands of small-scale farmers operating with varying degrees of success, they have transformed the farming sector in irreversible ways.

Today, there are still 5m ha under large-scale farming, some of it in very large holdings... There are perhaps only 2000-3000 white-owned commercial farmers still operating, with most having been displaced along with substantial numbers of farm workers. Most land today is under small-scale farming, whether as communal areas or resettlements. Estimates vary, but around 7m ha have been taken over through the Fast Track Land Reform Programme (FTLRP) since 2000.[31]

Farming is no longer synonymous with white commercial land ownership. The majority of land is now owned by black Zimbabweans. This change has come at a huge cost that could have and should have been avoided. Zimbabwe has taken some massive steps back in the journey towards economic development. At a human level the cost incurred in terms of suffering brought about by the collapse of health, education and other social services is immeasurable.

The real lesson to be learned from Zimbabwe is that political settlements which give political power and defer economic redistribution only delay the inevitable future struggle for diminished economic resources by a poor majority that can eventually turn violent. Elite concentration of wealth is only sustained for as long as the interests of the elites and the politicians in charge are absolutely aligned. To the extent that there is a divergence of agendas, particularly during times of drought, economic hardship and political tension, elite interests will be sacrificed to pacify the masses. There will come a time when majority interests can be suppressed no longer, and a powerful enough pressure-cooker environment is created. These majority interests can explode into mass revolution against the status quo. By the time this happened in Zimbabwe President Mugabe, in his self-interest, had no other choice (that kept him in power) but to ride the wave of rebellion by enthusiastically supporting the black majority in their quest for land.

The loss of just under 4 000 white farmers and their families has been tragic both to the farmers concerned and the Zimbabwean economy in general. Sadly the bulk of the pain has been carried by poor people who have experienced food shortages and price increases compounded by hyper-inflation, and the economically vulnerable labourers who have lost their livelihoods as farm workers.

> Food production, particularly maize, has been down in most years compared to 1990s averages ... due to the dislocations of land reform and the establishment of new farms, as well as poor input supply and repeated drought. Food imports and emergency relief have occurred each year since 2000, although the 2009 maize harvest was estimated at 1.24m tonnes, reducing the need for emergency measures. The displacement of around 150 000 permanent farm worker households, formerly resident and working on the large-scale commercial farms along with a comparable number of temporary workers, many of them women, is another major policy challenge.[32]

If asked today, one would be willing to wager that many of the 4 000 white farmers who lost their land would have agreed to finance the transfer of a portion of their massive farms in exchange for the peace of mind of living in harmony with fellow black Zimbabweans and continuing their own very profitable operations. Many of them are currently uprooted and living in different parts of the world doing agricultural consulting on other people's land. Ultimately South Africans in a similar economic position should want to avoid this fate.

The Arab Spring and the perils of youth unemployment

The term 'Arab Spring' refers to a wave of demonstrations and protests that have occurred in the Arab world since December 2010. These revolutions have swept through countries such as Tunisia, Egypt, Libya, Bahrain, Syria and Yemen. In each country they have taken different forms and displayed varying degrees of violence, the worst of which was in the civil wars in Syria and Libya. Leadership in all of the affected countries was seen as corrupt, undemocratic and therefore illegitimate by protestors. The effects of these protests have been profound, changing the way power is distributed in a region traditionally dominated by authoritarian regimes.

Often people looking at the reasons for dissatisfaction within certain societies do not differentiate between the impacts of inequality and inequity of income and wealth distribution as the root cause of the perception of societal inequity, as already discussed in the South African context. As Fouad Ajami eloquently states, 'Arabs did not need a "human development report" to tell them of their desolation. Consent had drained out of public life; the only glue between ruler and ruled was suspicion and fear.'[33]

The reason why this distinction between inequality and inequity is so important to keep in mind is that inequality was actually decreasing or stabilising in all parts of northern Africa and the Middle East that experienced this so-called 'Arab Spring'. 'In Tunisia, inequality declined in the 1980s, increased in the 1990s, and has been constant since. In Egypt it has been on the decline. Just before the revolutions, the level of inequality was high but not outrageous in both countries: in Tunisia it was almost the same as in the United States, and in Egypt, it was lower. Broadly constant Gini coefficients meant that everyone's income increased by about the same percentage – the rising tide lifted all boats.'[34]

This is not to say that young people were not suffering in Tunisia and Egypt. Indeed youth unemployment in both countries as well as neighbouring countries such as Algeria was at unacceptable levels. In Egypt, for instance, even though the economy was growing at above 6 per cent at the time of the uprising, 18 per cent of the population still lived below the poverty line and even official unemployment numbers were running at double-digit rates. 'Egypt is the Arab world's most heavily populated country and one of its youngest: two thirds of the population are under 30. However the young make up 90% of the nation's unemployed.'[35]

Young people who are badly affected by the idle numbness of

unemployment tend to blame corruption. These youths interpret corruption as being directly responsible for taking away opportunities from them. This pent-up frustration boiled over into a violent reaction from young Egyptians when President Hosni Mubarak attempted to pass on the presidency to his son. This form of hereditary rule, which for decades had been tolerated by citizens in the Middle East, represented a privatisation of state power and with it economic resources.

These protests were about freedom and economic well-being. The prospects of a better future for these young people and their parents were so poor that they were willing to risk going to jail or being killed to try and achieve positive political change. This trade-off analysis in the modern world of internet connectivity through mobile phones quickly becomes self-reinforcing, allowing crowd sourcing behind ideas at a pace that was previously unheard of.

> Arab governments have resisted full global integration and trade, media and other exchanges and maintained corrupt regimes... Opportunity filtered only to those with powerful connections, leaving millions educated, yet unemployed. In this demographic revolution, young Arabs are desperate enough that one Tunisian young man set himself on fire, followed by several others in neighbouring countries, and countless others defy government controls.[36]

From a South African point of view the lesson seems simple: young people's perception of inequity in society is more important than any statistic on income inequalities. Put differently, the country is only safe from violent protests for as long as young people buy into the way society distributes incomes. Equally important as a metric of stability is youth unemployment. The category of 2.8 million young South Africans whom Michael Cosser refers to as NEETS (not in employment, not educated and not trained), is the most worrying aspect in South Africa's unfolding economic development.[37]

The problem of youth unemployment in South Africa is acute and has worsened significantly over the last two years as a result of the recession. Employment of 18 to 24 year olds fell by more than 20 per cent (320 000) between December 2008 and December 2010, compared with an overall decline of 6.4 per cent. The unemployment rate among those under the age of 25 years old is about 50 per cent and accounts for 30 per cent of the total unemployment. Including those aged 25 to 29 years old adds another million to the unemployed.[38]

The problem of inequity is behind most of the rampant crime in South Africa and threatens to be the spark that can set off a spontaneous combustion of youth-led revolt. President Zuma's administration seems alive to this risk and is attempting to resolve it by proposing a youth unemployment subsidy. This is however an unsustainable solution to a fundamental problem which is rooted in labour market rigidity that makes it difficult to fire workers after hiring them, hence disincentivising corporations to take risky bets in the form of making new hires. Unemployment is also made worse by the failure of government to regulate competition in a way that gives small and medium enterprises an even playing field. SMEs employ more than 60 per cent of the workforce in South Africa; a failure to resolve this challenge could have dire long-term consequences for the stability of the country.

Venezuela and the perils of populism

'Contemporary politics in Venezuela begin with the so-called Caracazo of February 1989, an explosion of political rage by the under-class in Caracas and a handful of other cities against a neo-liberal program imposed by a once-popular president, Carlos Andres Perez, who had just been elected to do something entirely different. For two days Caracas degenerated into violence of the kind not seen in Venezuela since the nineteenth century, sparked off by an increase in bus fares but reflecting a much wider political discontent. A thousand people, perhaps more, were killed in the subsequent repression by the armed forces.'[39]

This environment of class warfare culminating in the riots was characterised as a tipping point which symbolised the inequity in the system in relation to the poor majority of the population. Ultimately this moment in history will forever be remembered for facilitating the emergence of Hugo Chávez to the political scene. In reality, policy errors by government officials representing the two dominant parties in Venezuela led to a series of economic reforms that were wildly unpopular.

Venezuela had been going through an economic crisis for most of the 1980s, which created severe fiscal problems for the state. The decision not to partake in the OPEC cartel (because of Venezuela's strategic relationship with the United States) led to Venezuela getting caught off-guard by a sharp increase in oil production by OPEC member states, which led to a decrease in oil prices and diminished oil revenues. Forced to seek IMF money, which was accompanied by structural adjustment policies, President Perez privatised companies, reformed the tax structure and generally reduced the role of the state in the economy. Included amongst these reforms was the elimination of a long-standing subsidy that had kept petrol prices (and consequently the price of public transport) artificially low. This resulted in a 100 per cent increase in petrol prices and despite the government's efforts to coerce public transport operators to the contrary, public transport went up by 30 per cent practically overnight. This was followed by a month-long period of protest characterised by looting, general civil disobedience and rampant lawlessness.

'When Hugo Chávez was first elected as president, in December 1998, the country had already suffered a prolonged crisis over many years. Mired in corruption, with the oil wealth dwindling, successive governments had imposed neo-liberal programs with scant success. Riots in 1989, attempted coups in 1992, the successful impeachment of the president in 1993, the collapse of the banks in 1994, and the implosion of the once-powerful political parties, were all signs of impending breakdown.'[40] In other words, Venezuela was slipping into peril.

Hugo Chávez fits all the stereotypes of a populist strongman. As a former paratrooper and a powerful public speaker possessing an uncanny ability to persuade other leaders to action in private meetings, he had led an unsuccessful coup attempt in February 1992, resulting in his arrest and incarceration. Chávez captured the imagination of the nation when he used his arrest as a podium to display authority over fellow coup plotters (by asking them to stand down), calm under pressure (by taking sole responsibility for the plot) and bravery by characterising the defeat of the rebels to be merely a momentary defeat, on national TV. He instantly became one of the country's most popular figures, capturing the imagination of a nation jolted by high crime rates, exorbitant levels of socio-economic inequality and rampant corruption.

As head of state Chávez has attempted to implement drastic populist policies that have helped make him an international pariah as well as a polarising domestic political figure.

> The Chávez government has greatly increased social spending, including spending on health care, subsidized food, and education. The most pronounced difference has been in the area of health care. For example, in 1998 there were 1,628 primary care physicians for a population of 23.4 million. Today, there are 19,571 for a population of 27 million. The Venezuelan government has also provided widespread access to subsidized food. By 2006, there were 15,726 stores throughout the country that offered mainly food items at subsidized prices (with average savings of 27 percent and 39 percent compared to market prices in 2005 and 2006, respectively). The central government's social spending has increased massively, from 8.2 percent of GDP in 1998 to 13.6 percent for 2006.[41]

Given these successes it is not difficult to see why Chávez remains a stubbornly popular politician domestically; what is not so clear is why these domestic successes have not translated into sustainable macro-economic growth.

The simple answer is that Chavez's policies have had a 'Robin Hood' quality about them. Steep sacrifices in the standard of living for the rich minority are required in exchange for an increase in the standard of living for the poor majority. The nature of the sacrifices by the rich in Venezuela has been delegitimised by the fact that these were forced on them by what the elite view as undemocratic means (manipulating the electorate to push through constitutional reforms), and compounded by gross mismanagement of the economy. Paradoxically, such populist policies have created macro-economic distortions which have hampered growth and ultimately caused the economy to contract, especially as oil prices have come off their pre-financial crisis highs. The administration's draconian nationalisation of industries which had significant foreign interests isolated Venezuela from its old allies, forcing it to carve out alliances with Cuba, Russia and China. For example, the petroleum industry – which had been state-owned since the 1970s but was moving in the opposite direction towards privatisation before Chávez took office – as well as the cement industry and commercial farming, were prime targets.

Hugo Chávez is reviled by most members of the wealthy class in Venezuela. They view him as a despotic populist who has abused his position to extend his term in office, centralised political power and weakened the inherent checks and balances within the federal system by vesting more authority in his national government structures.

> Eleven years after the 1999 constitution making, despite the political rhetoric and exuberant spending, which wasted the immense fiscal income of a rich state in a poor country, no effective reform of the state has been achieved. Instead of social and participatory democracy, the process resulted in the configuration of a centralized, militaristic, and concentrated authoritarian regime that seeks to impose a socialist model of society with a democratic veil – centralized populist programs and institutions that pretend to be participatory have almost completed the destruction of the direct representative democracy.[42]

In other words, economic progress for the majority of poor people in Venezuela has come at the price of a loss in democratic functionality. People are freer in the socio-economic sense, but they are robbed of some of their civil liberties.

Despite some statistics showing an improvement in the lives of ordinary people, the Chávez administration has overseen an overall economic meltdown which has continued to stifle the ability of the government to carry out its ambitious socialist agenda. According to *The Economist*, GDP in Venezuela declined by 5.5 per cent in 2010 and consumer prices were up 31 per cent, signalling a new era of hyperinflation, yet the country remained the number 8 oil-producing nation in the world. 'The chief cause of Venezuela's travails has been Mr Chavez's pillaging of PDVSA, the state oil firm. He has packed it with loyalists, starved it of investment and used it for social spending, cutting its output from 3.3m barrels per day (b/d) in 1998 to around 2.25m b/d, according to industry estimates. Of that some 1m b/d is sold at subsidised prices at home or to regional allies, leaving just 1.25m b/d for full price exports.'[43] The drastic reduction in full-price oil production has been compounded by other serious policy errors, such as the nationalisation of almost 100 businesses in so-called strategic sectors of the economy and pegging the bolivar (the Venezuelan currency) at 2.15 to the dollar.[44]

The populist approach has been a poisoned chalice for Hugo Chávez, giving him domestic popularity but international isolation, allowing him to increase the quality of life of the majority at the expense of macro-economic rationality. He will have at best a mixed legacy that falls short of his revolutionary aspirations. His experience should serve as a warning to would-be populist leaders all over the world – not least South Africa. The rhetoric of governing exclusively for poor people at the expense of the wealthy class of society is seductive and can get one elected. The reality of governing from that platform is entirely different, almost always leading to revolutionary dreams being deferred. An equally important lesson for South Africans is the fragility of selective prosperity and the lightning-like speed with which societies move from relative prosperity to peril. Populist leaders are propelled to power by insensitive, uncaring and ultimately short-sighted elites who believe that they are untouchable because of their wealth and stature in the economy. Time and time again history has proved that this hubris is likely to be followed by regret.

The thread which connects individual citizens living in societies in peril is their shared loss of faith in the facilitative capacity of democratic institutions to generate acceptable socio-economic transformation. The need for socio-economic transformation is almost always triggered by unjust economic distribution of wealth and incomes. The tipping point arises after a protracted period of societal inequity, usually magnified by an event interpreted by ordinary citizens as having the potential to make their already unbearable situation even worse. This tipping point is usually triggered by arrogant elites who display their opposition to marginal changes that could improve the lives of poor people in their societies. Signs of this elite arrogance are often visible for many years prior to the actual tipping point.

I believe South Africa is flirting dangerously close to being a society in peril. Current levels of inequality of both income distribution and wealth are unsustainable; so is the level of corruption that continues to go unpunished. The events in the Marikana mining community have awoken some elites to the immediacy of the potential socio-economic catastrophe. For the first time since apartheid, South African police were ordered to shoot to kill protesters (mine workers protesting for higher pay). The national outrage generated by this show of police brutality threatened to bubble over into widespread riots. This is a moment for leaders to lead. Humility and far-sightedness by South Africa's elite are necessary to transform a country in danger of degenerating into a state of peril into one that is a more civil society.

11

A More Civil Society

South Africa's history would have doomed many a nation to the ranks of failed states, but so far, it has shown a stubborn resilience against this fate. Through a period of over 70 years a slow process of organic, bottom-up integration amongst those who were opposed to apartheid helped remove racial barriers on the one side of the two societies that would integrate in 1994. This was facilitated in no small part by pragmatic partnerships that formed between communists and African nationalists, romantic relationships across racial group lines and faith-based initiatives recognising the humanity of black people and the inhumanity of the apartheid system. All three of these interactions facilitated inter-racial trust building.

Through the Anti-Apartheid Movement black people became increasingly unapologetic in their requirement that their interests, values and aspirations rank equal with the rest of the population as a prerequisite for integration. This culminated in a negotiated settlement predicated on the full integration of the two societies (one living comfortably under apartheid, fearing majority rule, and another living under the guidance of the Anti-Apartheid Movement, anxious about the possibility of a post-apartheid minority power grab). A sleight of hand by elites negotiating the integration in

1994 robbed the newly integrated society of the opportunity to make that integration economically sustainable. Failure to remove the remaining barriers in the way of black people to fully participate in the economy made it difficult for a society to emerge that was not only characterised by equal political rights but also by equal economic opportunity.

Liberation and integration

Steve Biko defined his vision for integration in a newly democratised South Africa as follows:

> Once the various groups within a given community have asserted themselves to the point that mutual respect has to be shown then you have the ingredients for true and meaningful integration. At the heart of true integration is the provision for each man, each group to rise and attain the envisioned self. Each group must be able to attain its style of existence without encroaching on or being thwarted by another. Out of this mutual respect for each other and complete freedom of self-determination there will obviously arise a genuine fusion of the life-styles of the various groups. This is true integration.[1]

What Steve Biko believed was at the heart of true integration was equality of opportunity, which he refers to as a 'provision for each man, each group to rise and attain the envisioned self'. He knew then and we have learned all too well since his death that sustainable integration is facilitated within society when the aspirations of its citizens are accommodated by the removal of barriers to their ability to work towards the attainment of their dreams, however modest or ambitious those dreams may be. This allows individuals and groups the full freedom to express their liberty in ways that are consistent with their community values and cultural norms. It is from this comfort zone that individual, community and group cultural norms and values can be shared within the wider society, thereby enabling this society to become fully integrated. At no stage can a society integrating on the basis of the domination of a minority set of values and cultural norms view itself as sustainable. Societal sustainability depends on broad enough ownership of those norms and values that are shared.

For too many privileged white liberals in South Africa, liberation put an end to any excuses for blacks not to live up to the promise these liberals spotted in them. This has resulted in many cases of white liberals feeling disillusioned by the new South Africa and its failure to live up to the impossibly high expectations of 1994. This dynamic played itself out in the form of premature promotion of inexperienced black executives to corporate positions that they would unsurprisingly fail in. Or in the form of early black empowerment transactions that empowered a handful of black entrepreneurs in the hope that the proceeds would somehow trickle down to poor South Africans. Or in the initial tolerance of clearly unqualified and under-prepared civil servants in the misguided belief that deployment would morph towards a state of meritocracy.

What may be at the centre of these instances of white liberal disappointment may be the dread that there is no magic wand to be waved. The inability of even President Mandela to work this miracle has left only hard work, national soul-searching and prolonged sacrifice by the rich – together with numerous annual reminders, in the form of public holidays, of the wrongs of the past – as the only way to heal South Africa's wounds. Making matters all the more difficult for inexperienced new black entrants into the business world is that South Africans attained their freedom in a global environment where ruthless competition had become the singular ground rule. A nation's lack of competitiveness was a gain for a more competitive nation interested in exporting the same goods or services in a new, more open and thus increasingly zero-sum game of international trade.

The liberation of South Africa coincided with a period accelerated by the fall of communism, driven by a form of capitalism where the consumer defined the society through his or her materialistic aspirations. In this era not only was the customer always right; she also had the right to shop anywhere, any time and in any language of her choosing. This era was the beginning of a period of global prosperity that was characterised by rampant accumulation of goods and services. Ordinary people used their increasing prosperity across the globe to acquire washing machines, dishwashers, microwaves, lawn mowers, computers (with internet connectivity) and various other previously unattainable products, in order to make their lives easier. This unleashed the talents of women in most societies into the workplace, as they got reprieve from household duties and consequently had more free time to develop their talents.

For middle-income families, the ability to afford vacations, holiday homes and second cars created unprecedented quality of life, bringing meaning to their workplace aspirations. At the upper end of the income distribution curve, rich families through liberation in 1994 got access to luxury goods and services in South Africa for the first time, bringing to an end the necessity to travel overseas in order to live on par with their global peers. These trends helped create the wide disparities in lifestyles in South Africa between people of close physical proximity.

The rainbow nation that President Mandela had in mind was not specific about whose culture should be the dominant one, which set of values should anchor society. It was however predicated on the rainbow nation's orientation being unashamedly African. It demanded that for the first time in its history South Africans collectively begin to sever the association of all things modern, progressive and civilised with the Anglo-Saxon world alone. The rainbow nation was founded on the principle that it should be a society characterised by parity in the value of each man and woman, as defined by the constitution. To achieve such parity, the role of African customs, African customary law and the role of traditional leaders had to be recognised not merely in the constitution but also by the broader citizenry as legitimate aspects of modern society. This parity was supposed to start first and foremost in the

231

distribution of rights, and these rights were to extend towards a distribution of opportunities to freely express one's liberty.

President Nelson Mandela put it this way:

> We enter into a covenant that we shall build a society in which all South Africans, both black and white, will be able to walk tall, without any fear in their hearts, assured of their inalienable right to human dignity – a rainbow nation at peace with itself and the world... Our single most important challenge is therefore to help establish a social order in which the freedom of the individual will truly mean the freedom of the individual. We must construct that people-centred society of freedom in such a manner that it guarantees the political liberties and the human rights of all our citizens.[2]

Given the emergence of a consumer-centric culture that came to define key societal principles such as the value of talent, what it means to have progressed, and who is deemed successful, those not achieving according to this new set of metrics were marginalised by society, and incapacitated from progressing by the systemic rigidity. This newly established consumer-centric ideology clashed with traditional African values such as ubuntu, impinged on the ability of citizens to continue to lead faith-based family-centred lifestyles and diminished the community-orientated recreational habits of the past. This pattern of cultural disturbance and a re-framing of societal norms was by no means unique to South Africa; societies across the world were impacted both positively and negatively by what has become known as globalisation.

Those societies that have become the clear winners in the new era of globalisation have managed to create a framework of integration between emerging global values and their traditional local values. Their value systems operate squarely on their own terms through various mechanisms, some by luck and others by planning and dogged determination. For example, the Chinese refuse to accept unrestricted global media advertising in their society for fear of the negative outcomes that uncensored advertising will have on their value system (and the future of the Chinese Communist Party). German, Italian and French societies, though able to operate well in English, use language as an anchoring tool for their traditional values, forcing the world to translate their global marketing strategies to local audiences with firmly grounded local values.

Even American society has had to adjust to the effect of globalisation: as much as US culture and values are being exported around the world, the inevitable consequence is that it has opened itself up to global competitive forces that cause havoc to its internal functionality and challenge its way of life. This affects what kind of US President they choose, the ethnic orientation of their corporate executives and the make-up of their corporate shareholders and sovereign treasury holders, leading to national anxiety and discomfort about the loss of sovereignty.

Ironically America prepared itself to successfully compete as a nation in the globalisation era through actions taken as far back as the 1960s when President John F Kennedy and later President Lyndon Johnson linked racial oppression and inequality of wealth as two key factors making the United States less competitive. In a speech delivered by President Johnson shortly after the death of JFK, he popularised the term 'Great Society' by stating the following:

> The purpose of protecting the life of our Nation and preserving the liberty of our citizens is to pursue the happiness of our people. Our success in that pursuit is the test of our success as a Nation... Your imagination, your initiative, and your indignation will determine whether we build a society where progress is the servant of our needs, or a society where old values and new visions are buried under unbridled growth. For in your time we have the opportunity to move not only towards the rich society and the powerful society, but upward to the Great Society.[3]

From 1963 till 1970, as the new policy measures adopted under

233

the Great Society banner took effect, Americans living below the poverty line dropped from 22.2 to 12.6 per cent.[4]

Given the massive transformation going on at home from the 1990s onward, South Africa lacked the space to undergo the necessary soul searching to come up with a sustainable holistic local strategy to deal with globalisation. As a result, many of its negative consequences have had to be countered in sporadic disaggregated efforts while the society has sought to find its feet. Slowly, over the last 18 years, the South African society has started to reassert itself and more clearly define under what terms it seeks to enter the global stage. This self-definition process has sometimes been led by the presidency, but more often has been organically formulated in everyday social integration.

In 1996, as the future leader of a country suffering a national identity crisis, Deputy President Mbeki was timely in his unambiguous declaration that he is an African:

> I owe my being to the hills and the valleys, the mountains and the glades, the rivers, the deserts, the trees, the flowers, the seas and the ever-changing seasons that define the face of our native land... Today, as a country, we keep an audible silence about these ancestors of the generations that live, fearful to admit the horror of a former deed, seeking to obliterate from our memories a cruel occurrence which, in its remembering, should teach us not and never to be inhuman again... My mind and my knowledge of myself is formed by the victories that are the jewels in our African crown, victories we earned from Isandlwana to Khartoum, as Ethiopians and as the Ashanti of Ghana, as the Berbers of the desert.[5]

With these words Mbeki facilitated the final steps towards self-actualisation of the rainbow nation, by forcing all who live within South Africa to confront their African roots and heritage.

This African heritage also necessitated an acceptance of a value system anchored on the principle of ubuntu by white, Indian and coloured South Africans who may have otherwise been reluctant to do so. President Mbeki also created, in his vision of an African Renaissance, a blueprint for South African participation in globalisation as a partner to its neighbours on the African continent, drawing strength from their collective wealth in their dealings with major trading partners such as China, America and the European Union, which have become the accepted way forward by a previously Eurocentric white South African business community.

South Africa is getting closer to seeing itself as a nation of multiple blended cultures that are fused into one national identity. To date that fusion is not nearly as smooth or as pervasive as the aspirational rainbow nation would like to acknowledge. At face value, aspects like the adoption of the 11 official languages, the acceptance of all religious practices and the dominance of an African imprint on popular culture give the country the aesthetic qualities of a cultural melting pot. What has not quite escaped the observation of most citizens is the uneven nature within which South African integration has occurred. The fact that the upper echelons of society remain largely unpenetrated by African culture is reflective of the economic distribution of wealth in the society as well as the make-up of the elite class and its unique cultural orientation.

One way of correcting this is by bringing the dream of a pluralistic culture to reality by putting greater emphasis on indigenous languages in the education system, in the support of artistic expression in indigenous African languages and in the conduct of official ceremonies. Neville Alexander advises:

> Language policy in education has to promote inter-group communication and understanding. The best way of doing so is via mother tongue-based bilingual education and the promotion of individual multilingualism (or plurilingualism) rather than by means of reliance on a *lingua franca* only. This is the rationale for the official language education policy of 'additive bilingualism' (i.e., the addition of another language and maintenance of the first/mother language). This is now being re-baptised 'mother tongue-based bilingual education' as it is argued that this formulation is more easily comprehensible

to non-specialists. It also has the advantage that in a context of continuing suspicion about the value of mother tongue education, it suggests very clearly that the objective of the system goes beyond the use of the mother tongue as a language of learning in that it points to the learning of additional languages and to their use as languages of teaching.[6]

What is being suggested here fits with a more holistic vision of a nation whose languages and the cultural nuances expressed through these languages are shared by all citizens. There is no reason that the dominant indigenous language in every school district cannot be taught alongside English and Afrikaans. This will not only enrich the communication between the children in these districts but better prepare them to live in a society where diversity of language and culture is a fact of life.

Even though many people of colour have successfully penetrated South Africa's elite, the institutions of the elite have remained, despite their public utterances to the contrary, characterised by a western orientation that fails to transform along with the rest of society. This has led to the often stated observation that South Africa is like an island of Europe on the African continent. Given that elite institutional frameworks are intrinsically exclusionary, it will be a difficult task to facilitate transformation at this level. Having said that, transformation of South Africa's elite institutions is essential to retaining the stabilising effect that comes from the ability of middle-class people of all skin colours to climb the economic and social ladder to the top of society.

Great societies typically only create one stumbling block in the ability of each citizen to attain their dreams, and that is that they have to out-compete fellow citizens in the attainment of these goals, or alternatively join forces with them to form alliances. Embodied in this social compact is the openness by elites to accepting fellow citizens of whatever hue into institutions occupying the upper echelons of society. The dynamism generated by this constant refurbishing of all ranks of society with hard-working men and women who have risen to the top, sometimes at the expense of lazier members of society, creates an environment that allows individuals the ability to generate a personal road map to success. Such a 'sink or swim' ethos is moderated by a willingness to help those unlucky few who have been incapacitated by circumstance to have a decent life, through a social safety net, while never compromising on a societal commitment to helping the children of poor people leapfrog the achievements of their parents through the use of the education system.

A truly great society constantly opens opportunities at both ends of its economic spectrum, assisting new entrants at the bottom end through the creation of equal access to education and an economic environment that generates jobs and rewards hard work. At the top end of the economic distribution curve, elites open their doors to new members who are included purely on the basis of their ability to generate wealth by the application of their unique talents and hard work. The two ends of the spectrum are joined by their common membership of a broader society that they all cherish, leading to a culture of helping the less fortunate that uses solidarity and social entrepreneurship as an extension of a value system which embraces the principle that even though we are not all given the same gifts as human beings, we are all equal in the eyes of our maker.

The great tragedy of South Africa's negotiated settlement is that it left the majority of its citizens as the incapacitated masses who have to be helped out by a government-run social safety net within a limited fiscal environment. To sit back and ignore the injustice of such a system is not in the majority of South Africans' nature. The good news is that many are refusing to let this status quo remain unchallenged. South Africans have made a decision that government is incapable of dealing with this situation alone and that business is not always capable of meaningfully or directly participating in the solution, so they as wealthy families, private citizens and corporate leaders have taken it upon themselves to use social entrepreneurship and the spirit of charity as the vanguard in the fight to create a more just, balanced and a more sustainable society.

On 18 July 2009 President Jacob Zuma announced the inauguration of Nelson Mandela Day. This was designed to be a day when all South Africans will celebrate the spirit of Nelson Mandela through charity, by donating 67 minutes of their time to a worthy cause. As an illustration of ubuntu, no better symbol could have been conjured up. Since then, private citizens, corporate leaders, students and members of civil society have joined hands annually to make this day truly worthy of the great man it was named after. Most astonishingly, this day has been accepted globally as leaders around the world institute Mandela Day in their respective countries as a way of celebrating the values that Nelson Mandela stood for. By effectively exporting ubuntu, South Africans can draw pride from the way they have influenced other societies dealing with similar socio-economic challenges.

Three emerging trends are serving to facilitate a fully integrated, people-centric and more community-conscious South African society. Firstly the improvement in the quality of life of 'born frees' and the effect that they have on their family structure and the broader society in general. Secondly the re-emergence of religion, particularly through charismatic churches, and the effect this has on individuals' personal conduct. The third trend is in the energisation of the field of charitable giving by social entrepreneurs. These three trends are linked: if harnessed by society and supported by business and government they have the potential to create profound long-term change.

'Born frees'

This is a term often used to describe children born post-liberation. It is typically used somewhat patronisingly in the South African political environment, where one's status in the ANC often depends on 'struggle credentials'. South Africa has technically been a free country since 1994. Anyone who is 18 years old or younger today is born free. It also happens to be true that anyone below the age of 18 is considered a child by the constitution, so at the time of writing, all 'born frees' in the South African context are children. Given that children make up approximately one third of the population, an analysis of their welfare, future outlook and economic prospects tells us a lot about post-apartheid South African society.

Our Bill of Rights is clear: 'A child's best interests are of paramount importance in every matter concerning the child.'[7] This is typically the foundational principle guiding the law in its application towards the awarding of decisions in custody battles between parents. In the battle between two separate societies engaged in a broader social integration while fighting for the custodianship of power and money within South Africa, justice has at least partly been upheld. The interests of the nation's children have been deemed to be of paramount enough importance by the warring elites for them to agree to a child-centred social grant framework aimed at protecting the nation's most vulnerable citizens. In comparison to the typical post-liberation African society, South Africa's social welfare system provides grounds for exceptionalism in the governance record of the ANC.

At first glance the statistics do not paint a favourable picture. According to a Unicef study, 11.9 million of the 18.6 million children in South Africa live in poverty.[8] Almost 1.4 million live in households that rely on streams or rivers as their main source of water, with a similar number (1.5 million) living in houses that have no toilet facility at all.[9] Sadly 1 400 mothers die in the neonatal period annually; these accompany 22 000 neonatal deaths each year, more than 43 per cent of which were probably avoidable.[10]

Just 43 per cent of children are exposed to any early childhood development programmes. More than half the nation's children arrive at Grade 1 never having been exposed to any formal learning process. Seventeen years after liberation, the lives of black children are still very much affected by the race group of their parents. A black child is 18 times more likely to live in poverty, 1.5 times less likely to be exposed to early childhood development, half as likely to have access to adequate sanitation and water, 12 times more likely to experience hunger and only half as likely to complete secondary education as a white child.[11]

During President Mbeki's second term his government put an emphasis on building a child-centred social grant programme to make life for children a little easier. As a result of these efforts reported hunger amongst children more than halved between 2002 and 2007, declining from 31 per cent to 15 per cent.[12] Today over 9 million children receive social grants, making South Africa a society with one of the largest (relative to GDP) social security frameworks for children in the world. Given that this support is used almost exclusively for subsistence purposes, and that the nation is producing over 1 million children per year without rapid economic growth, there is an inherent lack of sustainability in the national social grant system.

Having said this, a UN study reveals some undeniable short- and medium-term benefits of the current social grant programmes:

> Economic theory suggests that social grants by raising incomes, affect education in three ways: first to the extent that there are financial barriers to school attendance – purchasing school supplies, uniforms, tuition, transportation, etc – the boost in disposable income provided by social grants could help pay the otherwise unaffordable costs of attending school... Second a grant could relieve the opportunity cost of school attendance; with a cash transfer in hand a family might be more able to forgo a child's contribution to household income (or food production in the case of subsistence farmers) in favour of making a long-term investment in education. Third, by indirectly increasing the resources available to schools, the quality of education may improve, making education a more attractive option to households.[13]

Those against the social grant framework chosen by the government would be hard pressed to find a short-term mechanism better able to bring some meaning to the freedom these children were born into.

The social grant system would be greatly enhanced by the introduction of some level of conditionality into the system, not as a way of excluding those already qualifying but rather as a way of building in sustainability through a 'mini-contract' between the citizen and the state. The best example of this has to be the Brazilian social grant system, which attached conditionality in both the Bolsa Escola programme initiated in 2001 by the Education Ministry and the Bolsa Alimentaçao initiated by the Health Ministry in 2001. 'The basic idea was linkage of school attendance to transfer [the Bolsa Escola] payments to poor parents, or more frequently, a single female parent... Bolsa Aliementaçao had as its target group families with less than half a minimum wage per capita. In return for income transfer, there were explicit obligations, such as prenatal examinations, vaccinations, and nutritional advice from an expanded corps of local health workers.'[14] This conditionality serves to foster a social accountability amongst recipients of grant funding, encouraging behaviour that significantly enhances the future prospects of their children.

'In 2009, there were 12 million learners who were taught by 386 587 teachers in 24 693 public schools; 386 098 learners taught by 24 557 teachers in 1 174 private schools...'.[15] If one accepts the painful fact that nearly 80 per cent of South Africa's public schools are dysfunctional (see Chapter 9) and that all independent schools produce at least a decent level of education, that means there are roughly 2.4 million children receiving better than acceptable levels of schooling in South Africa. The medium-term challenge is to increase this number to 10 million. For the 2.4 million learners at private, independent (previously known as Model C schools) and functional public schools the opportunities for decent work, sustainable entrepreneurship and fulfilling civil service jobs are endless. Like other children around the world, 'born frees' are raised with ready access to technology. They live without fear of new concepts because they fundamentally embrace change. They have a more distant recollection and/or experience of racial bigotry and therefore are less likely to be bitter about the past.

These are the real born frees in the sense that they have no limit to their ability to achieve their aspirations – or, as Steve Biko put it, to reach their 'envisioned self'. They are also typically the least interested in scapegoats for personal failure, the most integrated and cosmopolitan South Africans. They give hope and meaning to the dream of a rainbow nation. By virtue of their cross-racial group friendships they force their parents into the new South Africa, creating life-long inter-racial family friendships that are vital to helping build a non-racial society. Supporting the expansion in the number of 'born frees' and their quality of education will cement the gains of the last decade and a half and help usher in an era where South Africa is led by post-apartheid leadership free of the burdens of the past.

The re-emergence of religion in South African society

South Africa has always been a nation that cherished religion. In the apartheid era the country was run within the framework of Christian Nationalism, which was an all-encompassing form of Christianity that dominated the education system (each day was started with prayer). The presence of other religions was merely tolerated but certainly not encouraged. After 1994 the constitutional framework accepted by the majority of South Africans entrenched the right of all citizens to worship a God of their choosing. This has led to the country becoming a nation whose religious tolerance is revered around the world. Based on the 2011 census an analysis of South Africa's population groups reveals that 79% of the population is Christian, 1.5% are Muslim, 1.2% practise Hinduism and 0.2% practise Judaism. Amongst black people the predominant form of Christianity is the independent and indigenous Zion Christian faith practised by over 19% of black Christians. Based on the 2001 census black people had the highest rate of unbelief with roughly 17.5% saying they had no religion.

Congregations around the major cities have seen a boom in new churchgoers, largely from the emerging black middle class. Given the complexities of operating in today's unequal society and the challenge of raising children in the midst of insidious violence many young black couples have returned to faith-based lives as a way of fortifying their family units. Even though traditional marriage is widely practised throughout the country according to specific ethnic customs, the union between a man and a woman is rarely forged outside of the church. Children are almost always baptised, forcing parents to introduce a religious framework early in their lives. This trend has done much to begin repairing the damage done to extended family networks through the late 1990s and the early 2000s.

Arguably the most powerful facilitator for young people to return to Christianity has been the emergence of charismatic churches that offer non-traditional methods of worship to a younger crowd in search of a more personally relevant message from God. It is more than a little ironic that black South Africans have become attracted to a form of worship that for many years helped downtrodden African Americans rise into one of the most prosperous African communities in the world. Part of the message is centred on dealing with material wants and needs and the role that prayer and hard work plays in the attainment of one's goals. Though many may see this aspect of charismatic churches as spiritually shallow and even opportunistic, the truth is that these churches provide basic lessons in hard work, thrift, personal financial management and estate planning that few institutions can give to newly emerging middle-class black people.

Many of the young black people attracted to charismatic churches are from homes where there were no mentors to guide them morally and motivationally in terms of their ability to self-actualise. The sense of community and group bonding created by the church has led to the establishment of home-cells and book clubs that are used by charismatic churches to overcome their inability to have one-on-one interactions due to their massive congregations; these increase camaraderie, personal accountability and in the long run will help chip away at the insecurity felt by first-time breadwinners as they enter the world of work.

There is a danger that some charismatic churches promote an unhealthy focus on the materialistic gains that will arise from dedicated worship of Christ. Often these churches are driven by the personality of one spiritual leader, creating an additional danger of a cult of personality. By promoting false hope about the prospects for overnight success through prayer and tithing, some of these churches take advantage of a vulnerable congregation that is often desperate for an improvement in their economic circumstances. More discerning worshippers will make charismatic churches that have a holistic focus on spiritual growth more popular. The sheer number of charismatic churches provides choices and opportunities for comparison, creating a 'spiritual market place' within which worshippers can 'shop around' for a spiritual home.

More than any other trend, these churches have facilitated the role of faith-based family-orientated lifestyles amongst the emerging middle-class youth. This has greatly improved their spirit of solidarity, the inclination to give to the less fortunate, the sense of national service and community obligation, allowing them to become more well-rounded, multi-dimensional citizens. Ultimately this will help produce a better cadre of leadership for the nation's numerous institutions, allowing for social transformation that is based on a sound value system.

Social entrepreneurship and its effects

Nobel Prizewinner Muhammad Yunus, in his visionary book pioneering a new kind of social business, describes the need within other human beings to help the least fortunate as follows: 'Charity is rooted in basic human concern for other humans.'[16] These roots are very deep in both pre-1994 societies and seem to have remained firmly planted in the newly integrated society post-democracy. The spirit of ubuntu, or people-centricity, has survived the constant barrage of individualistic emerging values to retain its status as a central organising principle for many South Africans, leading some to dedicate their lives to the betterment of fellow citizens.

One of the positive aspects of South Africa's history of anti-apartheid activism was the birth of multiple civil society institutions, many of which managed to continue operating under modified mandates post-liberation. Another factor increasing civil society activity in South Africa is the fact that the country has high barriers to entry in business (largely because of the multiple oligopolistic industries which have been net job shedders) and politics (based on the dominance of the incumbent political party), forcing many people to seek independent vehicles through which they can effect change. With respect to NGO funding, 'it is estimated that income generated through donations, grants, sales, membership dues, fees for services (contracts/tenders with government and the private sector) plus interest on investments is in excess of R16 billion per annum (US$ 2.3 billion). In 2007, R3 billion was contributed through corporate social investments. It is probable that more than 2 million people volunteer their time, talent and expertise to NGOs annually, with an estimated worth of a further R5.1 billion in sweat equity.'[17]

There are between 100 000 and 120 000 civil society organisations in South Africa, of which 37 000 are registered as not for profit organisations.[18] They provide a million sustainable jobs and 100 000 of them help the government deliver more than half of its welfare services.[19] The scale and scope of these organisations' activities cover areas such as HIV and AIDS, poverty alleviation, environmental programmes, gender issues, faith-based initiatives, housing and other areas of need.

Even for a nation with as many socio-economic problems as South Africa has, nothing should stand in the way of an army of 2 million volunteering patrons to overcome, particularly when government and business seem so willing to extend their arms in partnership to these volunteers and their organisations. The trouble in South Africa is that a glut is being created in the fiscal budgets of the treasury by using a method of wealth transfer that requires taxing private individuals and private sector corporations, then spending these tax proceeds on poverty alleviation by government departments. This often leads to late payments to local, provincial and national government departments, whose under-spending of their budgets is based on capacity constraints and the negative outcomes of corruption. To allow for this bottleneck to be decreased requires a more professional civil service and a decentralisation of the redistribution mechanism by allowing some direct corporate spending in the poverty alleviation arena.

These measures have to be rooted in the understanding that the incumbent administration can benefit politically by unleashing South Africa's 2 million-strong volunteer force, financed by enhanced corporate sector spending, to cement economic redistribution in a sustainable form. The political will for compromise has to be grounded in a three-way bargaining framework between labour unions, government and private sector. This three-way social compact has to be drafted and managed in a way that allows these three stakeholders to simultaneously claim to be forwarding their individual agenda while participating in the creation of broadbased economic freedom for poor South Africans. This will be a once-in-a-lifetime opportunity to erase the sins of the past while facilitating the attainment of the dream of a Great African Society.

12

Towards a Great Society

South Africa's path as a society headed into peril can easily be diverted into the direction of a great society. The ease with which the country can make that adjustment is not because of happenstance; it is enabled by a series of policy choices made by different leaders over the last century. These policies have ultimately built a prosperous nation with strong institutions and a wealth of critical infrastructure. As was demonstrated in Chapter 3, successive administrations focused on a set of domestic investments that enabled the country to access, transport and export minerals to willing international buyers. Throughout the apartheid period investments were made in critical domestic infrastructure to counteract the increasing isolation of the country and legitimise the government's separate development policy. As a result there was a steady increase in both the quantity and the quality of infrastructure available per person between 1960 and 1985. The real per capita value per person rose from R18 360 in 1960 to R41 055 in 1985.[1]

The first democratic government led by President Mandela and the subsequent administrations led by Presidents Mbeki and Zuma have all had the foresight to continue to build on this critical infrastructure at as fast a rate as was deemed responsible by their economic teams. The net result is that South Africa has a critical public infrastructure whose replacement value stood at R1 556 billion in 2009.[2] The Zuma government has announced plans to spend close to R1 trillion by 2020. This amount, which includes all infrastructure spending proposed through state-owned entities like Transnet, Eskom, Sanral and the DBSA, will take the total value of national infrastructure to north of R2 556 billion.[3]

It is in the area of harnessing and unlocking sufficient human capital to generate the economic dynamism needed to take advantage of this wealth of public infrastructure that South Africa has failed. Consequently the biggest national challenge is finding ways to facilitate the growth of companies that can create the 5–10 million new jobs needed to bring the country's unemployment to acceptable levels.

Analysis of the causal relationship between poor education and lack of economic progress has so far been avoided, not because policy makers are unaware of its roots or the way the problem manifests itself in the distribution of jobs in the economy, but because of an inability to fund the remedy and action the tough political steps required to deal with its root causes.

South Africa is not alone in this dilemma. Brazil, a country that shares some of our socio-economic challenges (inequality, urban slums and high crime and HIV rates), has had to learn the same painful lessons. 'Education has the largest explanatory power when disentangling the sources of income inequality. A variety of studies indicate that variation in educational attainment of the household head explains more than a third of total inequality. No other factor – age, gender, region, family type, race – has a third as large an effect.'[4] Brazil made three key policy interventions that helped improve its overall quality of education. Firstly, it put significant emphasis on improving the numbers of students at primary school level, resulting in a 40 per cent increase in primary school enrolment between 1980 and 1994.[5] Secondly, Brazil drastically improved the quality of its public school teachers by creating a National Fund for Primary Education Development and for

Enhancing the Value of the Teaching Profession (Fundef) which helped decrease the number of teachers without university training. Thirdly, close attention was paid to measuring the proficiency of students on a national basis to serve as feedback for the quality of students being produced by the system. The government partnered with the United Nations Development Programme to do comprehensive nation-wide sample tests of student proficiency in Portuguese and mathematics every two years for fourth, eighth and twelfth graders.[6]

In South Africa a second equally serious taboo negatively affecting policy making is the inability to deal with the reality that even with a helping hand in the form of access to quality education, citizens will still perform at differentiated levels, necessitating different types of higher learning institutions (FETs for some, apprenticeships for others and universities for a small number of learners). This reality will always produce a dichotomy between so-called white-collar and blue-collar job seekers. The type of social engineering that should be sought after is not to prevent this segmentation, but to allow it to happen more efficiently and without any racial prejudice.

The 'theory of the case'[7] in this book is meant to create the rationale for a shift in the burden of economic redistribution – away from the exclusive realm of the public sector's welfare regime of social grant programmes, and towards a more balanced, shared and sustainable social safety net with equitable private sector participation. The hypothesis is that South Africa's socio-economic realities have been created by a combination of the apartheid legacy and policy-making errors by the democratically elected government post-1994.

The private sector was complicit through its lobbying for conservative macro-economic policies which were beneficial to them in the short term (post-1994) but to the detriment of the country in the long term (through the lack of economic dynamism, which resulted in minimal FDI, resulting in economic stagnation for many and real unemployment for close to 40 per cent of working-age

South Africans). This hypothesis concludes that the elite domination of the economy by a small upper-middle class (of both black and white South Africans) is unsustainable and is likely to result in a populist revolt in the medium term that will have grave consequences for all of South African society, including business.

So far policy makers in the Zuma administration are proposing that the state should identify market failures such as the land redistribution process and the failure of transformation in the mining industry and increase the costs to the holders of these assets through taxation. The economic theory behind this is that government can target taxes to diminish 'rent seeking behaviour' by these owners of assets and that the government would use the tax receipts to finance programmes that will work towards poverty alleviation. To date a land tax has been mooted to try and tax those land owners who are in possession of agricultural land that is not being used productively. Similarly, in the mining industry a tax on 'super profits' is being advocated by some policy makers.

The danger with this approach is that the risk of policy failure through inappropriate or outright adverse incentives is high, which could lead to reduced private sector investment in these industries, as well as increased tax avoidance. The bigger challenge for the state is avoiding a situation where policy makers will be complicit in creating a siege mentality within the corporate sector, where chief executives are constantly looking over their shoulders in fear of the next redistributive tax proposal. Not only does this encourage cynical behaviour; it also discourages visionary corporate stewardship.

The Re-engineering South Africa Fund

Corporate leaders, union bosses and policy makers have to make a commitment towards a process that will result in a sustainable once-off redistribution programme that will restore certainty about the method of restorative justice and allow the respective decision makers to adopt a partnership mentality to solving national socio-economic challenges. South Africans have to 'walk together', in the words of the Dinokeng Scenarios,[8] by adopting redistributive policy measures underpinned by a massive social investment fund that will see the private sector invest R500 billion (roughly 10 per cent of the market capitalisation of the JSE) in mandatory equity grants that will translate into permanent BEE credits to invest in a Re-engineering South Africa Fund. This fund will facilitate three essential ingredients in the design of a great society: personal security, labour force competitiveness and upward economic mobility.

At the heart of this solution should reside a humble acceptance from all major stakeholders in South Africa that working together for change is the only way to protect the national balance sheet from the gross devaluation that will come from a populist backlash. The private sector needs a fast-growing South Africa powered by a highly skilled work force in order to generate greater shareholder value. Government hopes to cut unemployment by more than half from its current officially acknowledged level of 24 per cent towards a rate in the low teens. Labour unions want to see more decent work being produced in both the public and private sector, but more importantly would like to promote the economic welfare of members and their families. Shareholders of many companies would like to live lives without fear of crime. Poor citizens want an opportunity to work and the ability to dream of limitless possibilities for their children. Yet there are growing capacity constraints from a fiscal and bureaucratic standpoint, limiting the ability of the government alone to deliver on all these agendas. Without humility, foresight and sacrifice none of the stakeholders will be satisfied with the results. Therefore the following set of proposals is intended to create the framework within which societal bargaining can take place, paving the way for a shared prosperity.

❏   First, the country requires an increase in personal security for all South African citizens by investing heavily in critical infrastructure for primary healthcare that will underpin the basic

251

healthcare needs of South Africa's most vulnerable citizens, mothers and their young children.

❏ Second, the private sector needs to adopt failing urban public schools and create new urban charter schools to fast-track the creation of a level playing field in primary and secondary education.

❏ Third, a significant investment in mixed-use housing is needed to solve the urban housing crisis and put an end to shack dwelling.

❏ Fourth, the private sector should dramatically increase its spending on technical skills training and professional leadership development necessary to create a competitive work force that will drive productive output in the economy.

❏ Fifth, the Re-engineering South Africa Fund should make available loan guarantee instruments to facilitate expansion capital for SMEs in order to spur sustainable job creation on a national scale.

These investments should be matched by a new set of R500 billion worth of investments by government, focused on currently marginalised areas with critical needs:

❏ First, government should invest in equalising the quality of rural school infrastructure at the primary, secondary and tertiary levels.

❏ Second, retraining and/or pensioning all public school teachers who fail to attain an adequate grade on a national standardised test.

❏ Third, significant investment is needed in rural economic

infrastructure, creating where necessary special economic zones that can be sources of rural job creation.

❑ Fourth, significant investment has to be made in professional-ising the civil service by setting high entry standards to pub-lic sector employment and supporting those standards with a skills upgrade of current and future government employees, at the local, provincial and national levels.

❑ Fifth, government needs to invest in a land reform programme that is geared to stimulate small-scale commercial farming in order to create food security and employment growth in rural areas to help stem the tide of urbanisation.

Chapter 8, Economic Freedom and the Comrades Marathon, dis-cussed the challenges that come with accounting for how many of South Africa's economic transformation goals have been met to date. Consensus is that there is a gap between what was desired by the original BEE policies and the resulting set of outcomes from the suite of BEE legislation. At the one end of the spectrum the view is that the gap is between 1.8 per cent (being the un-geared equity portion of all BEE stakes in listed JSE firms) and 25 per cent, which is the minimum percentage of ownership in black hands targeted by government in almost all sectors (except for the exemption given to financial services). At the other end of the spectrum is the view that there has been 17 per cent of equity transfer into black hands in the form of direct and indirect ownership. Yet most South Africans intuitively know that neither of these figures comes close to capturing the amount of hard work needed to redress the scale of inequality currently besieging the country.

Far-thinking corporate citizens should be willing to invest in a social stability insurance instrument – the Re-engineering South Africa Fund – to correct historical imbalances once and for all. This would be in the form of a series of equity grant donations directing proceeds from dividends, share sales and increased equity value

253

through trusts set up by each corporation. These equity grants should be made by way of a fresh issue of shares at par value to a trust set up by the corporation having as its sole activity the management of proceeds into social investments. The trust will choose from a set of five high-priority social investments (urban primary healthcare, urban charter schools, urban mixed-use housing, increased technical skills development spending and a SME loan guarantee programme). The granting of permanent 'once empowered, always empowered' status by the Ministry of Planning in the Presidency should follow a project appraisal process and agreement to annual audits to be performed by reputable audit firms on the quantum and status of these private sector investments.

There is a significant challenge created by the inability to quantify the individual company contributions to BEE to date (the two different positions are whether BEE has delivered 1.8 per cent or 17 per cent in equity benefits so far). R500 billion is suggested as the compromise investment. There is far less known about the scale and equity value of South Africa's unlisted sector, creating the potential for a free-rider situation where listed firms subsidise unlisted firms, generating significant incentives to de-list and deterring new listings. As with the multiple waves of BEE legislation, the complexity of this solution might allow legal professionals the opportunity to blunt the real impact on firms, resulting in unsatisfactory outcomes.

It goes without saying that narrow-based economic empowerment – using investment holding companies for wealth generation that relies on the capability and honesty of its shareholders to redistribute this wealth through various interposing structures to previously disadvantaged persons in the broader economy – does not generate transformative results at anywhere close to the level required. We also know through lessons learnt that where possible firms and individual shareholders will play the system, falsely amplifying the amount of transactional equity benefits to 'previously disadvantaged groups' in order to reduce the cost of economic transformation to themselves. At the risk of becoming a society in peril, South Africa cannot repeat these policy mistakes and fail yet again to significantly transform the economy in a way that shares benefits across all race groups.

Given these challenges and the risks involved in any misstep, simplicity and uniformity across industries is necessary to ensure meaningful and satisfactory economic wealth transfer. I believe that many of these complexities can be avoided with a once-off grant of 10 per cent of all non-black-owned[9] firms' equity to newly established trusts independent of the firms' existing auditors. These trusts should be run by no fewer than three professional trustees who should have either legal or accounting expertise to qualify for trusteeship. These trusts' activities should be regulated by the Ministry of Planning in the Presidency to ensure that they exist exclusively for the donation of proceeds of dividends and/ or share sales to one of five areas designated as areas of critical national need.

None of the funds from these trusts should be used as manage-ment fees or for the trusts' operational expenses. Trustees need ei-ther to be paid directly by the firms that set up the trusts or to work pro bono. The shares held by the trusts have to rank pari-passu – that is, equitably and without preference – with those of the other shareholders. In private firms where the existence of multiple classes of shares is still prevalent, the majority shareholders should be given the burden of proof (as a condition for the BEE credits) that their trust is not unduly prejudiced by the existence or crea-tion of alternative classes of shares. Failure to comply or attempts at playing the system should be met by an immediate disqualifica-tion from public sector procurement of any kind pending inves-tigation by the Public Protector into the affairs of the infringing corporate. There should be no industry or nationality carve-outs (in other words international shareholders should not be shielded from compliance with these rules) for this policy. Equality in treat-ment will facilitate swift adoption and discourage the use of stall-ing tactics.

I propose the **establishment of 'charter schools'** completely owned, operated and funded by private entities as the first area of critical need. These schools should be free from all government regulation in terms of teacher and administrative salaries, to allow them the ability to compete for skilled teachers with market-orientated salaries and incentive structures. As a mechanism of fast-tracking the levelling of the playing field, government should select, based on the results of the competency examination process outlined in Chapter 9, the poorest-scoring 10 per cent of urban schools in South Africa and 'auction these off' to corporate sponsored trusts, who would upon 'buying' the schools, take responsibility for them and run them as chartered schools. These schools should have first-rate teaching infrastructure and a new, motivated and qualified set of teachers.

Additionally the legislation should allow private entities to invest in the establishment and operation of new urban schools on the same conditions and with the same incentives as outlined above. The Adopt-a-School Foundation, with Cyril Ramaphosa as its patron, has already proven that the model can work, adopting ten schools so far, creating a safe and vibrant learning environment for students in those communities.[10] Other initiatives by John Gilmour in the form of LEAP Science and Maths Schools[11] have created institutions that retrain underperforming grade 10 to 12 students for tertiary level by significantly boosting their maths and science skills. Projects such as the Oprah Winfrey Leadership Academy for Girls[12] and African School for Excellence[13] have taken a different model by building new, private school institutions in underprivileged communities from the ground up. These are just a few examples of the social entrepreneur-driven models that need to be heavily supported by capital from the Re-engineering South Africa Fund in order to replicate their successes and by legislative changes that would make it easier for these success stories to grow.

These schools should be managed and operated in accordance with state guidelines when it comes to curriculum. It is important that they meet the high education standards set by private schools while having the ability to enrol students without tuition and on a first-come, first-served basis (with a preference for neighbouring students), like public schools. This should dramatically reduce the burden on the public school system, lowering learner-to-teacher ratios. Firms will need to use the same rules that prevent discriminatory enrolment in public schools to ensure that equal access reduces the effects of the 'ovarian lottery' that damns young children to failure on the basis of where their parents live. It is important that schools in urban areas be uplifted quickly to reduce the effects of unequal distribution of opportunities currently scarring the psyche of South African society.

In recognition of the efforts necessary to support the implementation of National Health Insurance (which has an estimated cost in the region of R125 billion by 2012 and R250 billion by 2025), a second area of critical need is the **construction and maintenance of primary healthcare centres** close to or in urban 'townships' and in rural areas focusing on the provision of quality healthcare to mothers and their young children. Government simply does not have the capacity and expertise to roll out the required healthcare infrastructure to make the dream of equal access to healthcare attainable. To support government in this regard, corporations through their trusts need to be able to either adopt (through the upgrading of existing poorly capacitated healthcare facilities in the form of PPPs) or construct from scratch and manage new healthcare facilities in any urban centres where there is a demonstrated shortage of public health facilities. Children who enjoy good health facilities are out of school less often, which is a key facet of levelling the playing field in the distribution of education. The ability to give mothers the peace of mind that they can have a safe pregnancy and birth and that their newborns will be adequately taken care of, has been proven all around the world to be one of the leading causes of a reduction in birth rates. High infant mortality rates are incongruent with aspirations to become a great society.

One of the major challenges to the security of all South Africans is the persistently high crime rates which usually manifest themselves in violent crime. These crime rates have complex causes and will never be permanently reduced to zero. However a major contributor seems to be the emasculation of black men who cannot provide an income for their families. As a result the majority resort to alcoholism and crime (for further analysis see Chapters 5 and 10). An **urban renewal programme** founded on the principle of decent, practically constructed mixed-use accommodation constructed with the involvement of unemployed people will go a long way towards introducing a feeling of social accountability through home ownership.

To make this programme work efficiently firms need to be able to invest through the Re-engineering South Africa Fund in new urban developments by offering developers equity capital for their projects in exchange for transforming aspects of their planned developments into low-income accommodation (apartments, townhouses or houses depending on the theme and style of the development). This equity should be injected as an acquisition of a piece of land or finished accommodation at a price per square metre identical to other parts of the development profile so as to avoid subsidisation of otherwise commercially unviable schemes. Having said this, to the extent that turning significant parts of new developments into new housing for poor people will help make a scheme more bankable, then the result is a win-win situation for developers and the society at large. The Ministry of Planning should fast-track any re-zoning applications that would be necessary to facilitate low-income housing within already approved prospective property developments.

The candidates for occupancy for these new houses need to be taken initially from neighbouring RDP scheme lists (which are supposed to operate on a first-come, first-served basis). These home owners should be enrolled by the chosen construction company of the developer (as a quid pro quo for winning the new construction business) in an apprentice programme through which they can be trained to perform any tasks related to the construction (bricklaying, painting, plumbing, cleaning, security and site preparation) of the new urban housing development. This job experience and training will hopefully enable them to participate in other new construction opportunities, facilitating their entry as wage-earning members of society. The resulting injection of pride in being able to work on the construction of one's home is an important part in restoring broken self-confidence which negatively affects so many households in South Africa.

Additionally a programme to guarantee up to 40 per cent in the form of an equity contribution towards the first bond (through an interest-free instrument that can be repaid at the end of the mortgage period) necessary for working, first-time black home owners to acquire their homes should be set up to support the entrance of young people into the urban housing market. This guarantee fund should be available to all bond-issuing institutions through a random selecting lottery system (in which candidates fulfilling the criteria are automatically entered by the financial institution through which they apply for a bond) for the purpose of simulating an equity contribution to allow credit to be given to people who ordinarily would not qualify because of an inability to put in a significant own contribution.

Bond affordability tests should still be carried out to ensure that the mortgage holder can pay the monthly bond payment. This facility should be used to pay for existing houses and newly constructed houses in any urban centre. The cut-off should be for houses not more than R300 000 in value (a figure that should be annually adjusted to account for the effects of inflation), to facilitate the emergence of a young lower middle class home-owning sector that is fully invested in the future of the society. This guarantee should come with a precondition of an own contribution of R6 000, or 2 per cent of the value of the house (whichever is lower), which will serve to show some seriousness on the part of the home buyer. To put this in context, the average 'construction and construction material' cost to the owner of a shack is around R6 000.

Many corporations currently have skills development programmes that comply with the Skills Development Act. Yet skills shortages continue to be at the top of most firms' list of concerns for the future. In this regard a new **ongoing education culture to strengthen technical and managerial training** should be financially supported by business, through the Re-engineering South Africa Fund. To ensure that this essential aspect of private sector development is not overly represented in their Re-engineering South Africa Fund commitments, a maximum of 10 per cent of each firm's equity grants can go to this area. Having said this, even if firms up-skill their employees for purely competitive reasons (to out-compete their fellow corporate competitors) the net result is positive for the economy in the form of shared benefits from national productivity gains.

The government of Singapore, for example, has found useful ways to stimulate the private sector use and the quality of vocational schools in their country. 'Singapore has offered vocational training as a viable option for students who are not academically inclined and made a determined effort to erase the gap between general and vocational education. Through planning and effective use of employer feedback, Singapore has attempted to match the skills offered by vocational schools with the needs of the private sector... The authorities persuaded firms to train twice the number they required and gave them the first pick of the graduates. The surplus was used to attract new investors.'[14]

Corporations should be free to use whatever further education and training (FET) suits them and their employees' needs. The funding of tuition and all ancillary educational expenses should be provided on a free-of-charge basis to previously disadvantaged employees (in accordance with the definition in the Codes of Good practice currently regulating implementation of the BBBEE policy). These benefits should not in any way reduce the employees' total cost to the company. If an employee moves jobs within two years of finishing such a programme the new employer should be compelled to reimburse the old employer, to discourage free riding.

The challenge that South Africa has so far been unable to overcome has been the availability of **sufficient expansion capital**

for Small and Medium Enterprises. It is well publicised that the majority of new jobs are currently created by SMEs, meaning that the future of job-creation efforts is tied to the ability to fund the growth of new and existing SMEs. Although South Africa has a well-developed set of capital markets with a large (compared to peer group countries) private equity capacity (in terms of access to funds, sophistication of the investment vehicles and number of private equity fund managers), its funding for SMEs, especially equity risk capital for growth, remains below the expectations and needs of the sector.

The reasons for this shortage of funds are complicated and not easy to quantify. First, there are easier opportunities for most funders than to invest in the high-risk equity return prospects of an SME. Secondly, South Africa has a concentrated banking sector that is very tightly regulated, in terms of loan loss provisions, by the South African Reserve Bank. This makes for a conservative lending culture that requires a large margin of safety in prospective investments. It also creates a disincentive for traditional banks to provide risk capital to this sector, pushing up the average cost of capital to SMEs because of a lack of competition to the niche providers of SME finance. Failure to properly fund SMEs leads to their stagnation, usually in the form of lifestyle businesses that employ less than a handful of people and often fail to survive the death, illness or relocation of the founder.

The Re-engineering South Africa Fund should arrest these trends by creating a pool of guarantee instruments to be tapped into by any organisations funding credible SME expansion capital. Entrepreneurs are often short of pools of between 30 and 40 per cent equity needed to attract debt in order to fund their expansion plans. By issuing irrevocable guarantees for this equity capital the fund will facilitate billions in fresh SME debt capital from multiple sources, ensuring the stimulation of a vibrant job-creating community of companies. These guarantees should be exercisable to the holders of the security for the life of the debt period to ensure the stability of debt structures for the SMEs. Minimum equity contributions of 2 per cent of the guaranteed amount from the entrepreneurs should be required to weed out chance takers; conversely, each entrepreneur should only be allowed to use the guarantee instrument once to avoid narrow-based benefits.

This facility should be open to SME owners of any nationality whose staff is and continues (through the life of the guarantee) to be made up of at least 50 per cent South African citizens. The nationality of entrepreneurs and their executive teams should not obscure the vital job creation opportunities created by the location of these firms in South Africa. Above and beyond contributing capital, large companies should find active ways to encourage, mentor and cultivate the management of SMEs in their procurement chain, a practice currently being perfected, for example, by Anglo American through their Anglo Zimele Fund,[15] which is one of the most successful enterprise development programmes in the country.

Role of the public sector in leading South Africa towards a Great Society

In recognition of the enormous burden being shifted off its annual budgets by R500 billion in corporate social investments through the Re-engineering South Africa Fund, government needs to match the corporate sector with a targeted set of investments aimed at putting money into neglected high-priority areas. These investments need to be accompanied by a commitment to a zero-tolerance stance on corruption demonstrated by consistent accountability demanded of all public officials. A **Silent Truth and Reconciliation Commission on Corruption** should be used to swing the pendulum back in favour of the real principals (who are the voting public) away from the agents (who are government bureaucrats) in the way that social mandates are fulfilled through public institutions.

I suggest having an amnesty period that encourages government officials who know they have taken part in corrupt transactions to voluntarily resign. To make this work the period within which one can be eligible for amnesty has to be short (12 to 24 months) and the sanction should be immediate retirement with benefits subject to an agreement (enforced by blacklisting amnesty holders) to never work in government or participate in any company that the government procures goods and services from. This amnesty should be a lifelong legally guaranteed exemption from prosecution for any crimes committed during the pre-amnesty period, and the tax ramifications related to those crimes. This should be managed on a confidential basis (similar to the way South African Revenue Services currently conducts its work).

This amnesty period should be followed by a **corruption crackdown** that will lead to the arrest and prosecution of all those non-compliant with the amnesty in order to win the public's and the private sector's faith in the institutions of government. After the institution of the Silent TRC, there should also be zero tolerance on conflicts of interest by government officials. Joining government or participating in business transactions should be a binary decision that potential civil servants have to make prior to their appointments.

Having set the process in motion for a cleaner, more transparent civil service, government needs to turn to a few critical areas that need transformation. Firstly, it should acknowledge the large gaps in administrative and management skills (relative to the requirements of a well-run civil service) besetting most government employees, and resulting in a crisis of maladministration, waste and inability to spend budgets in local, provincial and some national departments. Government needs to fix this problem in three critical ways.

❏   The first step is to put an end to the policy of deployment at any level of government.

❏   Next, government needs to take steps to ensure that meritocracy in the selection of new government officials provides more qualified and better experienced candidates.

❏ Thirdly, government needs to more robustly enforce the performance management framework that all government officials have currently agreed to in their employment contracts. It is important that government recognises as a national management principle that bad performers need to be weeded out and good performers should be rewarded and promoted.

This shift in the selection and incentivisation of public sector officials needs to be accompanied by an **investment in public sector skills development**.

I propose a government employee skills development/training programme funded through the PIC, as a manager of capital for the Government Employees Pension Fund. Initially the funding should be an upfront R10 billion rand commitment with annual top-up commitments of R2 billion. In order to ensure efficient leverage of capital, the funding for this programme should operate in the same manner as most corporate bursary schemes. The employer (in this case government through funds administered by the PIC on behalf of government employees) finances the studies of the employee on condition that the employee passes the course and serves a minimum term of service (usually three to five years). Should the employee leave the service of the employer prior to completion of the minimum term of service and join the private sector, the new private sector employer should be obliged to repay the scheme (or 'buy out' the employee) with interest. If the government employee fails the course, he or she should be compelled to repay the scheme through salary deductions over a set period. That education and skills development is a privilege, not a right to be taken for granted, is an important principle to be upheld even while addressing historical imbalances.

A significant aspect holding South Africa back from producing quality graduates out of its education system is the prevalence of bad teachers in the public education system, largely because of the legacy of Bantu Education (explored in detail in Chapter 9). To deal with this challenge, I propose that **incompetent teachers should be pensioned off and retrained to join other professions**. This measure has so far been avoided because of its political sensitivity and potentially large costs. Given that South Africans are contributing more than R100 billion per annum to an education sector which is overseeing a system where 80 per cent of its public schools are deemed dysfunctional, I would argue that we cannot afford not to make the investment in retiring incompetent teachers.

To measure competence, I suggest that all teachers should complete a **compulsory examination geared toward establishing where they stand relative to private school teaching standards**. The principle is that equality of education cannot be achieved without equal access to quality teachers. The current asymmetric allocation of quality teachers to the private schools and substandard teachers to public schools needs urgent address to get a return on the billions spent on education annually. Government should institute a standardised test for teachers, which is modular with specific emphasis on the core knowledge set needed for the discipline they are teaching benchmarked against private school teachers. Those teachers who achieve a percentage mark within 10 per cent of the pass mark of the standardised test should be given the opportunity for intensive training and retesting within a year of their first test (this retraining should be funded by some of the R10 billion upfront PIC money).

Those public school teachers who achieve the targeted pass mark required by the standardised teacher's examination should be eligible for increased salaries and benefits (such as preferential access to cheap housing finance) that should aim over time to narrow the wage differential between private and public schools. Those teachers who fail should be asked to join a voluntary retrenchment programme that will include a reasonable pension and a funded skills development programme. Those who do not should be dismissed even at the risk of a constructive dismissal CCMA claim.

Teachers' unions should be encouraged to accept this proposal as a solution to a national emergency that is beyond political manipulation. If necessary, draconian action by the government to ensure enforcement of such a policy would by definition be altruistic in its motivation and should be popularly supported. South Africa cannot afford to continue to protect non-performing teachers at the expense of poor children from poor families and communities.

Likewise, as proposed in Chapter 9, qualified teachers who for whatever reason are no longer employed within the teaching profession should be encouraged through financial incentives (personal income tax breaks and housing subsidies) to take part in the competency examination process and, should they pass, be employed by schools in areas where there are teacher shortages. The current Home Affairs foreign national teacher's allocation for visas and permanent residency should be tripled from 4 000 to 12 000. Those teachers should also be encouraged to take the competency exam and their immediate families should be offered permanent residence status as an incentive for their qualification for teaching in the public and charter school system.

These two potential sources of teachers are currently discouraged from joining the teaching profession because of the difficult working environment created by the protection of mediocre incumbent teachers. The teaching profession should be returned to practitioners who love the engagement with and stimulation of young minds and taken away from those who view teaching as an easy profession for people who are incapable of doing anything else. At a corporate level, companies should be encouraged, through tax write-offs and BEE credits, to supply some of their staff members as supplementary teachers serving two to three years' national service whilst new teachers are recruited and trained.

With the introduction of the charter school system facilitating a massive corporate sector investment into urban public schools, attention should be focused on drastically and swiftly improving the quality of rural public schools. The government should seek to obtain a significant low-interest **World Bank loan to equalise**

educational infrastructure disparities. This would entail placing rural government schools on par with private schools or 'Model C' schools in terms of infrastructure and teaching materials available to teachers and learners alike. In addition there would need to be a focus on providing boarding facilities to aggregate services for disparate small villages and communities.

This investment should be made across the board from primary schools to tertiary institutions to ensure the availability of critical educational infrastructure such as computer labs, digital and physical libraries, tablet computer technology and modern furniture that would provide equally stimulating learning environments for as many people in the country as possible. Those who do not favour World Bank loans as a matter of principle need to consider that China would not have succeeded in pulling more than 400 million people out of poverty as quickly as it did had it not used both World Bank funding and more importantly the intellectual capital of World Bank programme experts in executing projects of high national priority. South Africa simply cannot afford not to take on debt of this kind for this long-term investment in its critical resource.

As a further education initiative, the government should commit to tripling its financial contribution to **Further Education and Training Colleges** (FETs). To leverage its capital, government should allow salary deduction codes currently only extended to universities to also apply to FETs, allowing a crowding-in effect of responsible private sector capital to finance those citizens seeking ongoing education. FETs are the lifeblood of industrial economies, facilitating the technical training of employable professionals who can be immediately eligible to mentor apprentices, thus facilitating fast and efficient skills transfer.

The government needs to declare certain rural areas **special economic zones** (SEZs), which should be allowed to function in a manner that takes into account the economic crisis many of these regions are going through. The aim of these special economic zones is to generate rural job creation. The lack of rural job opportunities is placing too much pressure on urban centres, thereby ensuring unbalanced, unsustainable distribution of growth on a national basis, heavily skewed towards a few urban nodes. There must be an understanding from the beginning that government's job is to play a facilitative rather than leadership role in the shaping of the direction of economic development in these SEZs.

These zones should be characterised by a moderated set of labour laws that take into account the need to create conditions for corporate investments in these otherwise destitute areas. This moderation of labour laws should include (but not be limited to) a relaxation of the provisions of the current labour law barring dismissal of employees at the discretion of the employer, a reduction by 30 per cent of the minimum wage, a removal of the overtime compensation provision and the ability to use labour brokers. In rural areas, which often have unemployment rates above 50 per cent, any salary is decent; the current minimum-wage provisions in these rural areas rob poor people of the opportunity for attracting investments in the neighbourhoods using the only resource they have to offer in exchange – cheaper labour than their urban counterparts.

In keeping with the plans documented in the New Growth Path, government should support these SEZs by the creation of critical infrastructure in these regions. Major ports near rural SEZs should be upgraded; national highways passing through these nodes need to be augmented, thereby connecting manufacturing facilities and factories through road and rail arteries that facilitate easy logistics. Rail lines passing through these areas need drastic upgrade. Transnet should be implored to significantly and swiftly upgrade the quality, quantity and the service of its rolling stock in order to unblock bottlenecks.

The aim of this prioritised infrastructure investment needs to be to facilitate domestic and foreign private sector investment into economic activity that will create jobs in rural areas. There needs to be a balance between creating the potential for white elephants and the principle of 'if we build it they will come'. The best way to manage these tensions is through co-ordinated planning with private sector chief executives, facilitating binding agreements between the parties. To make sure that plans do not get mired in the pre-feasibility stage, government needs to set aside and/or favourably amend rules that force developers to undergo onerous environmental impact assessment periods which are often far in excess of peer group countries and only serve to protect the status quo.

The last major area of investment by the government needs to be in the area of **small-scale rural commercial farming.** The willing-buyer willing-seller premise of land reform presupposes that there will be capital to buy farms from existing owners. It also presupposes that the new buyers will be capable of running operations that are economically successful enough to justify the price paid to previous owners plus the cost of capital to acquire the new owner's farm. The suggested approach is a 50-50 joint venture formation where a management contract is given to a company run by professional farmers for a maximum five-year period, on condition that the management company actively trains and mentors the new farmers in proper agricultural academies.

It is important that the government does not replace one set of large commercial farmers with black farm owners who will take the role of 'landed gentry' using their newly acquired estates as vacation farm houses. The theory that only large commercial farmers can be successful in South Africa is simply not true. All farmers, large or small, need training and basic farm management skills and access to sustainable finance for their farming operation, but the argument that large farmers are inherently more efficient should not inform policy makers' decisions. 'In reality, nearly a century of research by agricultural economists all over the world has produced a counterintuitive stylized fact: small-scale farmers generally use land, labor, and capital more efficiently than do large-scale farmers who depend primarily on hired labor. This "inverse farm size–productivity relationship" implies that agriculture generally is characterized by diseconomies of scale, which means that redistributing land from large farmers to family farmers can bring efficiency gains to the economy.'[16]

Government should support these new owners with conditional low-interest loans (at about half the prime rate with two- to four-year interest holidays) that are administered directly by the Land Bank and indirectly in the form of loan guarantee instruments to corporate agricultural lending institutions. The beneficiaries of this new funding have to be willing to work on the farm for the life of the term of these new loans (which should be 7- to 15-year loans). The structure of these investments should be similar to private equity leveraged buy-outs where the old farm is transferred into a new company and a valuation of the land and immovable assets is established by a credible third party. New shares should be issued on a 50-50 basis (the government should provide 78 per cent of the capital directly or indirectly on behalf of the new black farm owners) with the new farm issuing debt equivalent to 98 per cent of its value (with the balance being made up of a 20 per cent vendor financing by the original farm owner and a 2 per cent own contribution from the new farm owners), which the debt holder subscribes to using the shares of the farm and its assets as security.

This will ensure that the old and new farmers will have joint responsibility for debt servicing and that the obligations taken on are reasonably (based on the farmers' experience) expected to be serviced. Thirty per cent of the cash value of the new farm should be distributed to the old farm owner as a realisation of value that his or her family has created and the balance should be used for upgrading of the farm and an investment in farming operations (purchase of fertiliser, farm equipment, new irrigation facilities, acquisition of neighbouring land and farm management skills transfer through agricultural academies). By facilitating these sorts of voluntary partnerships the government can further the agenda of agricultural transformation while supporting commercial farming and generating wealth for a new class of committed farmers.

As a regulator of markets, the government has powers that can sometimes be more effective than the investment of capital in catalysing growth. Most of these powers lie in the framework of rules that government puts in place to regulate private sector activity. A coherent national economic blueprint is necessary to ensure that clarity and complementarity characterise government regulations. Most important is the recognition by government that its most important role is that of a referee and not a player.

The government should use its diplomatic muscle to aggressively **promote South African corporate interests on the African continent**. This can be achieved by equipping the Department of International Relations and Cooperation with able commercially minded diplomats to assist in identifying opportunities for corporate South Africa on the continent and create the basis for win-win pan-African trade agreements. To this end, I propose that South Africa invests in additional capacity to support the diplomatic missions on the African continent with well-trained, experienced and business-savvy diplomats. Contrary to popular belief, one of the best ways of stimulating more opportunities for business abroad is to be more open at home to competition. South Africa needs to achieve this through investment in a stronger, bolder and more assertive Competition Commission which should be better resourced to explore unfair barriers to entry into critical industries, and not merely focus on cartel behaviour or predatory pricing.

The South African Reserve Bank should encourage **more SME-orientated corporate banking licences**, preferably for African (outside of South Africa) banking groups, to encourage the introduction of more debt-based expansion capital for entrepreneurs, which is likely to have the effect of cheapening the average cost of capital for all entrepreneurs in the SME community as local banks and financial institutions have to adjust to more competition from both the public sector and pan-African financial institutions. Government should create opportunities for South African banks, law firms, accounting, construction, architecture and engineering firms to prosper from the economic growth of neighbouring countries such as Nigeria, Angola, Ghana and Kenya.

In order to achieve this, the government should **encourage pan-African business persons and the corporations that they own to set up corporate headquarters in South Africa** through more

271

relaxed immigration policies for professionals and preferential tax policies, as an indication to African governments that South Africa is prepared to open up its own market to competition. This will encourage the standardisation of legal contracts and accounting practices that will make South African law firms and accounting companies more popular. Being this open and encouraging to pan-African corporate competition at home should be followed by a full-scale diplomatic charm offensive with an unapologetic agenda aimed at the promotion of South African business interests on the African continent.

The government should supplement its commitments made in the New Growth Path with a phased reduction in corporate taxes from 30 to 20 per cent in recognition of the accelerated upfront direct corporate sector investment in the Re-engineering South Africa Fund. Government should give firms investing in the pro-gramme full BEE scorecard credits on a once empowered, always empowered basis. Government also should agree to rearrange its procurement policies to evaluate corporate qualification for pub-lic sector procurement based on corporate contribution to the Re-engineering South Africa initiative.

Finally the Reserve Bank needs to **eliminate exchange controls** as they pertain to investments on the African continent, encourag-ing cash-rich South African companies to earn higher returns on equity in faster-growing markets on condition that they do not use this loophole as a back door to international capital expatria-tion (outside the African continent). The PIC should be allowed to invest a third of its capital in pan-African stocks, bonds (both sov-ereign and corporate), third party managed private equity/venture capital funds and infrastructure investments. This will unleash more than R300 billion worth of investable capital (from the PIC alone) on a pan-African basis, giving South Africa huge diplomatic leverage that complements its existing use of the DBSA and IDC as investment vehicles to remain a dominant force for positive eco-nomic development on the African continent.

It is possible for South Africa to demonstrate through a period of active shared sacrifice over the next 20 years that a nation can move from being scarred by racism, imperialism and a systematic subjugation of a majority by a minority, to one that represents a post-racial, meritocratic and peaceful society that generates its growth through responsible, mutually beneficial economic development partnerships with its fellow African neighbouring states. To prepare the nation for this reality South Africans have to embark on a period of redistribution of both personal security and educational opportunities as an acknowledgement of its wretched past. Building a people-centric society characterised by its equality in opportunity granted to all citizens and thereby facilitating an era of shared prosperity through a globally competitive economy will be the greatest way South Africa can honour the men and women who died fighting for its liberation.

Notes

Chapter 1: The Elusive Rainbow Nation

1 J Smith and B Tromp, *Hani: A life too short*. Johannesburg: Jonathan Ball, 2009, p ix.

Chapter 2: The Making of South Africa

1 H Giliomee, *The Afrikaners*. Cape Town: Tafelberg, 2003, p 21.
2 F Fukuyama, *The Origins of Political Order*. London: Profile Books, 2011, p 252.
3 D Welsh, *The Rise and Fall of Apartheid*. Johannesburg: Jonathan Ball, 2009, p 37.
4 DM Tutu, *No Future without Forgiveness*. New York: Doubleday, 1999.
5 R Wilkinson and K Pickett, *The Spirit Level: Why more equal societies almost always do better*. New York: Bloomsbury Press, 2010, pp 18–19.

Chapter 3: A Pre-owned Society

1 T Pakenham, *The Boer War*. London: Weidenfeld & Nicolson, 1979, xix.
2 H Giliomee, *The Afrikaners*, 2nd ed. Cape Town: Tafelberg, 2009, p xiv.
3 PJ Steytler, 'The renaissance of traditional ownership of land', Butterworths *Property Law Digest*, November 2000.

4 *Ibid.*

5 Giliomee, *The Afrikaners*, p16.

6 Welsh, *The Rise and Fall of Apartheid*, p 29.

7 *Ibid*, p2.

8 Giliomee, *The Afrikaners*, pp 290–1.

9 Packenham, *The Boer War*, p xv.

10 T Mbeki, 'The historical injustice', Speech delivered at a seminar held in Ottawa, Canada, 19–22 February 1978, p 5.

11 Welsh, *The Rise and Fall of Apartheid*, p 5.

12 M Mbeki, *Architects of Poverty: Why African capitalism needs changing.* Johannesburg: Picador Africa, 2009, p 46.

13 Welsh *The Rise and Fall of Apartheid,* p 30.

14 Steytler, 'The renaissance of traditional ownership of land'.

15 Giliomee, *The Afrikaners*, p 318.

16 M Mbeki, *Architects of Poverty*, pp 75–7.

17 Giliomee, *The Afrikaners*, p 341.

18 Welsh, *The Rise and Fall of Apartheid*, p 8.

19 A Butler, *Democracy and Apartheid: Political theory, comparative politics and the modern South African state.* Basingstoke: Macmillan, 1998, p 70.

20 M Mbeki, *Architects of Poverty*, p 47.

21 J Cargill, *Trick or treat: Rethinking Black Economic Empowerment.* Johannesburg: Jacana Media, 2010, pp70–1.

22 N Nattrass and J Seekings, *Class, Race and Inequality in South Africa.* New Haven: Yale University Press, 2005, p 100.

23 Giliomee, *The Afrikaners*, pp 344–5.

24 *Ibid*, p 597.

25 A Hirsch, *A Season of Hope: Economic reform under Mandela and Mbeki.* Pietermaritzburg: University of KwaZulu-Natal Press, 2005, p 2.

26 C Rustomjee, 'Pathway through financial crises: South Africa', *Global Governance Journal*, no 12, 2006, p 431.

27 P Green, *Choice, not Fate: The life and times of Trevor Manuel.* Johannesburg: Penguin Books, 2008, pp 374–5.

28 R Richards, *Bullets or Ballots.* Cape Town: Mutloatse Arts Heritage Trust and STE Publishers, 2011, p 20.

Chapter 4: The Great Fraud

1 JA van Wyk, *Cadres, Capitalists and Coalitions: The ANC, business and development in South Africa*, Research paper no 1, Developmental Leadership Program, 2009. http://www.dlprog.org/ftp/download/Public%20Folder/1%20Research%20Papers/Cadres,%20Capitalists%20and%20Coalitions.pdf.

2 S Yusuf and K Nabeshima, *Some Small Countries Do It Better*. New York: International Bank for Reconstruction and Development/International Development Association/World Bank, 2012, p 32.

3 F Hendricks, *The Private Affairs of Public Pensions in South Africa*. New York: United Nations Institute for Social Development, p 1.

4 *Ibid*, p 2.

5 A Knecht, 'The 'Afrikaner Broederbond': From 'devil of apartheid' to an actor of change in the transformation process of South Africa?', in J Pretorius (ed), *African Politics: Beyond the third wave of democratisation*. Cape Town: Double Storey Books, 2009, p 61.

6 *Ibid*, p 60.

7 Butler, *Cyril Ramaphosa*, p 286.

8 Welsh, *The Rise and Fall of Apartheid*, p 526.

9 Article 7 (2)(h) of the Rome Statute of the International Criminal Court (last amended January 2002), 17 July 1998, A/CONF. 183/9.

10 Nattrass and Seekings, *Class, Race and Inequality in South Africa*, p 2.

11 *Ibid*, p 3.

12 *Ibid*, p 143.

13 *Ibid*, p 135.

14 http://www.history.ucsb.edu/projects/holocaust/Research/Proseminar/tomerkleinman.htm.

15 T Mbeki, 'The historical injustice', pp 12–13.

16 Hirsch, *A Season of Hope*: *Economic reform under Mandela and Mbeki*, p 23

17 M Gevisser, *Thabo Mbeki: The dream deferred*. Johannesburg: Jonathan Ball, 2007, p 498.

18 NC Gibson, *Fanonian Practices in South Africa: From Steve Biko to Abahlali baseMjondolo*. Pietermaritzburg: University of KwaZulu-Natal Press, 2011, p 63.

19 J Naidoo, *Fighting for Justice*. Johannesburg: Picador Africa, 2010, p 229.

20 *Ibid*, p 234.

21 *Ibid*, p 250.

22 Department of Finance Summary document, 1996, pp 1–2, quoted by Hirsch, *Season of Hope*, p 99.

23 S Yusuf and K Nabeshima, *Some Small Countries Do It Better*. Washington, DC: International Bank for Reconstruction and Development/International Development Association/World Bank, 2012, p 7.

24 D Hemson, 'In debt to apartheid', *Southern African Report*, vol 15, no 2, February 2000, p 30.

25 Hirsch, *A Season of Hope*, p 104.

26 Richards, *Bullets or Ballots*, p 58.

27 Gevisser, *Thabo Mbeki*, p 584.
28 Gibson, *Fanonian Practices in South Africa*, p xii.

Chapter 5: After 1994 – Unintended Consequences of the Settlement

1 Hirsch, *A Season of Hope*, p 235.
2 *Ibid*, p 237.
3 http://www.statssa.gov.za/publications/Report-03-03-01/Report-03-03-01.pdf.
4 *Ibid*.
5 *Ibid*.
6 A Fishlow, *Starting Over*. Washington, DC: Brookings Institution Press, 2011, p 130.
7 *Ibid*, p 136.
8 Nattrass and Seekings, *Class, Race and Inequality in South Africa*, p 235.
9 Hirsch, *A Season of Hope*, p 173.
10 Nattrass and Seekings, *Class, Race and Inequality in South Africa*, p 277.
11 Yusuf and Nabeshima, *Some Small Countries Do It Better*, p 124.
12 *Ibid*, p 124.
13 Green, *Choice, not Fate*, pp 419-20.
14 *Ibid*, p 454.
15 Hirsch, *A Season of Hope*, p 88.
16 *Ibid*, p 90.
17 C Paton, 'A looter continua', *Financial Mail*, 22 May 2010.
18 The Office of the Presidency, *Development Indicators 2009*; p 25
19 *Ibid*.
20 Yusuf and Nabeshima, *Some Small Countries Do It Better*, p 101.
21 D Hicks, *Dignity: The essential role it plays in resolving conflict*. London: Yale University Press, 2011, p 6.
22 Wilkinson and Pickett, *The Spirit Level*, p 77.

Chapter 6: An Imperfect Democracy

1 Gibson, *Fanonian Practices in South Africa*, p 2.
2 Electoral Task Team Report, Cape Town, 2003
3 *Ibid*, p 8.
4 *Ibid*, p 23.
5 Gibson, p 13.
6 A Butler, *Paying for Politics: Party funding and political change in South Africa and the global South*. Johannesburg: Jacana Media, 2011,

pp 15–16.

7 Democratic Alliance, http://www.da.org.za/newsroom.
   htm?action=view-news-item&id=9474.

8 J Knight, B Lingard and L Bartlett, 'Reforming teacher education
   policy under Labor Governments in Australia 1983–93', *British
   Journal of Sociology of Education*, vol 15, no 4, 1994, p 457.

9 Gevisser, *Thabo Mbeki*, p 657.

Chapter 7: Are We Capitalists or Communists?

1 L Callinicos, *Oliver Tambo: Beyond the Engeli Mountains*. Cape Town:
   David Philip, 2004, p 152.

2 *Ibid*, p 153.

3 http://www.sacp.org.za/docs/history/.

4 Gevisser, *Thabo Mbeki*, p 147.

5 *Ibid*, pp 148–9.

6 M Meredith, *Mandela*. Johannesburg: Jonathan Ball, 1999, p 130.

7 *Ibid*, p 131.

8 Callinicos, *Oliver Tambo*, p 281.

9 Gevisser, *Thabo Mbeki*, p 469.

10 Butler, *Paying for Politics*, p 253.

11 F Fukuyama, *The Origins of Political Order: From prehuman times to the
   French Revolution*. London: Profile Books, 2011, pp 64–5.

12 S Halper, *The Beijing Consensus*. New York: Basic Books, 2010, p 57.

13 South African Institute for Race Relations, www.sairr.
   org.za/services/publications/south-africa-survey/
   south-africa-survey-online-2009-2010.

14 A Arvanitis, 'Foreign direct investment In South Africa: Why it has
   been so low', http://www.imf.org/external/pubs/nft/2006/soafrica/
   eng/pasoafr/sach5.pdf.

15 Nattrass and Seekings, *Class, Race and Inequality in South Africa*, p 349.

16 Green, *Choice, not fate*, p 406.

17 AL Alfaro, G Bizuneh, R Moore, S Ueno and R Wang, *Microeconomics
   of Competitiveness: South Africa: automotive cluster*, Harvard
   Business School, 2012, p 14. http://www.isc.hbs.edu/pdf/Student_
   Projects/2012%20MOC%20Papers/MOC%20South%20Africa%20
   Automotive%20Final.pdf .

18 *Ibid*, p18.

19 Cargill, *Trick or Treat*, p xiii.

20 M Mbeki, *Architects of Poverty*, p 87.

21 South African capitalism: a new way of doing business, 22
   July 2005. http://www.sagoodnews.co.za/newsletter_archive/

south_african_capitalism_a_new_way_of_doing_business__3.html

22 S Halper, *The Beijing Consensus*. New York: Basic Books, 2010, p 32.

23 Economic Transformation Discussion Document, ANC 2010 National General Council, p 12.

24 South African Ministry of Economic Affairs, *New Growth Path Policy Document*, p 21.

25 Economic Transformation Discussion Document, ANC 2010 National General Council, p 12.

26 J Goldberg, *The Atlantic*, 8 September 2010. http://www.theatlantic.com/international/archive/2010/09/fidel-cuban-model-doesnt-even-work-for-us-anymore/62602/.

27 South African Ministry of Economic Affairs, *New Growth Path Policy Document*.

28 A Goswami, A Mattoo and S Saez, *Exporting Services: A developing country perspective*. Washington, DC: World Bank, 2012.

29 R McGregor, *The Party: The secret world of China's communist rulers*. New York: Harper Collins Publishers, 2010, p 17.

30 National Planning Commission, www.npconline.co.za/MediaLib/download/Diagnostic, accessed on 2 November 2012.

31 H Binswanger-Mkhize, C Bourguignon and R Brink, *Agricultural Land Redistribution*. Washington, DC: World Bank, 2009, p 12.

Chapter 8: Economic Freedom and the Comrades Marathon

1 S Nieftagodien and S van der Berg, 'Consumption patterns and the black middle class', Stellenbosch Economic Working Paper, February 2007.

2 R Loubser, 'Black SAns own at least 28% of available shares on JSE', politicsweb, 4 October 2011. http://www.politicsweb.co.za/politicsweb/view/politicsweb/en/page71654?oid=259431&sn=Detail&pid=71616.

3 *Ibid*.

4 *Ibid*.

5 Moneyweb. www.moneyweb.co.za, 14 September 2010.

6 A Ntingi and B Hlatshwayo, 'Blacks own less than 2% of JSE', *City Press*, 28 March 201 http://www.fin24.com/Business/Blacks-own-less-than-2-of-JSE-201003280.

7 *Ibid*.

8 www.sagoodnews.co.za/fast_and_quick_stats/index.html, 15 November 2012.

9 'Business unusual: Perceptions of corruption in South Africa', *HSRC Review*, vol 10, no 2, June 2012. www.hsrc.ac.za/

HSRC_Review_Article-316.phtml.

10 Transparency International, *CPI 2010 Report*. http://www.
transparency.org/cpi2010/in_detail.

11 BR Evans, *The Cost of Corruption: A discussion paper on corruption,
development and the poor*, TearFund, nd, p 1. http://www.tearfund.org/
webdocs/Website/Campaigning/Policy%20and%20research/The%20
cost%20of%20corruption.pdf

12 *Ibid*, p 5.

13 *Ibid*, p 1.

14 African National Congress Youth League, 'Towards the transfer
of mineral wealth to the ownership of the people as a whole: A
perspective on nationalisation of mines', Discussion document, 2009.

15 A Bishop, 'Civil servants wages eat into ability to build crucial
capacity', IOL Business Report, 25 January 2011. http://www.iol.
co.za/business/opinion/columnists/civil-servants-wages-eat-into-
ability-to-build-crucial-capacity-1.1016845.

16 G Dench (ed), *The Rise and Rise of Meritocracy*. Oxford: Blackwell,
2006, p 134.

17 A Sen, *The Idea of Justice*. Cambridge, Mass: Belknap/Harvard Press,
2009, p 19.

18 T Besley, *Principled Agents?: The political economy of good government*.
Oxford: Oxford University Press, 2006, pp 98–9.

19 *Ibid*, p 99.

20 *Ibid*, p 46.

21 The Presidency, Support programme for accelerated infrastructure
development, August 2010, p v.

22 K Cloete, 'R8.7bn of wasted expenditure tallied up by Govt',
Moneyweb, 21 January 2011. http://www.moneyweb.co.za/mw/view/
mw/en/page497784?oid=525472&sn=2009%20Detail.

23 World Bank Group, *South Africa: Second investment climate assessment*,
July 2010.

24 R Grobbelaar, 'Motlanthe: teach ethics to kids', TimesLive, 18 August
2011.

25 *Ibid*.

26 Dench (ed), *The Rise and Rise of Meritocracy*, p 9.

27 *Ibid*, p 162.

28 *Ibid*, p 27.

29 *Ibid*, p 137.

Chapter 9: The Original Sin

1 C Kros, *The Seeds of Separate Development: Origins of Bantu Education*. Pretoria: Unisa Press, 2010, p xiii.
2 M Cameron, 'The introduction of Bantu Education in Cape Town 1948-1960', in *Studies in the History of Cape Town*, Centre for African Studies, University of Cape Town, 1988, p 12
3 *Ibid*, p 45.
4 *Ibid.*
5 P Christie and C Collins, 'Bantu Education: Apartheid ideology or labour reproduction', in P Callaway (ed) *Apartheid and Education: The education of black South Africans*. Johannesburg: Ravan Press, 1984, p 60.
6 Cameron, 'The introduction of Bantu Education in Cape Town 1948–1960', p 46.
7 Christie and Collins, 'Bantu Education', p 63.
8 O'Meara, *Volkskapitalisme*, p 37.
9 *Ibid*, p 81.
10 Kros, *The Seeds of Separate Development*, p 27.
11 *Ibid*, p 62.
12 Christie and Collins, 'Bantu Education', p 64.
13 *Ibid*, p 134.
14 S Burger, *The History of Education in South Africa IV*, MyFundi.co.za. http://myfundi.co.za/e/ The_history_of_Education_in_South_Africa_IV.
15 Department of Education, *Education in South Africa: Achievements since 1994*, 2001. http://www.info.gov.za/view/ DownloadFileAction?id=70282.
16 PA Black and SG Hosking, 'The teacher crisis in South Africa: quitting, shirking and inferior substitution', *South African Journal of Economics*, vol 65, no 4, 1997, pp 232–6, p 234.
17 Department of Education, *Education in South Africa: Achievements since 1994*, 2001.
18 J Adler, 'Mathematics teachers in the South African transition', *Mathematics Education Research Journal*, vol 6, no 2, p 101.
19 *Ibid*, p 102.
20 J Heystek and M Lethoko, 'The contribution of teacher unions in the restoration of teacher professionalism and the culture of learning and teaching', *South African Journal for Education*, vol 21, no 4, 2008.
21 *Ibid*, p 1.
22 *Ibid*, p 4.
23 Black and Hosking, 'The teacher crisis in South Africa', pp 232–3.
24 *Ibid.*

25 *Ibid*, p 133.
26 SJ Howie, *Third International Mathematics and Science Study*. Pretoria: HSRC, 2001, pp 9-10.
27 *Ibid*, pp 11-12.
28 J Knight, B Lingard, L Bartlett, 'Reforming teacher education policy under Labor governments in Australia 1983–93', *British Journal of Sociology of Education,* vol 15, no 4, 1994, p 452.
29 *Ibid*, p 456.
30 *Ibid*, p 5.
31 Department of Education, *Education in South Africa: Achievements since 1994*, 2001.
32 *Ibid*.
33 Howie, *Third International Mathematics and Science Study,* p.15
34 Department of Education, *Education in South Africa: Achievements since 1994*, 2001, p 19.
35 Proceedings from the Academy of Sciences Forum, Critical issues in school mathematics and science, 30 September to 2 October 2009, University of Pretoria. http://www.assaf.org.za/wp-content/uploads/2011/04/STEM-FINAL-WEB.pdf.
36 mg.co.za/article/2012. Black access to varsity: What's the full story. Last viewed 2012 November 15th.
37 Proceedings from the Academy of Sciences Forum, Critical issues in school mathematics and science, 30 September to 2 October 2009, University of Pretoria. http://www.assaf.org.za/wp-content/uploads/2011/04/STEM-FINAL-WEB.pdf.
38 S Segar, 'Crippling shortage of maths and science teachers', *Daily News*, 28 May 2012. http://www.iol.co.za/dailynews/news/crippling-shortage-of-maths-science-teachers-1.1305920.
39 X Mbanjwa, 'Crisis looms as teachers quit in droves', IOL News, 7 June 2010. www.iol.co.za/news/south-africa/crisis-looms-as-teachers-quit-in-droves-1.486341.
40 *Ibid*.
41 M Mangome, 'Teachers quitting their jobs "not a crisis"', IOL News, 4 December 2008. http://www.iol.co.za/news/south-africa/teachers-quitting-their-jobs-not-a-crisis-1.427827.
42 Report of the Task Team for the Review of the Implementation of the National Curriculum Statement, Final Report, October 2009, p 11.
43 Department of Education, *Education in South Africa: Achievements since 1994*, pp 24-5.
44 Report of the Task Team for the Review of the Implementation of the National Curriculum Statement, pp 8-9.
45 Yusuf and Nabeshima, *Some Small Countries Do It Better*, pp 117–18.
46 President Obama, Address on education, Urban League 100th

Anniversary Convention, 29 July 2010
http://www.whitehouse.gov/blog/2010/07/29/
president-obama-education-status-quo-morally-inexcusable.
47 Press release issued by Equal Education, 22 July 2011.

Chapter 10: Societies in Peril

1 M Mbeki, 'South Africa: Only a matter of time before the bomb
explodes', *Leader*, 12 February 2011. http://www.leader.co.za/article.
aspx?s=23&f=1&a=2571.
2 *Ibid.*
3 T Mbeki, State of the Nation Address, 1998.
4 E Hassen, *The Balance Between Growth and Redistribution: Revisiting the
call for a basic income grant*, All Africa.com, 4 February 2011.
5 South African Social Security Agency, *Annual Report 2009/10.*
6 South African Social Security Agency, http://www.sassa.gov.za/Child-
support-grant-673.aspx.
7 *Ibid.*
8 South African Government Services. http://www.services.gov.za/
services/content/Home/ServicesForPeople/Socialbenefits/oldagegrant/
en_ZA
9 *Ibid.*
10 K Bloom, 'A forgotten township where only one murder
counts', *The Guardian*, 19 November 2010. http://
www.guardian.co.uk/commentisfree/2010/nov/19/
forgotten-south-africa-township-one-murder.
11 M Oosthuizen, 'Estimating poverty lines for South Africa',
Development Policy Research Unit, University of Cape Town, 2008.
12 M Leibbrant and I Woolard, 'The evolution and impact of
unconditional cash transfers in South Africa', A Southern Africa
Labour and Development Research Unit Working Paper, no 51, 2010,
SALDRU, University of Cape Town, p 5.
13 A Harber, *Diepsloot*. Johannesburg: Jonathan Ball Publishers, 2011, p 2.
14 South African Police Services, *Crime Report 2010/2011*, p 9.
15 *Ibid.*
16 'Crime statistics show marginal improvement', *Mail & Guardian*, 20
September 2012.
17 South African Police Services, *Crime Report 2010/2011*, p 11.
18 Wilkinson and Pickett, *The Spirit Level*, p 134.
19 K Karamoko and H Jain, *Community Protests in South Africa: Trends,
analysis and explanations*, Local Government Working Paper Series 2,
Cape Town: Community Law Centre, UWC, 1 July 2011, pp 1–2.

20 *Ibid*, pp 9–10.
21 *Ibid*, pp 11–12.
22 *Ibid*, pp 14–15.
23 *Ibid*, p 24.
24 *Ibid*.
25 *Ibid*.
26 Harber, *Diepsloot*, pp 18-19.
27 C Mushimbo, 'Land reform in post-Independence Zimbabwe: A case of Britain's neo-colonial intransigence?', Master's thesis, Graduate College of Bowling Green State University, 2005.
28 *Ibid*, p 23.
29 *Ibid*, p 30.
30 I Scoones, *Zimbabwe's Land Reform Myths and Realities*. Johannesburg: Jacana Media, 2010, p 2.
31 *Ibid*, p 3.
32 *Ibid*, p 5.
33 F Ajami, 'The Arab Spring at one', *Foreign Affairs*, vol 91, no 2, March/April 2012.
34 B Milanovic, 'Inequality and its discontents', *Foreign Affairs*, August 2011. http:/www.foreignaffairs.com/article/68031/branko-milanovic/inequality-and-its-discontents.
35 M Somerset-Webb, 'Egypt's youth unemployment problem has erupted – but what about Britain's?', *MoneyWeek*, 31 January 2011. http://www.moneyweek.com/blog/merryn-somerset-webb-egypt-youth-unemployment-and-britain-00311.
36 J Lehman, 'The 21st century Arab awakening?', YaleGlobal Online, 2011. http://yaleglobal.yale.edu/content/21st-century-arab-awakening.
37 M Cosser, 'Not a "NEET" solution to joblessness', *Mail & Guardian Online*. http://mg.co.za/article/2010-08-02-not-a-neet-solution-to-joblessness.
38 South African Treasury, 'Confronting youth unemployment', Discussion paper, National Treasury, 2011.
39 R Gott, *Hugo Chávez and the Bolivian Revolution*. London: Verso, 2005, p 4.
40 *Ibid*, pp 5–6.
41 M Weisbrot and L Sandoval, 'The Venezuelan economy in the Chávez years', Centre of Economic and Policy Research, 2008. http://www.cepr.net/index.php/publications/reports/update-the-venezuelan-economy-in-the-chavez-years/.
42 Brewer-Carias, A.R, *Dismantling Democracy in Venezuela: The Cháves Authoritarian Experiment*, Cambridge University Press, New York, 2010, p.19)

43 www.economist.com; February 24th 2011

44 *Ibid.*

Chapter 11: A More Civil Society

1 S Biko, *I Write What I Like*. Johannesburg: Picador Africa, 2004 (first published in 1978 by The Bowerdean Press, London), p 22.

2 N Mandela, Inaugural Address, Pretoria, May 1994.

3 L Johnson, 'The Great Society', 22 May 1964.

4 J Califano, 'What was really great about The Great Society', *The Washington Monthly*, October 1999.

5 T Mbeki, 'I am an African', 8 May 1996.

6 N Alexander, 'Language education policy: National and sub-national identities in South Africa', *Guide for the development of language education policies in Europe: from linguistic diversity to plurilingual education*. Language Policy Division DG IV – Directorate of School, Out-of-School and Higher Education Council of Europe, Strasbourg, June 2003. http://www.coe.int/t/dg4/linguistic/source/alexanderen.pdf.

7 The Constitution of the Republic of South Africa, The Bill of Rights, 1996 section 28(2).

8 *Unicef and the Ministry of Women, Children and People With Disabilities. A Review of Equity and Child Rights*, March 2011, p 13. http://www.unicef.org/southafrica/SAF_resources_factschildrens11.pdf.

9 *Ibid.*

10 A Motsoaledi, 'Maternal, Child and Women's Health Summit Keynote Address', 25 August 2009.

11 *Unicef and the Ministry of Women, Children and People With Disabilities*, p 21.

12 *Ibid*, p 12.

13 'South Africa: Study highlights impact of social grants', United Nations Office for the Coordination of Humanitarian Affairs. http://www.irinnews.org/Report/52401/SOUTH-AFRICA-Study-highlights-impact-of-social-grants.

14 A Fishlow, *Starting Over: Brazil since 1985*. Washington, DC: Brookings Institution Press, 2011.

15 South African Government Information. www.gov.za.

16 M Yunus, *Creating a World Without Poverty*, PublicAffairs 2007, p 8.

17 http://wiki.ngoconnectafrica.org/wiki/NGOs_in_South_Africa; Southern African NGO Network (SANGONeT), http://www.ngopulse.org/about.

18 *Ibid.*

19 *Ibid*

Chapter 12: Towards a Great Society

1 The Presidency, Support Programme for Accelerated Infrastructure Development, August 2010. www.btrust.org.za.
2 *Ibid.*
3 C Paton, 'Transnet helps Zuma deliver on his commitment to SA', *Business Day*, 13 February 2012. http://www.businessday.co.za/articles/Content.aspx?id=164746.
4 Fishlow, *Starting Over: Brazil since 1985*, p 129.
5 *Ibid*, p 88.
6 *Ibid*, p 94.
7 The 'theory of the case' refers to the comprehensive and orderly mental arrangement of principles and facts, which are conceived and constructed for the purpose of securing a judgment or decree of a court in favour of a litigant. The litigants in this case are poor marginalised people in South Africa.
8 http://www.dinokengscenarios.co.za/scen_overview.php.
9 Less than 51 per cent of its issued equity in the hands of black shareholders, using the modified flow-through principle suggested in the Codes of Good Practice in the BBBEE legislation.
10 http://www.adoptaschool.co.za/.
11 http://leapschool.org.za/.
12 http://www.owla.co.za/.
13 http://www.africanschoolforexcellence.org/.
14 Yusuf and Nabeshima, *Some Small Countries Do It Better*, pp 68–9.
15 http://www.angloamerican.co.za/about-us/anglo-zimele.aspx.
16 H Mkhize, C Bourguignon and R Brink, *Agricultural Land Redistribution: Towards greater consensus*. Washington, DC: World Bank, 2009, p 11.

Index